NEXT-LEVEL
Healthcare Leadership

*Advanced Topics for Healthcare
Administrators, Leaders, and Managers*

Laura Hills, D.A.

American Association for
PHYSICIAN
LEADERSHIP

AAPL books are available at special quantity discounts to use as premiums and sales promotions, or for use in corporate training programs. For more information, please write to Special Sales at journal@physicianleaders.org

This publication is designed to provide general information and is sold with the understanding that neither the author nor the publisher is engaged in rendering legal, accounting, ethical, or clinical advice. If legal or other expert advice is required, the services of a competent professional person should be sought.

13   8 7 6 5 4 3 2 1

Copyedited, typeset, indexed, and printed in the United States of America

PUBLISHER
Nancy Collins

PRODUCTION MANAGER
Jennifer Weiss

DESIGN & LAYOUT
Carter Publishing Studio

COPYEDITORS
Karen Doyle
Kerry O'Rourke

For Matt Hagadorn
and Sharif Farghaly,
my next-level sons-in-love

TABLE OF CONTENTS

ACKNOWLEDGMENTS

First, I would like to thank Nancy Collins for her steadfast belief in me year after year (after year) and for once again championing and guiding me through a book project. Thank you, Nancy, for making this book possible and for continuing to be an uplifting presence in my life. I am grateful to have witnessed the amazing things that you have accomplished in publishing. You stand as a role model for excellence and inspire that same excellence in others. Most of all, you are my friend. I am honored and grateful to be one of your authors.

Next, I would like to thank Dr. Marcel Frenkel for giving me that all-important opportunity in 1998 to write about staff development in *The Journal of Medical Practice Management.* Can you believe how far we've come, Marcel? Neither of us could have foreseen that this would become a 25-year+ writing gig for me (and we're still going strong), but how lucky for me that it turned out that way. You forever will be one of my heroes.

My sincere thanks go, too, to the extremely talented team that has supported my writing for many years and that has made this book possible. I've had the pleasure of working with Karen Doyle for many years, and she was an extraordinary copy editor. A huge, unpayable debt of gratitude goes, too, to the tremendously talented Jennifer Weiss, who provides the production support and copy editing for my writing. Thank you, Jen, for the countless things you do to ensure that everything chugs along smoothly, for catching my goofy mistakes, and for making such wonderful suggestions to improve my writing. Where would I be without you? I hope I never find out. Next, I'd like to thank Kerry O'Rourke for the time and effort she put into this project to ensure that my final draft was shipshape. And to the "Other Laura" in my life, the fabulous, the incomparable Laura Carter — you must be sick of my thanks by now, but I can't help myself. Thank you, thank you, once again for weaving my word-processed manuscript into design gold. I have no clue how you do what you do or how you keep track of the zillion and one things you do for a book-length project, but I am grateful down to my toes. It always and forever will be a joy and treat to work with you.

Additionally, I wish to thank the American Association for Physician Leadership for believing in me, for publishing another of my books, and for all you do to provide physicians and their organizations with the knowledge and skills required to become better leaders. We share the same passion for and commitment to this work and I am thrilled once again to have the opportunity to work with you. As professional associations go, AAPL is aces, and Peter Angood, MD, who captains the ship, is a sterling example of next-level leadership.

Finally, I wish to thank my husband Cornell Hills for his enthusiastic support of anything and everything I want to do, even my out-of-the-box ideas. You're more than the wind in my sails, my darling. You're the wind, the sails, the ship, the ocean, the world, and my life.

ABOUT THE AUTHOR

PHOTO BY STEVE BRANAGAN

Dr. Laura Hills has accomplished many things over a distinguished 40-year career but defines herself first and foremost as an educator. Her passion is to teach professionals how to lead and develop others, build better relationships, and communicate more effectively. She is well known for her books and articles, and notably has been the staff and leadership development columnist for AAPL's *Healthcare Administration Leadership & Management Journal and the Journal of Medical Practice Management* since 1998. Dr. Hills has grounded her work in a rigorous academic foundation. She holds a Doctor of Arts in higher education with a focus on adult learning and leadership and wrote and published her award-winning dissertation on leadership legacies. She lives in Baltimore, Maryland, with her husband Cornell Hills and is the mother of three adult daughters.

Also by Dr. Laura Hills

Hills, L. *Next-Level Healthcare Employees: Improving the Performance of a Good Team.* Washington, DC: American Association for Physician Leadership, 2023.

Hills, L. *The Problem Employee: How to Manage the Employees No One Wants to Manage.* Washington, DC: American Association for Physician Leadership, 2021.

Hills, L. *They'll Eat Out of Your Hand If You Know What to Feed Them: The 30 Essential Communication Skills that Give Highly Successful Career Professionals Their Edge.* Fairfax, Virginia: Blue Pencil Publishing, 2014.

Hills, L. *Lasting Female Educational Leadership: Leadership Legacies of Women Leaders.* Amsterdam and New York: Springer, 2013.

Hills, L. *Climbing Out of a Rut: Four Steps and 101 Secrets to Supercharging Your Career and Finding Greater Fulfillment and Reward in What You Do Every Day.* Fairfax, Virginia: Blue Pencil Publishing, 2012.

Sachs-Hills, L. *How to Recruit, Motivate, and Manage a Winning Staff: A Medical Practice How-to Guidebook.* Phoenix, Maryland: Greenbranch Publishing, 2004.

Sachs, L. *The Professional Practice Problem Solver.* New York: Prentice-Hall, 1991.

Sachs, L. *Do-It-Yourself Marketing for the Professional Practice.* New York: Prentice-Hall, 1986.

PREFACE

Today, each of us enjoys the fruits of excellent leadership that occurred long before we came to be. At the same time, we continue to deal with the legacy of lackluster and toxic leadership. Clearly, what leaders do and don't do matters and has the potential to outlive them. That is why leadership is such an awesome responsibility. My goal in writing this book is to help you lead as well as you can today and to leave behind you a magnificent leadership legacy.

I've studied leadership in graduate school and made it the topic of my doctoral research. I've stepped into various leadership roles over the years and felt the weight of that awesome responsibility on my shoulders. I've written countless articles on leadership, a scholarly book, and now this book. My guess is that like me, you have more than a casual interest in leadership and that you, too, have felt the weight of that awesome responsibility.

There are many approaches to leadership studies. For example, there are myriad training programs and workshops. We could fill an entire library with books about leadership and the inspiring stories of great leaders. We could bury ourselves in scholarship. I'm happy to say that that's not what we're going to be doing here. Instead, we will explore advanced leadership topics that would be useful to seasoned healthcare administrators, leaders, and managers. My approach in writing this book is how-to-do-it. So, though you will learn about the theoretical underpinnings or history of some of our topics, I promise you that that discussion will be brief. The lion's share of what you read will be extremely practical.

You will see, too, that I draw upon a great deal of research in this book. There's an extensive list of references in the back. Don't let that daunt you. I have written this book for you with an eye toward the what, why, and how of leadership. This work stems from a career writing for and speaking to healthcare professionals that spans more than 40 years. I've always been very pragmatic in my approach. This book is my way to teach you what I've learned about leadership over decades of work for and with people like you — what works, and what doesn't. The sources I have cited have informed and supported my work, but I have condensed and aggregated my learning for you.

You may choose to read this book from cover to cover. Or you may cherry pick chapters of particular interest. Some chapters will be relevant to your work right now, while others may be useful to you down the road. Read the book however best suits your purpose and interests. However, I urge you to set an intention for what you hope to gain from reading this book. Do this before moving on to Part 1. Then, keep your intention in mind as you read, and make notes along the way. When you're done reading — and this is most important — create and commit to one specific SMART goal before you put the book back on your real or virtual bookshelf. (SMART = specific, measurable, attainable, relevant, and time-bound.) For example, crafting a leadership legacy statement, the subject of this book's bonus chapter, could be your one and only SMART goal. Completing just that will make your reading this book worth your while. My hope, though, is that your reading motivates you to tackle more than one SMART goal. As you'll see, I've stuffed the pages with loads of good things for you to do after you read this book.

Before moving on, though, I'd like you to focus your attention on an age-old question about leadership. Do you believe that great leaders are born? Or do you believe that they are made? Researchers across the globe have tried to answer this question for as long as I can remember, and still, the scholarly literature suggests no conclusive answer. I've read the words of great leaders who have weighed in on this question, too, (Thank you, Vince Lombardi.). I can point to scores of authors, leaders, and talking heads who have something to say about this. But, after 40 years studying leaders and leadership, researching the topic, writing about it, consulting with and coaching leaders, even living leadership myself through various roles, I know for sure that Lombardi and many of the others were right; great leaders are made, and they are made through a whole lot of hard work. If I didn't believe that I would not have written this book.

Yes, some people are born with certain gifts that can foreground and strengthen their leadership. But I have learned and witnessed too much to believe that that's the end of the story. Genetics logic alone would suggest that outstanding leaders are born to families of leaders. If that's true, how can we explain Walt Disney, John D. Rockefeller Sr., or President Dwight

D. Eisenhower, to name just a few? There were no leaders in their families. In fact, Disney's father forbade him from participating in any work that was creative. Fortunately for us, he didn't listen. There are too many historical examples like that that do not support genetic logic, or at least, genetic logic alone.

We may never have a scholarly answer to this question. What we do know absolutely, though, is that it takes thousands of hours of deliberate practice to acquire mastery of a complex skill. That means that you can count the hours you spend reading this book toward your leadership mastery goal. That's excellent. However, I urge you also to read more leadership books and articles, take leadership courses, study successful leaders, take on new leadership challenges, ask questions, solicit feedback, and work with a mentor and/or a leadership coach. Learn as much as you can about leadership. Keep practicing and learning and growing as a leader. If you do, you will become the best version of yourself, and therefore, inevitably, you will become the best leader you can possibly be.

The ability to learn is arguably the most important quality a leader can have. I've done my best to help you learn about leadership in the following pages. Now, it's up to you. Soak up every bit you can. And who knows? Maybe someday, I will point to you as a shining example of outstanding healthcare leadership in one of my books or articles. I smile at just the thought of that as I sit at my desk and peek out the window on this gray, rainy day in Baltimore.

DR. LAURA HILLS
Baltimore, Maryland

Part 1:

Next-Level Healthcare Leadership

Next-Level Healthcare Leadership Begins with Self-Leadership

"Mastering others is strength. Mastering yourself is true power."
—Lao-Tzu, 500 BCE

Are you committed to leveling up your leadership? You're reading this book, so let's assume that you are, or at least that you are interested in leadership development. That's excellent. But before you go further into what to do and how to do it, let's pause for a moment to consider the importance of committing to next-level leadership. What are all the things that possibly could go wrong or get in your way? Why do so many leaders fail to commit to their own development? And why do so many of those who do make that commitment fail to live up to it?

Improving one's leadership is hard work, with *hard* being the operative word. It requires significant effort. You may discover things about yourself you'd rather not have known. You may not know how to go about improving yourself. Or you may lack the time, support, resources, and perseverance that the effort requires. It's so easy to plateau in one's leadership development when so many other things clamor or scream for your attention. Learning about leadership can help, but becoming a next-level healthcare leader will require much more of you than your good intentions, taking a course, or reading words on a page, even this page.

The place to begin your journey to becoming a next-level leader is with your own self-leadership. That's because becoming the best leader you can be is an inside job. Leadership focuses on how we influence others. Self-leadership, on the other hand, focuses on observing, understanding, and managing ourselves. That has to come first, and often it is the missing ingredient that keeps well-intentioned leaders from leveling up their leadership. Kara Dennison[1] explains, "Think about the inspiring leaders you know in business, politics, or your personal life. What sets them apart is their unchanging ability to motivate and guide themselves. They can do this even when faced with adversity." I've found this to be true, and I'll bet you have too. The most effective, inspiring, and visionary leaders we can think of have known how to lead themselves first, and because they do, they don't get derailed from their goals or their vision.

Are you new to or not well-versed in the concept of self-leadership? If so, this chapter will help. Maike Neuhaus[2] suggests, "We are not born with an instruction booklet, but if we were, I am sure the first chapter would explain the art of self-leadership." In the pages that follow, we will do precisely that. We will explore self-leadership, where the concept originated, its theoretical underpinnings, the behaviors and strategies of self-leadership, and, most importantly, how healthcare administrators, leaders, and managers can become better self-leaders. Dennison says, "Self-leadership influences and directs one's thoughts, behaviors, and actions to achieve desired goals." That may sound simple enough but make no mistake about it: self-leadership is a complex skill that requires strength, resilience, and a willingness to look inward without flinching or putting blinders on. Your ability to become a next-level leader will depend on a strong foundation in self-leadership. That said, let's begin now at the beginning, and understand what self-leadership is and what's behind the concept.

WHAT IS SELF-LEADERSHIP?

Self-leadership is the practice of understanding who we are, identifying our desired experiences and outcomes, and intentionally guiding ourselves toward them. It spans what we do, why we do it, and how we do it. Knowing our strengths and weaknesses is part of self-leadership. So, too, is acting like a grown-up, or acting with a high level of emotional intelligence. But as you'll see, there is much more to it than that.

Charles C. Manz[3] coined the term *self-leadership* in 1983. Manz[4] defined it further in 1986 as "a comprehensive self-influence perspective that concerns leading oneself toward performance of naturally motivating tasks as well as managing oneself to do work that must be done but is not naturally motivating." Some scholars back in the 1980s did not readily embrace the validity of Manz's concept or recognize its utility in practical settings. Nonetheless, Manz and Henry Sims[5] soldiered on and developed the insight in 1991 that self-leadership is a prerequisite for effective and authentic team leadership. Finally, more than 15 years later, in 2008, the team of Birdi, *et al.,*[6] concluded an important longitudinal study that found that more autonomous, self-leading workers are more productive, whether they are leaders or serve in other roles. That work gave strong empirical evidence to support the validity of Manz's self-leadership concept.

After Manz's first mention of self-leadership, discussion and examination of the concept remained predominantly in organizational leadership and management literature and contexts. Most people did not use it in their everyday vernacular. In 2019, however, Marieta Du Plessis[7] acknowledged the opportunity to complement Manz's concept of self-leadership with insights from positive psychology research, offering the following definition: "Positive self-leadership refers to the capacity to identify and apply one's signature strengths to initiate, maintain, or sustain self-influencing behaviors." Du Plessis emphasized the importance of value-based self-inspiration and self-goal setting in the self-leadership journey. The broader application of self-leadership becomes evident when we consider Du Plessis's definition. Today, self-leadership is widely accepted both in the literature and in common practice.

THEORIES THAT GROUND SELF-LEADERSHIP

Self-leadership's early definitions were based on three central theories:

1. **Self-control theory:** Charles S. Carver and Michael F. Scheier[8] suggested in 1981 that self-control is synonymous with self-management and self-regulation. It is important to note that, especially in the early literature, the terms *self-leadership* and *self-management* often were used interchangeably. Self-management now is considered to be a necessary but not entirely encompassing element of self-leadership in that it refers simply to the internally regulated management and execution of tasks (i.e., addressing the *how* of an action). Neuhaus explains, "In this case, the choice of the task itself and the underlying reason for the choice are externally regulated." In contrast, self-leadership includes an internally regulated choice, value alignment, and execution of the chosen activity (i.e., addressing the *how,* but also, the *what* and the *why).*

2. **Social cognitive theory:** Self-leaders do not operate in a vacuum. Social cognitive theory maintains that portions of an individual's knowledge acquisition can be directly related to observing others within their

environment. Albert Bandura[9] suggested in 1986 that social cognitive theory acknowledges the triadic interaction between our thoughts, our behaviors, and the sociopolitical environment in which we operate.

3. **Self-determination theory:** Self-determination theory describes the reciprocity between human motivation and a purposeful life. Edward Deci and Richard Ryan[10] suggested in 1985 that the theory highlights the role of internally regulated and intrinsic motivation as a driver behind self-leadership behaviors.

Self-leadership theory also plays well with at least two other widely accepted theories. The first is Abraham Maslow's hierarchy of needs, which, like self-leadership, focuses on one's intrinsic needs, particularly self-actualization. The second is Daniel Goleman's[11] emotional intelligence theory. The self-management and self-awareness components of self-leadership also are two pillars of the four pillars in Goleman's theory. (The other two are social awareness and relationship management.)

10 BENEFITS OF SELF-LEADERSHIP

Self-leadership is critical to next-level leadership because you will need it to accomplish your professional goals and become the best leader possible. Here are 10 of the most important benefits of self-leadership:

1. **Increased efficiency and productivity.** Self-leaders are masterful at prioritizing their work tasks. Dennison says that they learn how to "limit distractions and stay laser-focused" on their goals.

2. **Increased motivation.** Self-leaders adjust their goals to make them more personally appealing. They align their goals to their values and self-concept, which, in turn, makes them more motivating. Self-leaders also understand how to harness their willpower, which Neuhaus says is "a finite resource" but one that can be cultivated through self-leadership.

3. **Mental toughness.** Self-leaders are not squeamish about facing hard realities about themselves, and they are not wimps when trying to push through obstacles. They are tough and learn how to recover from setbacks and continue to strive toward their goals. Dennison says that the unwavering drive and mental toughness of self-leaders are infectious and that they will inspire followers to "up their game."

4. **Better planning.** High-performance planning requires leaders to ask themselves how they can perform optimally. Neuhaus says that

self-leadership requires "a particular form of planning, goal setting, and intention forming" beyond the tasks at hand.

5. **Stronger relationships.** Colleagues and followers regard the self-leaders among them as team players who are reliable and competent. They trust and respect self-leaders and know that they can count on them, which Dennison says is "the bedrock of high-performing, cohesive organizations."

6. **Greater self-compassion.** Self-compassion is treating oneself with the same care, love, and respect that you would give to a struggling close friend. It is a key ingredient in self-leadership. Neuhaus says, "Research shows that contrary to the popular belief that self-compassion leads to complacency, it actually increases motivation" among self-leaders.

7. **Better control.** Self-leadership will help you guide your actions, which will bring purpose to your leadership. Dennison says, "It allows you to take complete ownership of your life to make choices that truly match your strengths and aspirations." By mastering self-leadership, you will become the "author of your own story," Dennison says, rather than a passive player controlled by and reacting to external forces.

8. **Higher emotional intelligence.** Self-leadership skills will enable you to see yourself and your employees through the lens of increased emotional intelligence. Dennison suggests that a self-leader also is better equipped to "set boundaries, communicate expectations, and leverage team strengths."

9. **Better "bad day" recovery.** Bad days will occur less frequently when you lead yourself first. And when bad days do happen, self-leaders will be equipped with the skills they need to contain, manage, and minimize the bad experience.

10. **More balance.** Leaders' struggles, personality, and life aren't checked at the door when they walk into the healthcare organization each day. Self-leaders are better equipped to handle whatever happens both in their work and personal life, and to keep personal problems from spilling into their work.

OBSTACLES TO SELF-LEADERSHIP

Self-leadership requires self-awareness — the powerful combination of the will and the skill to see ourselves as we are. That's a huge obstacle for most of us. Tasha Eurich[12] explains, "95% of people think they are self-aware but only 10–15% actually are … On a good day, 80% of us are lying to ourselves about whether we're lying to ourselves." Why do so many of us lack self-awareness? Eurich offers several possible explanations:

- **Denial.** Some of us have become masterful at denying who we are and what we want because we have molded ourselves to fit others' expectations.
- **Avoidance.** Some of us find it hard to confront who we are and what we truly want. Or we can discover unpleasant experiences or things about ourselves, or others, that we'd rather not think about. It can be painful to shed light on these aspects of our lives, so we avoid doing so.
- **Poor feedback.** We may hold a powerful position, and the people we lead may not be honest with us. Or we may discount the feedback we receive because it conflicts with another reality of ourselves that we prefer.
- **Devaluing self-awareness.** Leaders generally are rewarded for results. Unfortunately, Eurich says, the quest for those results causes many leaders to misconceive self-awareness as a "soft skill" to develop in their spare time. However, Eurich warns, self-awareness should be front and center because it is "paramount to your success."
- **Leaders need two kinds of self-awareness.** These are internal self-awareness (understanding yourself from the inside out) and external self-awareness (understanding how people see us). While it may seem like these two kinds of self-awareness must be equally present in us, Eurich's research suggests that they are not. In fact, they operate independently from one another, Eurich says, adding, "Having one type of self-awareness and not the other can have some serious risks."

Most people don't spend a lot of time and energy working to improve their self-awareness. Unfortunately, those of us who do often choose a counterproductive method for going about it. We ask ourselves *why* something has happened, for example, "Why am I so upset about this?" Eurich warns, "*Why* questions tend to set off a ruminative spiral of thinking — single-minded fixation on our fears, shortcomings, and the bad things that happen to us which often turns off the rational processing portion of the brain." *Why* questions also can be misleading and, in some cases, dangerous for our mental health and well-being. Eurich suggests that we swap *why* questions for *what* questions. That will give us better answers, increase our self-awareness, and make us happier and more productive. For example, instead of asking, "Why didn't I get that promotion?" that we ask ourselves, "What can I do differently next time? What can I learn from this experience? What useful feedback can I get from this? What patterns can I uncover from what happened? What haven't I tried yet? And what is different now than it was before?"

Eurich also suggests that we will become more self-aware when we are discerning about who we ask for feedback. Eurich suggests soliciting feedback only from those who have our best interest at heart and who are willing to be "brutally honest" with us, and that we avoid those who are threatened by us or who "have their own issues." Eurich adds, "Don't ask questions that are too open-ended." Rather, confine feedback questions to specific goals and activities. Eurich says, "It's easy to look at the statistics and say, 'We're all doomed to live in a delusional world forever and ever.' But [what's] abundantly clear in all of our empirical research … is just how learnable and developable self-awareness really is." Ultimately, Eurich wants these findings to be a message of hope and says, "Most of us have a lot more work to do than we think, but if we are courageous enough and skilled enough and choose the right approach, we can make huge improvements and therefore improve pretty much every area of our lives."

15 COGNITIVE AND BEHAVIORAL SELF-LEADERSHIP STRATEGIES

While there is significant research in the broad subject of positive psychology, we will find relatively fewer studies of self-leadership. Neuhaus says, "There is still a general lack of self-leadership models and guiding frameworks…." Therefore, Neuhaus suggests, it may be helpful instead to focus on self-leadership strategies.

Following are 15 cognitive and behavioral strategies to help you reach the next level in your self-leadership. As you read about them, consider which ones are your strengths and which may be potentially holding you back or interfering with your leadership. Then, develop a short list of those to work on first. Recognize your preferred learning style and identify books, courses, coaches, therapists, study groups, mentors, and other resources that can help you improve.

1. **Become more self-aware**. As we've seen, Eurich's research found that most of us aren't as self-aware as we think we are. At a minimum, Neuhaus suggests, self-awareness includes knowing one's personality

traits, personal strengths and weaknesses, values, talents, and interests. Fortunately, everyone can learn to be more self-aware. Journaling, mindfulness practices, personality and skill tests, feedback from others, mentoring, coaching, and therapy are useful tools for becoming more self-aware.

2. **Identify desired experiences.** Most of us strive for happiness. However, our ability to predict what will make us happy is poorer than we think. Therefore, it is important for us to understand insights from happiness research as well as how to align our goals or desired experiences with our values. Doing so will enable us to identify opportunities and to live and lead in line with our values.

3. **Keep thoughts constructive.** We like to think of ourselves as cognitive, rational beings who make thoughtful choices. However, much of what happens inside our minds is anything but rational. Cognitive dissonance is an example of this. Another is that our ability to reason is inhibited when we feel stressed or are experiencing the fight-or-flight response. If you are prone to destructive thoughts, especially when things go wrong, you'll want to stop the negative self-talk and dysfunctional beliefs that are holding you back. (Examples: "I'm bad at this kind of work," "I'll never get everything done on time," or "I have no patience.")

4. **Plan and set goals.** Self-leaders know how to break bigger dreams into manageable milestones and then optimize each milestone into a goal. The goal-setting process includes SMART goals, contingency plans, documentation, accountability, and positive rewards for achieving goals.

5. **Keep your ego in check.** When you are in a position of leadership, especially a high position, it's easy to start believing your own press. However, Initiative One[13] warns, "The arrogant leader is not someone we want to follow. That's a leader who alienates their team, causes conflict, and incites drama, none of which is healthy for an organization." Effective self-leaders remain humble and recognize that leadership is about influence and impact, not authority. Learn to recognize the value of the team around you and reap the rewards of a team that respects your character and your willingness to work alongside them to reach a common goal.

6. **Optimize your motivation.** Self-leaders know how to adjust their goals to make them more personally appealing. They know how to align

their values with their self-concept. They also know how to optimize their motivation, for example, by using visualization and celebrating their successes.

7. **Develop confidence.** Most leaders doubt themselves from time to time. Initiative One warns, "The more you succeed, the more you're likely to wrestle with those feelings that you're not really who people think you are." Unfortunately, an ongoing lack of confidence can cripple your ability to inspire, motivate, and serve your team. Effective self-leaders unpack and examine their doubts to see the truth beneath them. They adjust their thinking so they can say to themselves, with confidence, "I am enough." Or, if they find that they are not enough for their leadership role, they identify what specifically is missing and work to improve those skills.

8. **Harness your ecosystem.** Do we learn our behavior mostly through our life circumstances, experiences, and the people around us? Or is our behavior mostly innate and inherited? Neuhaus says, "These days, scientists agree that the answer isn't usually found at either extreme end of the scale." Instead, we know that both nature and nurture influence the way we act. Harnessing your ecosystem is about proactively seeking support for your goals in the social, organizational, community, political, and physical environment in which you live and work.

9. **Deal with conflict.** Conflict is part of life and part of leadership. Initiative One says, "Effective leadership means embracing the fact that conflict has to happen — but that there's a way for conflict to be constructive. It means tough conversations. Sometimes it hurts." Self-leaders know how to avoid conflict when possible but also how to deal with it effectively when it is not.

10. **Self-regulate.** Effective self-leaders possess the ability to think before they act. They know how to manage or redirect their disruptive impulses and moods. Leaders who can regulate their emotions have greater honesty, which makes them more trustworthy to those they lead. However, self-regulation doesn't mean that leaders must repress or suppress their emotions. Scott Jeffrey[14] explains, "While sometimes we do need to suppress our initial emotional response in a situation, ultimately, we need to work with our emotional landscape so our feelings don't negatively influence our thoughts, attitudes, and behaviors." Self-regulation means being flexible and open to change. Jeffrey adds

that being okay with ambiguity is another defining characteristic of a self-regulated, mature self-leader.

11. **Recognize and release your anxiety and stress.** We all know that leadership can be stressful. Unfortunately, Initiative One says, "The fear, the self-doubt, the cascade of problems and expectations that leaders often face — it can all add up to a level of stress that puts your ability to lead in danger." Effective self-leaders learn to recognize the first inklings of their own stress. They also know their triggers and how they typically react to stress. They understand their thoughts and behaviors and develop healthy techniques for reframing their challenges and releasing their stress.

12. **Become more visionary.** You may think that some leaders are visionary and others aren't. However, everyone has the ability to be a visionary, and you can develop visionary skills. Sarah Kristenson[15] suggests that you learn to brainstorm and not overthink things. Rather, let your mind freely imagine what you would want to happen if everything were possible. Then, most importantly, Kristenson says, involve "the emotion you seek to feel in reality." Engage your five senses. Notice the tastes, smells, sights, textures (from feeling), and sounds that you will experience if your vision becomes reality. Be specific. For example, if you're thinking about how great it would be if you were to build a new building for your healthcare organization, imagine how you will feel when you walk through that building, how it will sound when you hear your own footsteps in the corridor, and what it will look like when you see the faces of the employees who will work in that building or the patients who will receive their healthcare services there. Imagine the smell of the products the custodians will use to wax the floors, the scent of the fresh flowers that will be delivered to the reception desk, and the aroma of the fresh coffee brewing in the cafeteria when you arrive at work in the morning. This level of sensory detail will make your vision real to you, which in turn, will ignite your passion. (See Chapter 3, "How to Become a More Visionary Leader," for more information on this topic.)

13. **Stay motivated.** We all have bad days and blah days. Initiative One explains, "It's easy to dwell on what isn't working and let it sap your energy. And that can be especially tough for a leader to work through because everyone's looking to you to be a cheerleader — a champion of forward momentum, enthusiasm, and the 'get it done' attitude."

Unfortunately, the expectation of you to be the chief motivating officer for your followers can be one of the most personally demotivating factors you deal with, Initiative One warns. Nonetheless, your team will look to you to lead, guide, and inspire them. Self-leaders recognize when their motivation is waning and have the skills they need to ramp it back up. They practice gratitude, set deadlines, create rewards for themselves, and remind themselves often why they do what they do. They recognize the first signs of demotivation or burnout and seek help when they need it.

14. **Cultivate grit.** Can you bounce back quickly from setbacks and power on when things get tough? Ashley Elizabeth[16] says, "Research indicates that the ability to be gritty — to stick with things that are important to you and bounce back from failure — is an essential component of success." Persevering, even against the odds, is about learning how to sit with your darkness and soften into the discomfort. Self-leadership may require you to adjust your view of failure so that it doesn't devastate and derail you. You may need to learn how to dig deep inside you for strength when things get hard. Neuhaus adds, "Grit is what can, more reliably than any other characteristic, distinguish the successful from the non-successful."

15. **Make hard decisions.** Overthinking and fear can get in the way of making good decisions. Initiative One explains, "You fear making the wrong decision. All the risks and 'what ifs' that can stop you in your tracks — from economic changes or market shifts, to the specter of job cuts or restructuring, to global crises." However, fear left unchecked can interfere with what you need to do and undermine your leadership. Initiative One says, "Leadership is full of tough decisions. Some gut-wrenching. It's the leader's job to stare those tough decisions down."

HOW TO DEVELOP A NEXT-LEVEL LEADERSHIP MINDSET

Exceptional leaders don't settle for the *status quo*. They continuously seek improvement by exploring strategies to adapt and refine their leadership plans. They leverage the lessons they've learned, from both their successes and their failures. As Monique Valcour[17] succinctly puts it, "Leading well requires a continuous journey of personal development." While most of us know this, a lot of people who occupy leadership roles sidestep the long and challenging work of deepening self-insight. Instead, they chase after the latest and greatest management tools, Valcour says, preferably the "'quick 'n' easy'" kind. For example, Valcour says, they may cling to personality type assessments that reduce employees to a few simplistic behavioral tendencies. Or they may attend short implicit bias workshops that do little more than serve as a Band-aid solution for systemic discrimination. These tactics are not inherently bad and may, in fact, be useful when combined with other efforts. However, they are not in and of themselves a shortcut to effective leadership. Rather, Valcour warns, they are a mechanistic approach that is more often a "dead end." Unfortunately, turning to what appear to be quick and easy fixes can misdirect leaders' attention away from the harder work of understanding and strengthening the link between their own behavior and employee outcomes.

As a leader, you must be careful not to search in vain for a magic tool or resource to help you lead others. Do remain open to new ideas and resources, of course. However, also think in terms of creating new practices and skill sets to increase your leadership capability. To do this, you'll need to develop your own leadership learning program customized to your specific learning needs and goals. Tools can be part of that effort, but none will take the place of your own fearless introspection, quality feedback from trusted individuals, and your continuous, committed efforts to change your behaviors and mindset to achieve greater leadership effectiveness. Like all next-level leaders, you must be willing to identify and challenge your assumptions, biases, and behaviors, even when doing so becomes humbling or even painful. You must be willing to focus fully on the meaningful outcomes that will make a difference to your healthcare organization and the people in it, but also to *you*. Authentic leaders believe in what they do and are fulfilled by their work. If you don't feel that way, you need to figure out why.

Your first thought as you consider your leadership development program may be to improve upon your weaknesses. That makes perfect sense, because so much of our education and self-development efforts focus on our mistakes and shortcomings. Certainly, there is merit in overcoming a powerful weakness that may be holding us back or crippling us. But what if we think about a next-level leadership mindset in a different, more positive way?

Tom Rath and Barry Conchie[18] argue that the best leaders invest in their personal *strengths* while building a diverse team to fill in for their weaknesses. Using a strengths-based approach to leadership, they say, each individual contributes unique strengths to create a well-rounded team. For strengths-based leadership work, though, leaders must become objectively and realistically aware of their own strengths. In fact, Rath and Conchie say, "Without an awareness of your strengths, it's almost impossible for you to lead effectively." Next-level leaders may study other leaders, famous or otherwise, for inspiration and encouragement. However, they don't try to make themselves into an exact copy of another leader because, as Rath and Conchie point out, "Serious problems can occur when we think we need to be exactly like the leaders we admire." Next-level leaders find ways to retain their "natural element" (i.e., their authenticity and strengths) in their leadership, Rath and Conchie say, adding that trying to fashion yourself into another Lincoln, Churchill, or Gandhi "practically eliminates the chances of success."

You have stepped into and occupy your leadership role for a reason. Perhaps you aspired to lead others and let that be known to people who had the potential to influence hiring and promotion decisions. Perhaps you studied leadership and gained a degree, certificate, or other relevant credential. Perhaps leadership was thrust upon you. However you became a leader, one or more people in your healthcare organization recognized your strengths and entrusted you with your position so you can apply those strengths to the enormous responsibility of leading others. The strengths they saw in you *are* in you, even if you don't see them or know what they are, even if you take them for granted. Do you recognize and appreciate your strengths? Are you using them as well as you can? Are you nurturing and building your strengths so they don't collect dust and atrophy? Remember: your strengths are what make you *you*. They may be the best part of you, and most likely, they are the best part of your leadership. Therefore, they are the place for you to begin your effort to become a next-level leader. Your first step will be to treasure and protect your strengths and make them the centerpiece of your own next-level leadership mentality.

There is more to learn about leadership than you can learn in a hundred lifetimes. In scholarly literature alone, there are more than 1500 definitions of leadership. My own doctoral dissertation reviewed dozens of leadership theories — the great man theory, situational leadership, servant leadership, trait theories, behavioral theories, participative theories, contingency theories, transactional theories, transformational theories, and more. There will always be new leadership studies, theories, and frameworks, as well as new leadership articles, courses, books, webinars, podcasts, blog posts, study groups, tools, instruments, mentors, coaches, and gurus. Some leadership concepts will turn out to be short-lived fads, whereas others will have more staying power. It's not always easy to know which is which. You cannot spend all your time studying everything there is to know about leadership or you'll never be able to get anything else done. On top of that, you're already in your leadership role, and unless today is your first day in it, you've already established yourself as a leader. The people you lead have an opinion of you, and expectations of you, and it may take work and time to change them. That means that you've got to start your next-level journey where you are, and they are, and be realistic about what you can learn and how quickly you can accomplish what you set out to do. The good news is that you *can* learn more about leadership and you *can* improve and change. Just don't try to soar too high too quickly or like Icarus, your wings may melt.

Self-leadership is an inside-out approach to leadership development: it begins with your commitment to improve and grow, and your willingness to work on yourself, warts and all. Be selective and focus on efforts that are likely to have the biggest impact on your leadership. The more you know, the more skills you develop, and the more self-aware you become, the more you will have to give. The people you lead will notice the changes in you and respond differently — and better — to you, even if you do nothing else. Matthew Kelly[19] wrote: "You were born to become the-best-version-of-yourself. This is your essential purpose. Embrace this one solitary truth and it will change your life more than anything you have ever learned."

Herein lies the essence of a next-level leadership mindset. The goal of self-leadership is simply to become the best version of yourself. We can fill an enormous library with the why's and the how's of leadership and run out of shelf space. Don't get so bogged down in the study and practice of leadership that you lose sight of what you're ultimately trying to accomplish. Hold your strengths dear. Treasure, nurture, and build on them. And remember that if what you are setting out to do were easy, everyone would do it. Leadership is hard work. Self-leadership is hard work, too. It can be unpleasant at times. Look for the grace in the challenges, setbacks, and frustrations. Forgive yourself for past leadership transgressions and for making mistakes as you learn. Most importantly, keep going. You will hit times in your self-leadership journey when you want to give up. That's when your grit comes into play. Most of us are a lot stronger and tougher than we think we are.

As you can see, next-level leadership is an advanced topic. What you gain personally in the pursuit of your own leadership excellence will be just as valuable as what you accomplish in your leadership role. Self-leadership requires that you examine your life — who you are, what you believe, your strengths and shortcomings, what you have to offer. It's about becoming the best version of yourself as a leader but also as a person. It's so easy to stagnate, to drift through life — so easy to put our own development on the back burner when we are busy and tired and pulled in 17 directions at once. But as Socrates famously said, "The unexamined life is not worth living."

Next-level leaders lead examined and worthwhile lives. In the end, there will be no better use of your time, energy, and talents than that. How do you become a next-level leader? Become a self-leader first, keep leading yourself, and your leadership will be well on its way to the next level.

THE EIGHT C'S OF SELF-LEADERSHIP

Psychotherapist Richard Schwartz,[20] the founder of The Center for Self-Leadership (now called IFS Institute), developed a concept of the "Self" that's different from the rest of mainstream psychology. "Self" in this context, Schwartz explains, doesn't mean only our sense of self or ego. Instead, Schwartz refers to our true Self (capital "S") as an organizing principle within us. Jeffrey says, "This Self already possesses all the qualities we seek to develop or integrate to become a mature adult, including confidence, openness, and compassion." The ultimate goal of self-leadership is to navigate through our various parts, tendencies, and prior conditioning so our Self can shine forth.

Schwartz developed a list of eight one-word qualities of self-leadership, all beginning with the letter C. Max Freedman[21] says that developing these eight qualities can help you to become "the self-leader you know you can be."

1. **Creativity:** The best leaders are imaginative. They come up with out-of-the-box solutions to both new and old problems. Freedman says, "That's creativity in a nutshell: bringing something to life that wasn't there before." In Schwartz's concept of "Self," we often access peak creative experiences (flow states) where we become fully absorbed in what we're doing, accompanied by feelings of enjoyment, spontaneity, and inner freedom.

2. **Clarity:** Self-leaders learn to see situations as they are, without allowing themselves to skew the picture to make it prettier. Jeffrey says, "Clarity gives us the ability to pierce through distortions (delusions) from extreme beliefs, emotions, and preconditioning to perceive situations accurately." Clarity provides us with greater objectivity because we become objectively aware of our personal biases without being influenced by them.

3. **Calmness:** Leadership can be stressful even if you love what you do. In the most overwhelming moments, calmness is the hallmark of a self-leader. Freedman says, "It's on you to ground yourself when stressors emerge, and the same is true when your team is overloaded." Learn how to settle yourself and address your team's concerns and the path from start to finish will feel less chaotic and cluttered. Jeffrey adds, "With this calmness, you're able to manage challenging life situations in less automatic (preconditioned) and extreme ways."

4. **Curiosity:** Curiosity helps self-leaders to inquire into their true nature. With curiosity, they can learn about themselves and others without judgment. Jeffrey says, "Here, criticalness gives way to a sense of wonder, a quality Maslow observed in self-actualizing individuals." When leaders lean into and nurture their own curiosity, new ideas and innovative solutions will be more likely to come to them.

5. **Confidence:** Self-confidence gives leaders the ability to take risks and to handle whatever is thrown at them. Jeffrey says, "Confidence comes after having worked through previous traumas, setbacks, and failures." Confidence also will help leaders to feel comfortable in their own skin, and less fearful of making mistakes. Freedman adds, "Confidence is the soil from which the flowers of excellent team leadership grow."

6. **Connectedness:** You'll be much more likely to be a great leader if you feel a meaningful connection with your team and healthcare organization. Freedman suggests, "Take the time to discover the parts of your

organization's mission and vision statements that resonate with you. Get to know the people you work with, too." You'll wind up building bonds that make everyone — yourself included — enthusiastic about sharing ideas, collaborating, and pushing together toward the finish line. In a connected state, you will be able to relax your ego defenses and your need to control others. Jeffrey says, "This sense of connectedness allows you to navigate through life circumstances in a more intuitive, free-flowing manner."

7. **Courage:** Courage enables leaders to take responsibility for their actions and to make amends when they make mistakes. It gives leaders the strength to face external challenges and threats. Jeffrey says, "Courage is a vital quality for doing inner work, facing our shadow, and embracing one's hero's journey...."

8. **Compassion:** Compassion breeds deeper understanding and allows leaders to appreciate themselves and others without feeling the need to fix, change, or judge anything. Jeffrey explains, "Many of us approach change with self-criticism, which ensures we never change." When we have compassion for ourselves and others, we can learn and grow with understanding, kindness, and self-acceptance.

Julia Sullivan and IFS Institute[22] provide a simple free assessment tool called *The 8 C's of Self-Leadership Wheel* that can help you evaluate how much "Self" you have available to you right now: https://foundationifs.org/images/banners/pdf/The_8_Cs_of_Self_Leadership_Wheel.pdf

Part 2:

Advanced Topics For Healthcare Administrators, Leaders, and Managers

CHAPTER 1

Assessing and Changing Work Culture

Most healthcare employees readily agree that every healthcare organization has its own unique culture. However, culture as a concept is difficult to define. You can't see or touch a healthcare organization's culture. It's hard to describe succinctly what a culture is and isn't. And you and your employees may experience your organization's culture in significantly different ways. That's because any organization's culture is likely to be interpreted differently by diverse individuals. Unique events in people's lives affect how they act and interact with information, policies, and one another. Edgar H. Schein[1] suggests, "We recognize cultural differences at the ethnic or national level but find them puzzling at the group, organizational, or occupational level."

Nonetheless, you can and probably do see many physical manifestations of your healthcare organization's culture every day. In some ways, culture can be described as the overall environment that surrounds you in your healthcare organization. But more than that, and whether you realize it or not, your healthcare organization's culture powerfully shapes your employees' work enjoyment, experiences, relationships, and processes.

Think of your healthcare organization's culture as its unique personality. In a person, the personality is composed of the values, beliefs, underlying assumptions, interests, experiences, upbringing, and habits that shape and influence behavior. Likewise, in a healthcare organization, culture is made up of the values, beliefs, underlying assumptions, attitudes, and behaviors shared by the people who work in the organization. The result of a healthcare organization's culture is a set of behaviors that is motivated by rules for working together. Many of these are usually unspoken and unwritten.

Your healthcare organization's culture comprises all of the life experiences each member of the team brings to the organization. However, your organizational culture probably was influenced most by the people in your organization who are or were in leadership positions — your organization's founder, physicians, and key administrators — because they most likely shaped your healthcare organization's mission, vision, decision-making, policies, and planning strategies. Nevertheless, each member of the healthcare team contributes positively or negatively to your healthcare organization's culture and is in a position to deviate from or perpetuate the status quo.

HOW CULTURE IS EXPRESSED IN A HEALTHCARE ORGANIZATION

A healthcare organization's culture is not expressed as a hard number or a line item on the bottom of a report. However, it is a key ingredient that influences patient retention figures, collection ratios, production reports, and other important healthcare organization management data. Kim S. Cameron and Robert E. Quinn[2] suggest, "Most organizational scholars and observers now recognize that organizational culture has a powerful effect on the performance and long-term effectiveness of organizations."

Perhaps the best way to understand a healthcare organization's culture is to look at the ways that it may be expressing itself in the organization. For example, a healthcare organization's culture may be expressed through the employees' language, decision-making, symbols, stories and legends, uniforms, posture, facial expressions, meetings, and daily work practices. The objects chosen to grace a desk can tell you a lot about how employees view and participate in a healthcare organization's culture. Likewise, a healthcare organization's bulletin board content, patient newsletter, brochures, website, e-mail, and voice mail; the interaction among employees at staff meetings; and the way in which people do or do not collaborate speak volumes about a healthcare organization's culture. So, too, do the apportionment of space within the organization, wall décor, wall and flooring colors, furniture styles, magazines in the reception area(s), lighting, cleanliness, hours, salaries, bonuses, and even the assignment of staff parking spaces in the parking lot.

When healthcare organizations are examined from a cultural viewpoint, attention is drawn to various aspects of daily life that historically have been ignored or understudied. Joanne Martin[3] suggests, these include, " . . . the stories people tell to newcomers to explain 'how things are done around here,' the ways in which offices are arranged and personal items are or are not displayed, jokes people tell, the working atmosphere (hushed and luxurious or dirty and noisy), the relations among people (affectionate in some areas of an office and obviously angry and perhaps competitive in another place), and so on."

Your healthcare organization's culture may be strong or weak. If it is strong, chances are that most of the people working in your organization agree on its culture. If it is weak, the employees probably don't agree. Sometimes, a weak healthcare organization culture can be the result of many subcultures, or the shared values, assumptions, and behaviors of a subset of the organization. In other words, each department in your organization may have its own subculture. Within departments, the staff and the managers may each have their own culture. These departmental cultures may or may not support your overall organizational culture.

Ideally, your healthcare organization culture should support a positive, productive environment for you and the members of your team. However, it is important to remember that happy healthcare organization employees are not necessarily productive employees. From a leadership point of view, it is important to focus on those aspects of healthcare organization culture that will create a happy and positive work environment and will support and increase the organization's productivity and quality of care.

HOW TO ASSESS YOUR HEALTHCARE ORGANIZATION'S CULTURE

While you may admire and learn from the culture of another healthcare organization or another organization, you cannot duplicate that culture 100% in your healthcare organization. Ann Rhodes and Nancy Shepherdson[4] suggest, "Great cultures can't be replicated or copied; you must launch your own based on values you and your people determine are best for your organization." Therefore, while your healthcare organization's culture may share some of the qualities of other organizations, it will have its own distinct flavor and be uniquely yours.

You can obtain a picture of your current healthcare organization culture in several ways. However, before venturing forward, be sure that you're ready to take a long hard look at your culture. Your assessment may make you happy, puzzled, sad, or disappointed. However, whatever you learn from your culture assessment, your culture is what it is. To change your culture, your first step is to understand the culture that already exists.

It is generally a lot easier to assess another organization's culture than your own. When you work in an organization daily, many of the manifestations of your culture are likely to become invisible to you. You must be willing to take yourself out of the equation and look at your organization objectively. That means that you must become an impartial observer of your culture. Look at everything and everyone with the eye of an outsider. Pretend that you are a cultural anthropologist observing a group you've never seen before. Observe and make note of emotions, objects, artifacts, and interactions among people. Pay particular attention to:

- How space is allocated.
- What is posted or displayed on the walls.
- Other signage both inside and outside the organization.
- Objects displayed on desks or in other work areas.
- How common areas are furnished, decorated, and used.
- The tone and frequency of emails and other written messages.
- The tone, frequency, and volume of telephone calls.
- How staff members interact with one another and with patients.
- Sensory observations such as smells, sound volume, and textures.
- The general atmosphere of the reception area(s).
- Employee dress, hygiene, age, diversity, and other characteristics.
- Employee behaviors such as posture, facial expressions, and pace.
- Office location.
- Neatness and cleanliness.

Also notice what is not being said or done. For example, if no one in your organization smiles or mentions something that you think is important, that's an observation worth noting. Finally, try one or more of these three effective techniques for assessing organizational culture:

1. **Culture walk:** Step out of your usual role and literally take a walk around your healthcare organization as an observer. Look for the physical signs of your culture. You may have to take repeated walks, on different days and at different times, to get the most complete picture of your culture.

2. **Culture interviews:** Interview your employees individually or in small groups to get their insights about your healthcare organization's culture. Use indirect questions such as those suggested in the bonus feature at the end of this chapter. Observe and make note of your staff's behaviors and patterns of interaction throughout the interviews. Who speaks the most? Who speaks the least? Are you noticing any communication patterns?

3. **Culture surveys:** Craft your survey after you have completed your culture walk and/or interviews to get more detailed information. Provide space on your surveys for your employees to elaborate on their responses.

IDENTIFY YOUR DESIRED HEALTHCARE ORGANIZATION CULTURE

With a clear assessment of your current culture, you are now ready to identify your culture strengths and where you may be falling short. Examine your organization's mission, vision, and values. What vision does your healthcare organization have for its future, and how must your culture change to achieve that vision? Work with your colleagues to answer these questions:

- Where do we see our healthcare organization in 10 years? Who will be our patients? How does this vision mesh with the overall demographic trends predicted for our community?
- What are the five most important values we would like to see represented in our healthcare organization culture, now and in the future?
- Are these values compatible with our current healthcare organization culture? Do they exist now? If so, where? If not, why not?
- What needs to happen so that we can create a culture that supports where our organization wants to be?
- Do we have support for creating cultural change? Will our organization's leadership support the change both verbally and behaviorally? Do we have the funds and other resources we will need to change our culture?
- Do we have sufficient training to achieve the desired culture change? Are we able to provide training to communicate new expectations and to teach new behaviors?

WHY CHANGING CULTURE IS SO DIFFICULT

Before forging ahead, keep in mind that a culture change may be one of the toughest challenges a healthcare organization will ever take on.

Culture change requires people to be uncomfortable, to break out of long-established routines, and to change their behaviors. It often is difficult for employees to unlearn their old way of doing things, embrace the new ways, and consistently behave differently.

Chances are that your healthcare organization was formed some time back and that it grew and developed over a period of many years. Your healthcare organization culture also was formed during this time, and it probably grew in response to particular needs and values. For example, your current healthcare organization culture may match the style and comfort zone of your organization's founder who may or may not still be working in the organization today. Perhaps your organization's culture meshed well with the expectations of the patients you served at one time in the past. Or perhaps your culture was established and perpetuated by the management style that at one time prevailed in your organization. The organization of your past may be quite different from your organization today, and the individuals who formed the culture may no longer be involved. Nonetheless, the old patterns of thinking and behaving that started long ago may have become cemented in your organization and may be difficult to change today.

In general, employees resist a culture change for one or more of these reasons:

- **They see no need to change.** If your employees don't see the organization as broken, they probably won't see a need to fix it. People usually want and need a compelling reason to undertake a culture change. Financial hardship, the threat of legal action, or other threats to the well-being of the organization and its employees usually get people's attention.
- **The timing seems bad.** Employees may feel that there's too much going on right now for them to step out of their day-to-day concerns to think about larger issues like healthcare organization culture.
- **The change appears to be too costly.** It may seem to employees that it will take too much time, money, or both to justify changing the culture.
- **They don't know how.** The employees in the organization may think that a culture change is a good idea but not know how to change the culture, what to do, in what order, or when.
- **They mistrust the new direction.** The organization's employees may perceive the culture change as too risky, likely to cause a backlash, and

fraught with too many problems. They may feel that changing the culture of the organization could threaten their job security or that more will be expected of them without reward.

When the healthcare organization employees feel secure, realize and recognize that their current culture needs to transform, and understand what to do, they generally will be in support of the culture change. Therefore, it will be important to know what employees are worried about, what they need to move forward, and what feels unclear, murky, frightening, or overwhelming. Then with a combination of persistence, employee involvement, kindness, understanding, and training, it will be possible to change the culture of your healthcare organization.

HOW TO CHANGE CULTURE: 12 FUNDAMENTAL CHANGES

Conventional wisdom suggests that it can take up to seven years to change a work culture. However, it is possible to change a culture more quickly. The key is to change fundamentally the basic work systems and processes that created the organization that you have now. As you measure your success in changing your healthcare organization culture, look at what you accomplish one person at a time. Focus your attention on the success of individuals. By doing so, you will see a wave of optimism unfold as these individuals begin to build your new healthcare organization culture and bring others into the fold.

Below are 12 fundamental changes that can ultimately lead to a more significant change in your healthcare organization culture. Use them to develop and implement your culture change plan.

1. **Make your expectations clear.** Talk with your employees without using threats or coercion. Simply identify what has to change and why, and what is expected of the employees in the organization. Put the emphasis on individuals and on departments in each step. That may mean that what is expected of individuals may vary. However, each employee should understand their unique role and how they fit into a larger collaborative effort to change your culture.

2. **Stop doing things that run counter to your desired culture.** Every day, your existing culture is moving either closer to or further from the

type of culture that you want it to be. Identify systems and behaviors that are clearly moving you in the wrong direction. Make those your priority and focus on them first.

3. **Provide incentives for hard work and performance improvements.** Letting employees know that their behavior is noticed and appreciated can boost morale and change work culture. Establish performance recognition awards and give bonuses to deserving employees to reinforce behaviors that lead to the desired culture change.

4. **Change your compensation system.** Is your existing compensation system perpetuating your existing culture? For example, does the way you make decisions about salaries and raises affect the degree to which staff members bring up problems to their administrator, assist with putting improvements in place, provide service to your patients, and detect and correct deficiencies? Employees are constantly evaluating what they and others are earning against the daily efforts they are making. Change your compensation system to reward the employees who support your desired work culture.

5. **Reward success in other ways.** Title changes, parking spaces, office locations, and other perks linked closely to culture change successes also can ensure the long-term success of your culture change.

6. **Align work systems with the desired culture.** Review your systems for promotions, staff scheduling, and task assignments to be sure that they support your desired culture. For example, don't reward individual performance if the requirements of your desired organizational culture specify teamwork.

7. **Practice effective communication.** Keep employees informed about the culture change process. Be explicit about what is expected. Be sure your employees see meetings, postings, and other communications as valuable.

8. **Create value statements for each employee.** Have employees put your mission, vision, and values into words that state their impact on each of their particular jobs. For example, a front-desk receptionist's value statement might be: "I live the value of quality patient care by listening attentively whenever a patient speaks to me in person or on the telephone." This exercise gives employees a way to relate your desired culture to their specific job duties.

9. **Review your physical structure.** Does the way you apportion and use your physical space support your desired culture? For example,

if your desired culture is one of trust and confidentiality for every patient, then your space must support that. Can your receptionist speak to patients in confidence without being overheard by others in your reception area? If not, you will need to change your structure to support your desired culture.

10. **Change your hiring process.** Is your current hiring process designed to help you attract, identify, and retain people who think and behave in a manner that is consistent with your desired culture? If not, you are moving further from your change goals with each new hire. Change the way you recruit, interview, and hire your employees so you can employ individuals who will support your desired culture.

11. **Acknowledge and celebrate success.** As a leader, culture change will be dependent upon your acknowledgement of success. Even a brief moment of one-on-one acknowledgment from you will ensure that your employees know that you noticed what they did and that it was important to you and your organization.

12. **Engage in ongoing constructive dialogue.** Everyone in your health-care organization should feel that their input matters. Establish regular opportunities for your employees to share complaints and suggestions with you and with one another, without fear of reprisal.

HOW HEALTHCARE ORGANIZATION CULTURES ARE FORMED AND PERPETUATED

Before it is possible to change a healthcare organization's culture, it will be helpful for you to understand how any organization's culture is typically formed and perpetuated. Here are three ways:

1. **People shape the culture.** The personalities and experiences of the staff create the culture. For example, if most of the people working in your organization are outgoing, the culture is likely to be open and sociable. If employees display photos depicting your organization's history, your culture is one that values history. If doors are kept open, and few closed-door meetings are held, your culture is unguarded. If negativity about your organization or its administrator is widespread and your employees complain often, a culture of negativity will take hold.

2. **Culture is negotiated.** One person working alone in a vacuum cannot create a culture, and a culture cannot be handed down from on high. The

entire staff must work collaboratively to change the environment, the way work is performed, and the manner in which decisions are made in the organization. That means that culture change must be a process of give and take by all members of the healthcare organization team.

3. **Culture is learned through interaction.** Employees learn to behave in particular ways through rewards and negative consequences that follow their behavior. They learn culture by interacting with one another. Even a job applicant experiences a sense of culture during the interview process. An initial opinion of your culture can be formed as early as the first phone call or visit to your website.

––––––––––––––– **CHAPTER 1 BONUS FEATURE** –––––––––––––––

GREAT QUESTIONS TO ASK IN A CULTURE INTERVIEW OR SURVEY

It is usually difficult for most employees to put their healthcare organization culture into words. Indirect questions will help you elicit the most useful information. Below are examples of indirect questions you can ask during a culture interview or in a culture survey.

- How would you describe the employees who fail in your healthcare organization?
- What is a good question to ask a candidate seeking a job in our healthcare organization?
- Who is a hero in our healthcare organization? Why?
- What is one thing you would most like to change about our healthcare organization?
- What would you tell a friend about our healthcare organization if they were about to start working here?
- How would you describe your relationship with your coworkers?
- What kind of a boss is your boss?
- What television program reminds you most of our healthcare organization? Why?
- Who does most of the talking in our healthcare organization?
- How, if at all, does seniority play a role in our healthcare organization?
- How are decisions made in our healthcare organization?

- On a scale of 1 to 10, with 10 being the highest, what is the stress level in our healthcare organization on most days? What is the stress level on the most challenging days?
- What five adjectives would you use to describe our healthcare organization?

Servant Leadership in the Healthcare Organization

When many of us think of leading a healthcare organization, one of the first things that comes to mind is a traditional hierarchical structure. Alex Lyon[1] explains, "Traditional leadership sees the people lower in the pyramid of leadership, lower in this structure, serving the leaders above them." Traditionally, we may think of leadership as the top position on an organizational chart and as a rank. We assume that leaders, in general, use their power, control, and authority, mixed perhaps with a little bit of persuasion and inspiration, to direct, shape, and drive follower performance. In addition, we may think that the best way to measure leaders' success is by the goals achieved and the output produced. It often comes down to numbers. The Servant Leadership Centre of Canada[2] suggests that we may think that leadership is mostly about leaders — how to recognize and develop them, and how they can use their authority and influence most effectively. As Lyon puts it, traditional leadership is a "boss-centered" approach. Certainly, we've all known, seen, and studied traditional leaders throughout our lives. And, in fact, traditional leadership is alive, well, and still widely used in many organizations today, perhaps even your own.

Servant leadership, on the other hand, focuses neither on leaders' position in a hierarchy nor on their rank, authority, or control. It is a leadership philosophy that, as the name suggests, puts the leader's main emphasis on being of service to others. In this chapter, we will explore servant leadership and consider why and how it can be used effectively in the healthcare organization.

WHAT IS SERVANT LEADERSHIP?

Although the concept of leaders who serve their followers is an old one, the phrase *servant leadership* was coined by Robert K. Greenleaf[3] in 1970. Back then, Greenleaf predicted that his servant leadership concept was not one that most people would embrace readily. He wrote more than 50 years ago, "My thesis, that more servants should emerge as leaders, or should follow only servant-leaders, is not a popular one. It is much more comfortable to go with a less demanding point of view about what is expected of one now." Since then, however, Greenleaf's concept of servant leadership has gained acceptance, momentum, and a great deal of popularity. Edward Tzimas[4] explains that there has been empirical research and evidence to support the idea that leaders should consider servant leadership to "shape their teams and aim toward growth."

Greenleaf argued that the focus of servant leadership should be on others rather than on the self. In fact, self-interest should not motivate servant leadership at all, Greenleaf said. Rather, leadership should come from a higher, more selfless plane of motivation. In addition, Greenleaf suggested, serving others should be the prime motivation for and the very essence of leadership. A. Gregory Stone, Robert F. Russell, and Kathleen Patterson[5] explain, "Servant leaders develop people, helping them to strive and flourish. Servant leaders provide vision; gain credibility and trust from followers; and influence others."

THE POPULARITY OF SERVANT LEADERSHIP

Organizations of all shapes and sizes have adopted Greenleaf's servant leadership framework. According to Ben Lichtenwalner,[6] a list of companies that seek and value servant leaders includes 7-Eleven, Starbucks, Walmart, Marriott International, The Container Store, Chik-Fil-A, Kaiser Permanente, Keller Williams Realty, Nordstrom, Southwest Airlines, Wegmans, Whole Foods, and the U.S. Air Force, Army, Marine Corps, and Navy. Furthermore, among *Fortune* magazine's list of the top 100 companies to work for, 17 were listed as practitioners of servant leadership. That may not sound like that many until you realize that five of *Fortune*'s top 10 companies practice servant leadership. The Servant Leadership Centre of Canada explains, "All 17 of those organizations outperformed the market by over 50%, showing that servant leadership has a real impact on performance."

Servant leadership has gained popularity because it offers clear benefits to organizations. However, Tzimas warns, servant leadership may not come easily to everyone. In Tzimas's words, "Leadership can be challenging. It requires you to let go of ego and self-importance and lead for the greater good of the team and business overall. A servant leader requires an even higher ability to let go of self and increase levels of empathy, influence, courage, and focus on others." However, the extra effort to become a servant leader will be worth it. Tzimas suggests, "Servant leadership is still the most effective leadership strategy that suits a wide range of organizations and businesses today."

THE BENEFITS OF SERVANT LEADERSHIP

Some leaders naturally will be attracted to the servant leadership concept because it is in sync with their personal values. But even those who don't initially find the servant leadership concept appealing may be attracted to the many benefits it offers. For example:

1. **A high-performance culture.** Positive culture shift is an inevitable byproduct of servant leadership. Tzimas explains, that research suggests that servant leaders promote self-confidence and assertiveness, and that they build the potential of their teams. They also lead their employees to greater productivity. Interestingly, Tzimas notes, servant leaders more often use words like *we, our team,* and *us,* instead of *I, me,* and *I think.* Such inclusive language encourages an inclusive culture for all members of the team, Tzimas says. It also encourages the team to function as a whole, which, again, leads to high performance.

2. **High employee engagement.** Servant leadership builds a fast-growing environment of trust and mutual cooperation. People know what to expect and trust that their leaders care about them. Tzimas suggests, "They do not feel utilized or mistreated." Servant leadership balances professional skills with personal warmth and empathy, resulting in more highly satisfied employees. Tzimas adds that increased employee satisfaction squelches backbiting and unhealthy competition. It also helps everyone potentially to achieve a better work-life balance.

3. **Increased employee loyalty.** Servant leadership increases employee engagement and satisfaction, which, in turn, makes employees more loyal to their employers. Ontime Staffing[7] suggests, "A loyal workforce can reap numerous rewards for your organization as a

whole — including better retention and optimal performance." Loyal employees also are more likely to refer their friends and family to work in your organization, Ontime Staffing says.

4. **High morale.** Employees led by servant leaders feel highly valued. Fraser Sherman[8] explains, "They know you're looking out for them." That inspires them to work with more enthusiasm, which in turn boosts morale.

5. **Better collaboration.** Servant leaders emphasize collaborative decision-making, rather than a more traditional model in which decisions come from the top down. Sherman explains, "Listening to your employees instead of assuming you have all the answers can teach you a lot. Workers on the front lines often understand what they need much better than upper management."

6. **Bigger picture thinking and results.** Servant leaders rarely are interested in immediate gains. Tzimas says, "They have the power to foresee the long-term profits." Many surveys from all over the world have clearly proved that organizations that have servant leadership principles grow faster than others in the long run, Tzimas says.

7. **Better role models.** Servant leaders often are shining examples of how to treat others with empathy. J. Luthor[9] suggests that servant leaders model respect and genuine caring, which others will recognize, admire, and emulate. They also model how to behave ethically, Luthor says.

8. **Increased personal and professional growth.** Servant leaders empower others to recognize their inner potential. Tzimas suggests that they give others space to "nurture their creativity and talent." They also do what they can to help others develop and grow. They surround themselves with positivity, which enables them to maximize their own abilities as well.

9. **Authentic leadership.** Servant leadership is hard — if not impossible — to fake. Sherman suggests, "Living up to this model is a serious commitment." Insincere servant leaders will have a difficult time fooling their employees for long, because they're easy to spot, Sherman warns.

10. **Better understanding.** Servant leaders build relationships with employees primarily by listening closely and asking many questions. However, the questions go both ways. Mark Tarallo[10] explains, "Employees should feel comfortable asking the servant leader questions without worrying that the leader will feel badgered, threatened, or implicitly criticized." The combination of asking questions and

listening actively ultimately reduces misunderstandings and increases understanding, Tarallo suggests.

GETTING STARTED WITH SERVANT LEADERSHIP IN THREE STEPS

Although becoming a servant leader may sound straightforward, that is not the case. Josh Spiro[11] says, "As with most things, it's far easier to talk the talk than walk the walk." Ideally, it would have been best if servant leadership had been woven into the core founding values of your healthcare organization. But even if that didn't happen, you can take three steps now to begin your servant leadership journey:

1. **Revise your organizational chart.** If yours looks like a steep pyramid or tree with you at the top, upend it and put your team above you. You will still retain the final say on things. However, Spiro suggests, an upended or "flatter" organizational chart will illustrate your commitment to serving the needs of your employees. Next, be sure that your stakeholders are represented in your organizational chart. Most importantly, put your patients at the top of the chart and everyone who serves them below. A service-oriented organizational chart such as this will be the most efficient and powerful way for you to express the concept of servant leadership to everyone in your organization. Keep your revised chart handy and consult it regularly. Use it to keep your primary focus on serving the needs of others.

2. **Focus more on listening and less on telling.** Remain as open as you can to new ways of thinking about yourself and others. J. Zisa[12] explains, "We all have personal biases and prejudices even if we'd like to believe otherwise. Listening helps us serve by exposing prejudices that filter select words, warp messages, and prevent us from considering another point of view." Be prepared to discover new things about yourself and the way you lead. Brace yourself because some of those discoveries may be uncomfortable or painful. Zisa writes, "I had a great teacher who once said she loved to discover a prejudice because then she could work to overcome it." Zisa deeply admires this mindset because it accepts the fact that we don't always listen and we're not always open-minded. Yet, Zisa says, "We have the power to consciously change how we listen and interact with others."

3. **Revise your meetings.** Sally Percy[13] suggests, "Remember that the core ethos of the servant leadership style is the well-being and the development of people." Therefore, broaden your regular progress meetings with your employees. Focus on delivery of tasks and metrics as usual, Percy says, but also devote time and energy to discussing worklife balance and personal development. Likewise, expand the agenda of your performance evaluations and other one-on-one meetings to include career progression and lessons learned, and to exchange valuable feedback, Percy suggests.

INCREASING YOUR SERVANT LEADERSHIP SKILLS

There are many resources to help you learn more about servant leadership. Of course, a good place to begin is by reading Greenleaf's 1970 essay.[3] You also can read Greenleaf's books on servant leadership or those by other authors such as Ken Blanchard and John C. Maxwell. In addition, you may find it useful to visit the website of the Robert K. Greenleaf Center for Servant Leadership (www.greenleaf.org) and take advantage of their excellent blog posts and podcasts. Or conduct an online search and find your own articles and videos about servant leadership. If you've not done this before, you will be amazed by how much good material is available.

Servant leadership also is the focus of many educational programs. The Robert K. Greenleaf Center for Servant Leadership offers courses, as do many other organizations. Servant leadership also is a topic of study in several degree programs. For example, Gonzaga University offers a servant leadership concentration as part of its online M.A. in Organizational Leadership program. Shorter academic programs also focus on servant leadership, such as the servant leadership certificate programs at the University of Wisconsin Continuing Studies and at Cornell University's eCornell. com. Modern Servant Leader[14] has created a list of degree, non-degree, certificate, non-certificate, online, and campus-only programs that focus on servant leadership.

Finally, a good way to increase your servant leadership knowledge and skills is to learn and gain support from other servant leaders. Identify like-minded leaders locally or through your professional association who are willing to meet regularly and share challenges, resources, and best practices in servant leadership. If possible, find and work with a servant leadership mentor. The best way to keep your commitment to servant leadership will be through learning and support.

SERVANT LEADERSHIP: 10 POPULAR MISCONCEPTIONS AND MYTHS

Some leaders wrestle with or reject servant leadership because they don't understand the concept fully or they dislike the sound of it. Lichtenwalner explains, "The term *servant* itself disturbs many people otherwise advocating these principles." Here are 10 of the most popular misconceptions and myths about servant leadership:

1. *Servant* **implies subservience**. A popular misconception is that servant leaders give their support to and obey others unquestioningly. However, servant leaders are not blindly obedient. They ask questions before they will support anyone or anything, and they don't give their support until their questions have been answered satisfactorily. They also are willing to make difficult decisions. Lichtenwalner explains, "In order to effectively serve others, you must often do what is unpopular with followers."

2. **Servant leadership is a utopian concept that does not exist in the real world.** Skeptics believe that servant leadership sounds too good to be true, or that it is just a theory that can't be applied to real-life leadership challenges. However, Lichtenwalner, *Fortune*,[15] and others have demonstrated that servant leadership currently is being used with great success by some of the largest and most successful organizations.

3. **The focus is entirely on followers.** Many opponents of servant leadership mistakenly assume that servant leaders serve only their followers. However, Lichtenwalner points out that a servant leader must focus on serving all of the organization's stakeholders. These will include not only your followers or employees, but also your patients, partners, associates, colleagues, investors, community, and governing bodies.

4. **Servant leaders are upbeat all the time.** Tzimas explains, many people incorrectly assume that servant leaders "have smiles on their faces 24/7." However, servant leaders are not endlessly cheerful. They are fully developed people who express a wide range of emotions.

5. **Servant leadership is a religious concept that has no place in business.** Some servant leadership concepts are taught throughout the

Bible. A similar outlook is found across most major religions. However, Lichtenwalner argues, "The concept of servant leadership alone is secular in nature."

6. **Servant leaders are pushovers**. Tzimas suggests that a popular misconception is that servant leaders live to "take orders and fulfill demands of both peers and stakeholders." People often assume that servant leaders can be manipulated and pushed around. However, M. Fox[16] explains, "A servant leader isn't weak, but uniquely strong because he or she has made the effort to understand and prioritize the employee . . . Placing others' needs first doesn't make servant leaders pushovers, but rather earns them respect that employees thrive upon."

7. **Servant leaders focus too much on the present.** Servant leadership focuses more on the present and the future than on the past. However, Fox explains, that does not give employees a "free pass" when they fail to meet expectations. Servant leaders motivate with love, trust, and respect, Fox says, but they also tell others what they need to hear to grow, even when they can't admit it themselves.

8. **Servant leadership can't work because people can't be trusted.** This misconception is based on the erroneous assumption that most members of organizations are inherently dishonest. However, mistrust does not lead to creativity or initiative. J. Riley[17] warns, "It leads to closed doors and a silo mentality." That said, although servant leaders assume that they can trust others, they are not naïve. They have their eyes and ears open. They put safeguards in place and are quick to act if trust is breached.

9. **Servant leaders allow employees to decide what to do, when to do it, and how to do it.** Ken Blanchard[18] says, "If that's what servant leadership is all about, it doesn't sound like leadership at all. It sounds more like inmates running the prison, or managers trying to please everyone." Although leaders should involve experienced people in shaping a compelling vision, setting goals, and defining strategic initiatives, Blanchard says, the ultimate responsibility remains with the leaders themselves and cannot be delegated to others. Then, Blanchard says, "Once employees are clear on where they are going, the leader's role shifts to the task of implementation — the servant aspect of servant leadership."

10. **Servant leaders don't actually lead.** Another common misconception is that servant leaders don't lead but simply hold the space for the team

and remove obstacles. However, Rosetta Technology Group[19] explains that servant leaders are very much leaders. They have clarity of vision and a wide span of awareness, and they can help defuse the anxiety of the organization. Rosetta Technology Group says, "People follow leaders because the leader has made them feel like they are in good hands, and the direction is clear." Leaders also "create or maintain order" when it is needed, Rosetta Technology Group says.

--------- **CHAPTER 2 BONUS FEATURE** ---------

TEN CHARACTERISTICS OF SERVANT LEADERSHIP

Do you have within you what it takes to become a servant leader? Larry Spears[20] has identified 10 characteristics that contribute to the meaningful practice of servant leadership. Although Spears' list is by no means exhaustive, these are all characteristics that can be developed and improved.

1. **Listening.** Servant leaders are deeply committed to listening intently to others. They listen receptively to what is being said and notice what is not being said. Listening also encompasses hearing one's own inner voice. Spears points out, "Listening, coupled with periods of reflection, is essential to the growth and well-being of the servant-leader."

2. **Empathy.** Servant leaders strive to understand and empathize with others. They believe that people deserve to be accepted and recognized for their special and unique spirits. Spears says, "One assumes the good intentions of co-workers and colleagues and does not reject them as people, even when one may be forced to refuse to accept certain behaviors or performance."

3. **Healing.** One of the greatest strengths of servant leadership is the potential for healing oneself and one's relationship to others. Spears points out, "Many people have broken spirits and have suffered from a variety of emotional hurts." Although this is a part of being human, servant leaders recognize that they have an opportunity to help make whole those with whom they come in contact.

4. **Awareness.** General awareness, and especially self-awareness, strengthens the servant leader. According to Spears, "Awareness helps one in understanding issues involving ethics, power and values." The aware

servant leader can view most situations from a more integrated, holistic position.

5. **Persuasion.** Servant leaders rely upon persuasion, rather than on their positional authority, to make decisions within their organizations. As Spears puts it, "The servant leader seeks to convince others, rather than coerce compliance." The servant leader also is effective at building consensus within groups.

6. **Conceptualization.** Servant leaders seek to nurture their ability to dream great dreams. They think beyond day-to-day realities. However, Spears warns, "For many leaders, this is a characteristic that requires discipline and practice."

7. **Foresight.** Closely related to conceptualization is the ability to foresee the likely outcome of a situation. This can be hard to define, but easier to identify. Spears explains, "One knows foresight when one experiences it." Foresight is a characteristic that enables the servant leader to understand lessons from the past, realities from the present, and the likely consequence of a decision for the future. It also is deeply rooted within the intuitive mind. Spears adds, "Foresight remains a largely unexplored area in leadership studies, but one most deserving of careful attention."

8. **Stewardship.** Stewardship is holding something in trust for another. The servant leader's role is to hold their organization in trust for the greater good of society. Stewardship assumes a commitment to serving the needs of others. And, as Spears explains, "It also emphasizes the use of openness and persuasion, rather than control."

9. **Commitment to the growth of people.** Servant leaders believe that people have an intrinsic value beyond their tangible contributions as workers. According to Spears, "The servant leader recognizes the tremendous responsibility to do everything in his or her power to nurture the personal and professional growth of employees and colleagues." In practice, Spears suggests that this can include (but is not limited to) concrete actions such as making funds available for personal and professional development, taking a personal interest in others' ideas and suggestions, encouraging involvement in decision making, and actively assisting laid-off employees to find other positions.

10. **Building community.** In recent human history, there has been a shift from local communities to large institutions as the primary shaper of

human lives. Spears suggests that a great deal has been lost through this shift. Servant leaders are aware of this and seek to identify the means for building community within their organizations. Spears explains, "Servant leadership suggests that true community can be created among those who work in businesses and other institutions."

CHAPTER 3

How to Become a More Visionary Leader

When we think of visionary leaders in the business world, most of us turn our thoughts to a larger-than-life persona, such as Steve Jobs. Dave Cornell[1] suggests, "Perhaps no other individual in the corporate world is as well known for a visionary leadership style than Steve Jobs. He was a visionary in technology, in product design, and in marketing." Jobs was driven by a passion to revolutionize the consumer experience with game-changing technological innovations that created a near cult-like loyalty to his company and its products. Cornell says, "He compelled his teams to push further than they imagined possible by creating a vision that was awe-inspiring." Most business analysts would agree that Steve Jobs was an extraordinary, history-making example of visionary leadership, as would anyone who has ever shopped in an Apple store or come in contact with an iPad, iPhone, iMac, or other Apple products.

Will this chapter urge you to become the Steve Jobs of healthcare leadership? No, not unless that is your goal. Such extraordinary visionary leadership is a tall order, because a leader who has the vision, creativity, drive, talent, and success of Steve Jobs is extremely rare. However, this chapter does suggest that every leader can become more visionary and that there will be tremendous benefits to you and to your healthcare organization if you do. Unfortunately, Don Meinert[2] points out, "Few leaders think of themselves as proficient at what George H.W. Bush famously called 'the vision thing.'" They spend their time grappling with today's problems and don't devote enough thought to preparing for tomorrow's challenges. This is true even though developing a clear picture of the future has long topped executive polls as the most critical requirement for the job, Meinert says. But why is this so?

Being a visionary is most definitely within your reach. Rob-Jan De Jong[3] explains, "My take on the term *visionary* isn't larger-than-life, born-with-it-or-not. Instead, I believe it's something that can be developed, something that's practical and real, something that can be embraced by anyone willing to invest the time into it." I've thought deeply about why it is that more leaders aren't visionary and I believe that many if not most of them do not think that they've got that ability or can ever have it. However, that is not true. I'd like to illustrate this point briefly by drawing from my personal experience.

Years ago, I dipped my toe very casually into the world of golf so I could participate in my Rotary Club's annual golf tournament. I bought an affordable set of clubs, took an introductory package of eight lessons with a pro, read up on golf etiquette, hit a few buckets of balls, and played a few times. My game was poor at the tournament that year and by the next year, it didn't improve because the course was challenging and I devoted little time or effort to practice. What I learned is that you don't get much better at golf when you dabble in it as I did. I would have needed to take more lessons and devote much more of my time and effort to practice and play during that year if I had any hope of improving my game. The same is true of any complex skill set, including visionary leadership. De Jong says, "Sure, some of us are better than others as a result of practice combined with perseverance and natural ability. But practice and perseverance can take you a long way." Whether I had any natural ability in golf is unclear; what *is* clear is that I did not practice or persevere. When we think of becoming more visionary in leadership, I suggest that we consider the words of pro golfer Lee Trevino,[4] who famously said, "There is no such thing as natural touch. Touch is something you create by hitting millions of golf balls."

You can become a leader who provides authentic inspiration for your employees that is fueled by your own passion, energy, and commitment to your vision. However, that's going to require something significant of you, certainly effort much greater than I gave to my pitiful golf game. What can you do if you don't already have a clear vision? You develop one, which you can do if you are willing to roll up your sleeves and get to work. In this chapter, I share the practical, doable steps that you can take to increase your visionary skills. You do not have to commit to hitting Trevino's millions of golf balls, just a bucket of them to start. As you'll see, you can become more visionary, even if your vision into the future at this moment doesn't extend much beyond next Tuesday.

WHAT IS A VISIONARY LEADER?

Visionary leaders are forward thinkers who do not accept the status quo as the way things must be. Suzanne Lucas[5] says that they "see the potential for how the world should exist." They have their finger on the pulse of what is going on both inside and outside of their organizations, and they accurately assess both where things stand right now and how they got to be the way that they are. Then, they develop a vivid and exciting picture of what a better future can look like.

Visionary leaders exist in all levels of management and leadership, regardless of their industry or the title they hold. They do not necessarily work in the C-suite, although some most definitely do. They are curious, optimistic, and observant people who believe in excellence and despise mediocrity. They believe that change is possible, if not inevitable, that things can get better, and that we have the ability to shape our own future. They neither shy away from problems nor are afraid to tackle what Jim Collins and Jerry I. Porras[6] famously called *Big Hairy Audacious Goals (BHAGs)*. Some visionary leaders think outside the box, which was definitely the case for Steve Jobs. Others limit their visions to a better or bigger box, one that functions more efficiently, achieves better outcomes, and generates more profits. Thus, visionary leaders can be bold and revolutionary in their thinking, or they may simply envision their organizations improving and growing in extraordinary ways to become the best versions of themselves.

Of course, visionary leaders do not exist in a vacuum. They are effective only when they have the ability to describe their vision clearly to others in a way that doesn't make it sound like a pipedream or the pie-in-the-sky ravings of a lunatic. They build excitement about the way things can be and the goals that can be achieved. They may or may not be charismatic, although at least a little charisma would certainly help them. [See Chapter 11: "Leading Your Healthcare Organization with Charisma," for more information on this topic.] However, they will always find a way to get others interested in what they have to say and to jump on board. Otherwise, they may be visionaries, but they will not be leaders.

Visionary leaders develop the people they lead. They encourage innovation and collaboration by building a vision inspired by a common goal, one that is right not only for the marketplace and the bottom line but also for the people who work in the organization. They develop the core values of their teams and foster loyalty to their organization, vision, and one another. They encourage those they lead to be creative and to develop their skills, both individually and collaboratively. They help their followers to feel that they are part of something that is important and bigger than themselves, and they make their wins everyone's wins. Because of this, they encourage people to care about what they are doing and, usually, to work harder. Most of the time, they also improve workplace morale.

THE BENEFITS OF VISIONARY LEADERSHIP

We live in an ever-changing world where the speed of change seems to accelerate every year. Visionary leadership helps us counter the strain of the challenges and opportunities that we will face moving forward and enables organizations to survive and thrive under the weight of them. It ensures that we look to the long term, not only to day-to-day matters, so that our organizations will not be blindsided by events that could have been anticipated. It looks to more significant trends in technology, trade, the economy, demographics, the environment, global health, and politics to gauge how an organization can adjust to or in some instances drive these trends. Visionary leadership prevents leaders and team members from getting stuck with a reactive approach to development. Carl Lindberg[7] suggests, "Visionary leadership is important since it helps to address a fast-changing world and creates sizable long-term goals rather than small, short, and iterative goals." Additionally, visionary leadership can be the kick in the pants needed to get stagnant or slow organizations to accelerate their growth in anticipation of the future. That is why Indeed Editorial Team[8] suggests, "Organizations that are experiencing slow progress can benefit from the innovation and creativity of a visionary leader."

Visionary leaders also can make the organizations they lead more competitive. Lindberg says that visionary leadership creates the opportunity to "disrupt competition," as well as to understand the risks of being disrupted. It can help organizations to move into new markets, to shift in response to changing demographics, and to remain a contender despite intense competition and threats in the immediate landscape. Visionary leaders see things early, which helps them steer their organizations out of harm's way and toward opportunities. Meinert says, "The sooner you notice something that will impact business conditions, the faster you can react — which gives you a strategic advantage." Visionary leadership also can improve an organization's brand recognition. It can replace outdated practices with better ones and provide new and better solutions to problems. Indeed Editorial Team says, "Other companies may follow your company's lead, thereby making you a trendsetter and enhancing the recognition of your business."

Visionary leaders also foster unity in the workplace. They emphasize striving for a common goal, which helps to align individuals and departments of different perspectives and to get everyone rowing in the same direction. Indeed Editorial Team says, "This sense of unity strengthens workplace bonds and fosters teamwork and productivity." Leaders who are able to get everyone working enthusiastically toward a common goal instill cooperation and reduce silos. They are able to create a context for team members to see mundane everyday activities as part of something greater. Lindberg says that they can build engagement by "involving and inspiring people." The effect that visionary leaders have on the people they lead can be very dramatic, but that effect can and often does extend beyond the people employed by the organization. Lindberg says that compelling visions can provide a greater sense of purpose to an organization's customers, suppliers, investors, governing boards, and other stakeholders that participate in reaching them.

A final benefit of visionary leadership is that it can enable leaders to pass their organizations on to someone else by creating a culture that will outlive them. Visionary leaders can communicate their vision to others in a way that makes their vision everyone's vision, which can create lasting natural momentum within the organization's culture. Masterclass[9] says, "Employees and other stakeholders will carry on the vision even if the leader moves on or steps away." This is a major advantage over leadership that relies more heavily on a leader's individual traits and personality. Leadership that is 100% charismatic may result in an organization that is not able to move forward if the leader leaves. Visionary leadership, whether charismatic or not, ensures that the organization continues to strive toward its vision even when someone else must take the helm. [See the bonus chapter, "Crafting Your Leadership Legacy Statement: A Template," for more information on leadership legacies.]

CHARACTERISTICS OF VISIONARY LEADERS

Visionary leaders use a variety of skills to inspire growth and increase their chances for success. They share several striking characteristics:

- **Imagination.** Every vision begins with an individual who imagines a different future. Visionary leaders have agile, innovative, and curious minds. They ask, "what if?" and "why not?" when others don't. They question assumptions and dream big. They don't let the obvious obstacles deter them from their dreams, and they don't talk themselves out of them because they seem too difficult. They dream big and in great detail, even when at first their vision seems a little crazy or out of reach, even to them.
- **Emotional intelligence.** Visionary leaders have excellent social skills, self-awareness, and empathy toward others. Indeed Editorial Team says, "A high level of emotional intelligence strengthens team building, improves morale, and increases productivity in the workplace." It also enables visionary leaders to be more self-aware, which helps them to make rational decisions and to provide viable solutions in conflict resolution, Indeed Editorial Team says.
- **Risk-taking.** Visionary leadership is all about change, and change is never risk-free. Visionary leaders do take risks for themselves and their organizations, but very carefully. They understand the value of taking risks and know fully what is at stake. Indeed Editorial Team says, "They ensure extensive research and consideration go into assessing risk levels," and they don't take risks for the sake of just doing so. At the same time, visionary leaders aren't timid or overly cautious. They are bold when they must be to lead their organizations into the new and unexpected places that they envision.
- **Speaking and writing.** Visionary leaders express themselves well in speaking and often also in writing. They describe their vision and plan well and in detail, and they explain the value proposition. They can speak passionately and persuasively and convince others to come along with them on the journey. They focus less on their authority as a leader and more on inspiring people to want to follow them into the future they describe. [See Chapter 7: "Telling Stories to Lead, Teach, Influence, and Inspire," to learn more about how to inspire others.]
- **Listening.** There will always be naysayers to anyone who suggests change and innovation. However, Lucas says, "Visionary leaders don't just go forth ignoring all the naysayers and do what he or she thinks is best." They listen very carefully to what each person says to them, then choose carefully whether to act upon or to ignore the feedback they receive.
- **Strategic thinking.** Visionary leaders are passionate about their visions but they are not unrealistic about them. They think strategically, not

emotionally, when making decisions. Lucas says, "This makes the difference between the big idea guy and the visionary leader. If you're not willing to listen and accept advice, look at how the market is changing, and take feedback seriously, you won't succeed." Strategic thinking also means that visionary leaders develop plans that are practical and can work. Indeed Editorial Teams says, "Strategic thinking includes acquiring the right resources and putting the relevant measures into action to ensure that you and your team are in the best position to succeed." Visionary leaders may ask a lot of the people who work for them, but they strive to be humane. They understand the difference between giving it your all and asking people to push themselves to the breaking point.

- **Ownership.** Visionary leaders know that their ideas often involve a significant risk and that the people who follow them are taking a chance and a leap of faith. Therefore, they take responsibility for their vision and their actions. Lucas says, "This is not only when events go poorly — it's also to make sure that they don't go poorly in the first place."

- **Trustworthiness.** Visionary leaders have the trust of others before they try to lead them toward their visions. How do they gain that trust? Abbey Lewis[10] says, "It starts with creating a safe environment where people feel comfortable expressing themselves and taking risks. It means being transparent, reliable, and authentic." Visionary leaders also build trust with their followers by communicating clear expectations and by following through on their commitments, Lewis says.

HOW TO BECOME A MORE VISIONARY LEADER: 15 STRATEGIES

The following 15 practical strategies can help you become a more visionary leader. You may never do all of them, and you certainly shouldn't try to do too many at once. Commit to one or two right now and build from there. Work at these strategies and in time, you will become more visionary, both in your thinking and in your leadership.

1. **Gain an in-depth, targeted knowledge of the healthcare industry.** Visionary leaders know what's going on in their world. They strive to keep up with relevant developments both in their industry and more broadly. Indeed Editorial Team says, "This knowledge forms the foundation of every business decision, plan, and vision you have for

your company or team." However, the most effective visionary leaders do not consume information randomly. De Jong[11] says, "Many people do take the time to keep up with what is happening in the world and in their industry. They watch the news, read newspapers, and consult trade publications. But there's so much going on, and so much is changing rapidly, that it's hard to make sense of. And what makes it even harder is that the short term runs the agenda." De Jong suggests that leaders will have a hard time distinguishing "the signal from the noise" when they have to-do lists filled with items that need their immediate attention. Therefore, leaders must "prime" themselves to pick up early signals of change first by considering innovative, disruptive ideas for their organizations, their industry, and even the world. De Jong says, "By priming themselves with these ideas first, they get better at picking up potentially relevant information. Random consumption becomes more targeted, and the signal starts to emerge from the noise."

2. **Practice seeing things from the perspective of an outsider.** Visionaries know that the perspective of an outsider is key to analyzing current practices and to questioning those that are often overlooked or assumed by insiders. Life Coach Spotter[12] suggests, "Assuming an outsider's point-of-view leads to enlightenment. Visionaries use this intellectual practice to develop new ways of thinking at their organization and developing their vision." An outsider's perspective can help you reexamine the "sacred cows" in your organization, Life Coach Spotter says — the practices that you maintain because "we've always done it like that." As a weekly or more frequent exercise, identify one of your systems or practices or even one part of your physical environment and intentionally look at it from an outsider's point of view. Imagine yourself as a consultant to yourself or that you are one of your patients or employees. Ask, "Does this make sense?" and "Is this the best we could be doing?"

3. **Develop strategic networks.** Develop strategic relationships both within and outside your organization. Find out how other divisions and organizations work and learn from them. Ask them to describe their best practices, what resources are most and least helpful to them, and what mistakes they regret.

4. **Become more comfortable with uncertainty.** Part of imagining the future is imagining it in multiple ways and in all its complexities. Scenario planning significantly increases the chances of your

developing a fuller picture of what the future may bring. De Jong says, "It is a proven methodology that requires an existential open-mindedness, agility, and creativity that is extremely helpful in growing your visionary abilities."

5. **Build relationships with visionary thinkers.** Stillman[13] says that many visionary leaders admit that it is their friends, colleagues, and professional acquaintances that make them truly visionary. Look for people who, like you, are interested in fostering innovation. Indeed Editorial Team says, "As a visionary, you can leverage the ideas of those around you. It can help inspire new solutions and innovative ideas you may not have discovered by yourself."

6. **Improve your communication skills.** Visionary leaders need to gain the support of their followers. Therefore, invest the time and effort necessary for you to become an excellent communicator, one who not only is clear, concise, and easy to understand, but also persuasive and compelling. Take classes; work with a coach or tutor; join Toastmasters International; study how to communicate more effectively through reading, podcasts, and videos; and most importantly, practice what you learn and solicit and use feedback.

7. **Go for long walks.** Your mind processes lots of information every day, However, Stillman says, "If you allow it a quiet moment, it might reveal to you great advances which can revolutionize the company or even the entire industry practice." While any opportunity for quiet contemplation will be beneficial, you may make even better use of the time if you use it for long walks. Stillman says, "Charles Darwin, Friedrich Nietzsche, William Wordsworth, even Aristotle: the list of great minds that were also obsessive walkers is long." What is it about walking, in particular, that makes it so amenable to visionary think-ing? Ferris Jahr[14] explains, "When we go for a walk, the heart pumps faster, circulating more blood and oxygen not just to the muscles but to all the organs — including the brain. Many experiments have shown that after or during exercise, even very mild exertion, people perform better on tests of memory and attention." Walking on a regular basis also promotes new connections between brain cells, staves off the usual withering of brain tissue that comes with age, increases the volume of the hippocampus (a brain region crucial for memory), and elevates levels of molecules that both stimulate the growth of new neurons and transmit messages between them. Will other forms of exercise

or moving through space help to stimulate the same level of creative visionary thinking? Perhaps not. Jahr explains, ""Walking at our own pace creates an unadulterated feedback loop between the rhythm of our bodies and our mental state that we cannot experience as easily when we're jogging at the gym, steering a car, biking, or during any other kind of locomotion." When we stroll, the pace of our feet naturally vacillates with our moods and the cadence of our inner speech. At the same time, we can actively change the pace of our thoughts by deliberately walking more briskly or by slowing down, Jahr says. A good strategy is to pose a question to yourself about the future as you head out the door for your walk.

8. **Record your innovative thoughts.** Writing down your ideas takes them from being just a thought into being a real, feasible idea. T. Christensen[15] says, "In this way the creative ideas you have also become expandable; you will be able to physically see the idea, rather than just imagining it in your mind (seeing is believing)." Of course, you can carry a notebook or create an electronic file to capture your ideas. However, being able to see your ideas is the very first step toward acting on them. Therefore, De Jong suggests that you physically post your ideas on the wall of your office. Not only will these ideas become integrated in the way that you think, but "they'll also start to shine through in the way you lead," De Jong says.

9. **Become a student of culture and trends.** Before visionary leaders can predict what will interest and concern people in the future, they must understand what interests and concerns them today. Tarun Stevenson[16] suggests, "Very often teenagers set the trends of the future…In particular, 13-year-olds have a very good pulse on what's going on." Spend time learning about and understanding today's culture, and, when you can, stick close to what young people are doing and thinking. That way, Stevenson says, you will be able to make predictions and decisions that are based on "where people are heading" rather than where people "have been up till now."

10. **Study what futurists say.** Visionary leaders do not have to imagine the future by themselves but can draw from other sources. Simon Elias Bibri[17] says, "In recent years, scientists, sociologists, futurists, and researchers within different disciplines have developed qualitative and quantitative methods for rationally predicting the future." Generally, future study methods do not pretend to be able to predict the future.

Rather, they usually are designed to help people better understand future possibilities in order to make better decisions today. What separates futurists from the soothsayers, star gazers, and palm readers who came before? According to Bibri, futurists rely on rationality, not hunches; an awareness that the future cannot be known with absolute certainty; and the recognition that many different futures are possible, depending on the decisions people make in the present. When studying futurists, choose those who use reliable methods and data. Keep in mind that they are presenting possibilities, not promises or foregone conclusions. Andrea Gold[18] suggests, "Get a sense of the big picture from unrelated, broad, and narrow sources. Take it in. Don't make judgment." The more you learn about what visionaries suggest, "the better you can adapt your business and keep success in your sights," Gold says.

11. **Strengthen your intuition.** Intuition is that feeling you have when you instinctively know something. You may not know why you feel the way that you do, but your feeling is undeniable, even when it is not logical. Jeremy Sutton[19] says, "It [intuition] is not the result of a set of considered steps that can be shared or explained. Instead, while based on deep-seated knowledge, the process feels natural, almost instinctual." A strong intuition can be extremely helpful to visionary leaders. Gold says, "Pay attention to your intuition. It's often the source of innovative thoughts or insights." Lissa Rankin[20] suggests 18 ways to develop and strengthen your intuition. These are to meditate, start noticing all that you can with your five senses, pay attention to your dreams, get creative, consult oracle cards, test your hunches, consult your body compass, escape from your daily routines, spend time in nature, learn from your past, feel more and think less, engage in repetitive movement, align with your values, practice sensing into people before you know them, read books about developing your intuition, train your intuition, release your resistance, and start a new breath work practice.

12. **Develop your courage.** Visionary leaders are willing to venture into the unknown, which takes courage. Phil Cooke[21] warns, "Positioning your organization for the future can be challenging, frustrating, and, often, expensive. People hate change, and your team probably isn't paying attention to what's coming as closely as you are. Therefore, they will often fight it." However, visionary leaders are willing to fight to

protect what needs to change in their organization and stand ready to take the criticism that comes as a result. Minda Zetlin[22] suggests eight "tricks" to boost your courage. These are to ask yourself if you should take action to quell your fear, remind yourself that fear can harm you, remember that fear is just chemicals, enlarge your comfort zone, do something to engage your cognition, name your fears, meditate (or at least stop and breathe), and embrace your fear and then let it go.

13. **Foster and indulge your curiosity.** It is tempting for leaders to stick with strategies they know because they are comfortable and have worked in the past. However, that temptation also means that they may not seek out new methods or ways to solve problems. They also may miss important opportunities. For these reasons, curiosity is extremely important to visionary leaders. Kristen Meneghello[23] says, "I see successful leaders get curious about information in three ways. They seek information to uncover new possibilities. They become interested in other functions in the business. They request feedback about their own leadership." Ian Leslie[24] suggests seven ways to become more curious. These are to read widely and follow your interests, polish your mind with the minds of others, visit a physical bookstore or library and browse the shelves, be willing to ask dumb questions, put a lot of facts in your head (and don't rely on Google), be an expert who is interested in everything, and focus not only on puzzles but also on mysteries.

14. **Ask visionary questions.** According to Marilee Adams,[25] our mindsets are driven by the questions that run through our conversations and internal dialogue. Adams presents two mindsets and calls them the "learner" and the "judger." Learner questions focus on solutions and lead to understanding, progress, discovery, and possibilities. They also help to identify and shatter assumptions. Examples of learner questions are "What are we missing?" "Is there a better way?" and "What else may be possible?" as well as "What if?" and "Why not?" Judger questions are reactive and mostly unproductive. Two examples of judger questions are "Why aren't we outperforming the competition?" and "Who is at fault?" Adams assures us that we all have learner and judger moments. However, visionary leaders more often ask learner questions.

15. **Learn about inspiring visionary leaders.** There have been many inspiring examples of visionary leadership throughout history. Some were CEOs or business leaders. Others were leaders in social

movements, entertainment, government, and in other arenas. Learning about them can inspire you to become a more visionary leader and may teach you both about mindsets and strategies that can help you. Commit to reading biographies of or watching documentaries about inspiring visionary leaders. Of course, you can choose your own shining examples of inspiring visionary leaders to study. However, Cornell provides a short list to get you started: Sam Walton, Reed Hastings (CEO of Netflix), Richard Branson, Alan Mulally (former CEO of Ford Motor Company), Steve Jobs, Elon Musk, Mahatma Gandhi, Coco Chanel, Franklin D. Roosevelt, Henry Ford, Ratan Tata (one of the most influential leaders in India), and Warren Buffet. Additional sources suggest other inspiring visionary leaders worth studying, such as Dr. Martin Luther King Jr., Katherine Graham, Marie Curie, Madame C.J. Walker, Dr. Charles Drew, Bill Gates, Amelia Earhart, Oprah Winfrey, Walt Disney, Cesar Chavez, Mark Zuckerberg, Genghis Khan, Andrew Carnegie, Alvin Ailey, John Rockefeller, Estee Lauder, and Mary McLeod Bethune.

--------- **CHAPTER 3 BONUS FEATURE** ---------

10 COMMON MISTAKES VISIONARY LEADERS MAKE

Any leadership strategy has the potential to fail, and visionary leadership is no exception. Following are 10 of the most common mistakes visionary leaders make and what you can do to prevent them.

- **Too many ideas, not enough strategy.** Some visionaries find themselves constantly coming up with new ideas, wanting to experiment, and ready to jump onto the next venture on a moment's notice. Although such creativity is great, constant shifting will make it hard, if not impossible, for your team to settle into a rhythm and pursue ideas to completion. That will lead to frustrated employees and many projects being half done. Therefore, visionary leaders need to establish a clear and well-designed idea-to-action protocol. According to Sonita,[26] that means that you will need to define a framework with your team that evaluates first whether an idea is worth pursuing, and then, when is the right time is to do so.

Sonita urges, "Empower your team to be custodians of this framework and participate in the idea-vetting process." Then, when one of your ideas gets a green light to proceed, define the objective for pursuing it and, most importantly, the timeline, ownership, and how you will measure its progress and success.

- **Believing everything is wrong with everything**. The more time we spend dreaming about what ought to be in the future, the more broken-ness and corruption we will see in the present. If we are not careful, a downward spiral can begin. According to Welford Orrock,[27] "Over time concern turns into disappointment, disappointment turns into disillusionment, and disillusionment turns into disengagement." Although it is true that every person, every institution, and every system can be broken, it is not true that everything is wrong with everything. Orrock says, "When we become disillusioned to the point of disengaged, we have missed an opportunity to celebrate whatever good can be found amidst the brokenness and fail to explore new creative possibilities for healing." Visionaries who give in to negativity and despair may need help from others to bring them back to a more positive and constructive mindset.

- **Lacking alignment with middle managers.** Visionary leadership breaks down when middle managers aren't aligned with top management's strategic vision. This can cause strategic change efforts to slow or fail. According to Nufer Yasin Ates, et al.,[28] "Visionary leadership is not just important for senior managers; it also matters for middle and lower-level managers, who play a key role in carrying out strategic change. Their ability to inspire their own teams and create strategic alignment — a shared understanding of and commitment to the company's strategy — within them is a core element in successful strategy execution." When managers were misaligned with the organization's strategy in Ates et al.'s study, the dark side of visionary leadership became evident. The more these misaligned managers displayed their own visionary leadership, the less strategic alignment and commitment were observed among their teams. Ates et al. suggest that visionary leaders invest more time, effort, and resources in creating strategic alignment among their managers at all levels. They say, "Our experience working with companies around strategic alignment suggests it starts with creating strategic alignment among middle managers before strategy execution efforts begin." This alignment should not be a one-time effort, Ates *et al.* urge, but an ongoing dialogue. They add, "People will only take ownership of strategic change if they are consistently persuaded by its value."

- **Being unnecessarily cruel:** Visionary leaders sometimes can become so caught up in their visions that they put them before the people they lead. The result is that they can push their employees too hard, be uncivil to them, or treat them cruelly. For example, Tony Schwartz[29] says, after reading about Steve Jobs, Jeff Bezos, and Elon Musk, "What disheartens me is how little care and appreciation any of them give (or in Mr. Jobs's case, gave) to hard-working and loyal employees, and how unnecessarily cruel and demeaning they could be to the people who helped make their dreams come true." Why would these and other brilliant visionary leaders behave in such destructive ways? Schwartz suggests, "The first answer is that they can. Genius covers a lot of sins." Employees are willing to sacrifice a lot to work for a visionary. Moreover, a certain level of financial success and the resulting power can effectively excuse some who achieve it from the ordinary rules of civility and even humanity. Schwartz explains, "Mr. Jobs drove around without a license [plate] on his car, and he regularly parked in spaces reserved for the handicapped," as though the normal rules of social engagement did not apply to him. Visionary leaders can prevent themselves from crossing the line toward arrogance and cruelty by having a trusted accountability partner who reins them in. They also may benefit from working with a coach or other professional who can help them to walk the line between their drive and vision and the needs of the people they lead.

- **Having unreasonable expectations, especially about timelines.** Visionaries sometimes can become impatient. They usually want to see their visions realized as soon as possible, and in their excitement, underestimate what that "possible" exactly means. Sonita warns, "Whether it's due to being overly optimistic or simply unaware of the skills and effort needed, an unrealistic deadline will only leave your team feeling frustrated, rushed to perform, and producing subpar work." Your team's involvement is key to developing achievable action plans. Sonita says, "The secret here is to open the lines of communication with everyone involved to ensure you're taking their expertise and point of view into account."

- **Treating realists as pessimists in disguise.** Visionaries need realist friends who bring them back to earth by reminding them of the practical questions that must be answered and the challenges that must be overcome. Orrock warns, "Idealists often view them as pessimists in disguise. Even the term 'devil's advocate' can become a sly way of marginalizing their ideas." There is a difference between taking the present realities into account and being negative for negativity's sake. The mistake visionaries sometimes make is thinking that someone who says "it can't be done" or "people will never go for that" somehow lacks hope. Orrock says, "Remember, a visionary can be just as guilty of delusion as a realist can be of hopelessness." Rather than discrediting the voice of difference, invite that person into a deeper conversation about what immediate challenges they anticipate. Orrock says, "You can't get from A to Z without steps B, C, and D. The realist can help you with these next practical steps."
- **Assigning responsibility to a team member with no agreement, timeline, or role.** Assigning a task or responsibility to a team member without their enthusiastic (or at least informed) agreement is a common visionary leadership mistake that can cause a lot of problems. According to Sonita, "A clear scope of work and shared understanding of who owns key tasks or initiatives helps you and your team hold each other accountable and work together towards a common objective."
- **Thinking that what is most important to me should be most important to you.** As hard as visionaries may try to be objective and inclusive, dreams are influenced by personal experiences and values. One mistake visionary leaders sometimes make is thinking that their future is the best future. Orrock says, "This assumes a high degree of shared values and expectations…This is, in most cases, not a safe assumption." Therefore, visionaries must take care to listen to what people value. Orrock warns, "If we are unwilling to listen to and honor the values and expectations of the communities we serve, even if we sometimes disagree, we will risk leading them to places they do not want to go."
- **When something goes wrong, assuming that "it was clear."** A lack of clarity often results in mistakes. Sonita says, "Something is only clear once everyone has a shared understanding of it." Numbers are a great tool to ensure that you and your team are speaking the same language.

Use dates and metrics to check that everyone is on the same page. For example, Sonita says, "Having a team member understand her role is to 'grow the email list to 1,000 names by the end of Q3' is dramatically different than saying 'you're in charge of email marketing.'"

- **Expecting employees to know where your healthcare organization is going without clear communication.** As a visionary leader, it will be up to you to communicate your values, where you're going, and what your organization needs from everyone to get there. Sonita says, "Doing this gives your team a compass that lets them know what 'true north' is." It also enables you to spot who is truly aligned with your vision and belongs at the table.

Management Fads: How to Resist Shiny Object Syndrome

Do you know what's fun and exciting? *New.* We love new ideas and projects and go gaga over the latest gadgets and gizmos. We love "it" concepts, "it" strategies, and "it" technologies that everyone is talking, writing, blogging, podcasting, and swooning about. *Fresh* and *new* draw us every time, just as shiny objects draw a magpie.

In fact, our attraction to *new* drives a great deal of human behavior. For example, it can explain why we consume so many goods and services that we don't need, why we see a constant barrage of new diet and exercise products flooding our marketplace each year, and even why some among us seem unable to sustain long-term relationships. Kari Perina[1] suggests, "When something is fun, exciting, and new, you get a temporary hit of dopamine which feels good and rewards your brain." For many, the rush of something new is like the rush of an addictive drug. We are hooked and can't be without it. If you don't believe this, just go to a shopping mall on a Saturday afternoon, or watch a few minutes of home shopping television, or strike up a conversation with an 11-year-old to learn about the latest video games out there. Is it any wonder, then, that leaders find themselves veering if not jumping off course to pursue whatever new project or management trend is beckoning to them?

Psychologists have come up with a succinct way to describe our pursuit of the new to the detriment of the tried and true. They call it *shiny object syndrome,* our tendency to chase a new and exciting object rather than to stick to our original goals. It is a phenomenon rooted in constant distraction. Toggl Track[2] suggests, "Think of a small child who's happily playing with a toy — until their eye catches something shiny and new in the corner. What happens? In all likelihood, they promptly abandon whatever they were just playing with in order to go over and grab that irresistible shiny object." Leaders, too, can pursue shiny objects and abandon the old. Toggl Track explains, "Because they [leaders] always have an eye on what's next for their businesses, it's increasingly easy for them to constantly get distracted by whatever shiny object is lurking in the corner." Shiny object syndrome can and eventually will sabotage healthcare leaders, however, by constantly distracting them from the core mission of their organization, Toggl Track warns. This is especially true when the shiny object is a management fad.

THE HIGH COST OF CHASING MANAGEMENT FADS

A management fad is a diabolical shiny object in disguise. In fact, the term *management fad* is pejorative; it implies a short-lived philosophy and strategy for management that doesn't deliver everything it promised. A management fad may be extremely popular for a time, but it lacks staying power. The expectation is that the management fad of today will be replaced tomorrow as the next new management philosophy and strategy (shiny object) catches everyone's imagination, admiration, and acceptance.

Leaders usually have good intentions and buy into a management fad because they believe that it will help them improve their organizations. Then, if that one doesn't deliver the results leaders seek, they may very likely jump to another fad, then another, hoping that if this one doesn't work, the next one will. However, ricocheting your organization and employees from one management fad to the next can end up being a huge and extremely costly headache. Geoffrey James[3] suggests, "Companies have wasted trillions of dollars on these ridiculous but plausible-sounding ideas." In fact, management fads require a lot more than money; they also require a great deal more energy, time, and patience than most leaders expect. The cost is not only what it takes to implement the fads, but also, the lost work and opportunities that result when leaders and their employees lose their focus. Most importantly, employees can easily become fatigued and lose interest when fads are rolled out one after the next.

Specifically, M. Dsouza[4] identifies the following costs of chasing management fads:

- **Learning.** Fads require employees to learn new ways of doing things, which can take time away from other work and require costly training and support.
- **Tangibles.** Fads sometimes require costly new technologies and changes to the physical workplace.
- **Frustration and demotivation.** Fads require change because they ask employees to abandon what is familiar and comfortable and head into the unknown. You are likely to have employees who resist making the changes a fad requires, or who want to change but slip into the old ways of doing things for the sake of expediency, ease, or habit.
- **Confusion.** Employees may not know which parts of old fads to let go of as they embrace new ones. Dsouza warns, "A leader prone to shiny object syndrome can cause a team or organization full of disoriented people."
- **A graveyard of unfinished projects.** Your focus on fads may mean that old projects take a backseat. Repeat this a few times, Dsouza says, and you will end up with a collection of costly unfinished projects.
- **A jaded staff.** How many times can you get your staff pumped up about a new and exciting management strategy, philosophy, tool, or process? Not many. Pretty soon, your employees will regard fads as what they are — just the latest management flavor of the month. Jaded employees will do the minimum you require as they wait for the fad to lose its appeal, because they know that eventually it will.
- **A distracted leader.** A leader who shifts from fad to fad loses focus and misses opportunities. It's hard to quantify what that costs an organization, but we can safely assume that it's astronomical.

IS IT A MANAGEMENT FAD? LET'S FIND OUT

Have you ever heard of Management by Objectives or the One-Minute Manager? How about Management by Walking Around or Japanese Management or Total Quality Management (TQM)? Those were the popular management concepts when I began my career as a healthcare writer in the 1980s, so naturally, I wrote about them. Like so many of my readers, I thought that all of healthcare management's ills could be cured if only we could latch onto the right new approach. I will be the first to admit that there was and still is merit in each of these concepts. A fad becomes a fad because it is rooted in something that is appealing and logical. However, none of those concepts or strategies was the panacea my readers and I sought, which explains why we don't hear as much about them anymore. Once the newness of one management fad waned, off we went in search of the next new shiny object, and of course, we had no trouble finding it. It seems that there is a constant supply of new and better management mousetraps calling to us. Danny Miller and Jon Hartwick[5] explain, "Like fashion trends, management fads erupt on the scene, enjoy a period of prominence, and then are supplanted."

Although the term *fad* may seem dismissive, it's not. Miller and Hartwick suggest that some fads introduce sound, useful ideas that organizations incorporate into practice, even as the fad itself fades from the scene. But fads often fail to deliver on their promises, a factor that contributes to their short life cycles and rapid decline. So how do you know if the new strategy or concept you're considering is just another management fad? Miller and Hartwick offer nine criteria. Management fads are:

1. **Simple.** Usually, a few key points convey a fundamental message, Miller and Hartwick say, and concepts tend to be framed with labels, buzzwords, lists, and acronyms.

2. **Prescriptive.** Fads tell managers what to do, making action points easy to misinterpret or apply inappropriately.

3. **Falsely encouraging.** Miller and Hartwick warn, "Fads are better at raising hopes than delivering results, and they generally fail to specify clear-cut criteria for evaluating whether or not an implementation succeeded."

4. **One-size-fits-all.** Fads often claim universal relevance, but few management approaches are universally applicable. Trying to fit a management fad's round peg into an organization's square hole will never work, with devastating results. "Attempts to implement a mismatched approach can do more harm than good," Miller and Hartwick warn.

5. **Easy to cut and paste.** It's easy to implement a fad in part. However, partial implementation of a fad is a problem, because it means that certain fad features may be grafted onto standard operating procedures and localized within a few committees or departments. Miller and Hartwick warn, "Outside these pockets, it's business as usual — which means that fads rarely challenge the status quo in a way that would require significant redistribution of power or resources."

6. **In tune with the zeitgeist.** Fads resonate with the pressing problems of the day. Their laser focus on the concerns of the moment means that

they tend to apply to a few specific issues, and they may not address the fundamental weakness or soundness of overall business practices, Miller and Hartwick say.

7. **Novel but not radical.** Fads grab our attention by their apparent novelty. But their freshness is often superficial, and, because of that, fads don't challenge basic managerial values and assumptions. Miller and Hartwick warn, "Many [management fads] simply repackage or extend ideas or approaches that managers have long embraced."

8. **Legitimized by gurus and disciples.** Many fads gain credibility by the status and prestige of their proponents or followers, rather than through empirical evidence. Often, we see external consultants who specialize in implementation of the fad, and even certification and appraisal processes performed by external agencies. But we don't always see a body of empirical evidence sufficient to support a fad's claims.

9. **Too good to be true.** Management fads usually are simple to learn. However, if they seem too good to be true, Miller and Hartwick warn, they probably are.

HOW TO PREVENT OR CURE SHINY OBJECT SYNDROME: 15 STRATEGIES

As you can see, shiny object syndrome is a very human affliction, and it's all too easy to be lured into it. That's why so many leaders fall prey to management fads. However, shiny object syndrome is not a foregone conclusion or a terminal condition. The first step to preventing or curing it is to take stock of your past and current leadership practices. Take the quiz that serves as the bonus feature for this chapter to assess whether you have jumped onto one or more management fads or been distracted by other shiny objects. If you have, don't despair. Spend time thinking about what happened, the red flags you missed, the costs to you and your organization, and how you could have avoided being lured into the fad in the first place. When it comes to healthcare leadership, there is going to be no more powerful teacher than lessons you learn from your personal experience.

Next, learn to recognize management fads and other shiny objects for what they are and avoid getting sucked into them. That will require your commitment and patience. Here are 15 strategies that can help:

1. **Consider the timing and what's at stake.** Shiny object syndrome is most destructive when it's ripping your attention from something that's much more urgent or critical than the shiny object luring you. Is now a time when you can focus on something new? Do you already have numerous pressing projects demanding your time and energy? Have you given what's already on your plate sufficient attention? Toggl Track suggests, "Maybe you haven't given your current thing enough time and focus to get the traction it needs to reach its potential."

2. **Think before you leap.** Your own ability to think things through will serve as the most effective strategy to combat shiny object syndrome. Dsouza says, "Consider what you might have to overcome to make a new idea successful. Do not neglect the fact that the new idea will consume your time, leaving you with fewer hours. You might have to give up on the goal you're already chasing." Don't assume that you can spare the time, money, and effort required to implement a new management fad or other shiny object. Work the numbers to make certain that you can. If you can't, do not allow yourself and your organization to take the leap.

3. **Focus on the pros and cons.** Make an extensive list of all the pros of your current situation. If you have the desire to leave it and move onto something new, it's probably because you're hoping that the new shiny object will offer more pleasure and less pain than you are currently experiencing. That can mean that you may be blind to the benefits, positives, and pleasures of your current situation. Sam Stokes[6] suggests, "Keep listing out the benefits until you feel true gratitude for your current situation." Next, make a list of all the drawbacks of the management fad or other new shiny object that is beckoning to you. What challenges will arise when the shine of the new object fades? Stokes says, "Keep stacking the drawbacks until you no longer feel infatuated with the new shiny object, or until 'the shine' subsides."

4. **Focus on the 1/50 rule.** You will be more prone to being distracted by something new when you feel overworked and stressed. Keep shiny object syndrome at bay by focusing on what truly matters. David Finkel[7] suggests, "Choose one day a week where you block three to four hours out of your day to focus on the 1 percent that produces 50 percent of your results." Turn your cell phone off, step away from your email, and work on the A-level tasks and projects that matter most.

Avoid management fads and other shiny objects during this time. That will help you stay focused on what's most important, Finkel says.

5. **Challenge yourself to explain the benefits of those shiny objects.** Explain to someone else, preferably a skeptic, a clear reason that you want to pursue the new philosophy, strategy, or other shiny object beyond the fact that you think it will be exciting. Describe the metrics you can use to measure your results, project what you can expect, and explain how you are making your projections. As with any business decision, you should be able to point to a direct and measurable benefit of the activity. According to Toggl Track, "That simple exercise will help you weed out the frivolous shiny objects and focus on the strategies that actually move the needle for your business."

6. **Check your reasoning.** Sometimes leaders give in to management fads and other shiny objects because they are running away from something. Toggl Track suggests, "Sometimes frustration with your current business can lead to shiny object syndrome." It usually is easier and a lot more fun to jump into a management fad rather than to hunker down and work on fixing problems. We've all been there. The key is to be aware of this and recognize it when you experience it.

7. **Spend time on research.** Management fads often are described and extolled by eloquent, bright individuals. In a sense, these fads are sold by good salespeople. However, you can't make decisions for your organization based on a sales pitch. Look for the reliable, credible, and trustworthy research to support what they tell you. Anecdotes are lovely, but you need to know that the ideas being forwarded have worked for organizations like yours, with measurable results. You also need to know that these results have been replicated in numerous organizations.

8. **Face your most daunting tasks.** You will be most susceptible to management fads and other shiny objects when you are faced with a task or challenge that seems extremely difficult or time consuming. It's much easier to push your to-do list aside and work on something more exciting and rewarding, like a management fad. Therefore, Finkel suggests that you create a detailed action plan that breaks goals down into a manageable task list. Finkel explains, "The key is to pick one to three to focus on, and then invest a portion of your best resources, because you know that these are the areas that will really help you scale and develop your business." As you move toward the goal, you

will enjoy the satisfaction of checking things off your to-do list and staying on task. That will make shiny objects much less of a distraction, Finkel suggests.

9. **Wait out the idea.** When a new and exciting management philosophy or strategy arrives on the scene, it can feel a lot like you're falling in love. The attraction and spark you feel for a management fad can lead you to make an impulsive decision. Don't. Give yourself the time you need to diffuse your initial excitement so your reason can take over. Dsouza says, "What seemed like a brilliant idea may appear average within a short time."

10. **Build a community of trusted advisors.** You can get so wrapped up in a management fad that you aren't thinking clearly. That's especially the case when your emotions are involved and you're too close to the situation to think about it objectively. When in doubt, it's time to phone a friend, so to speak, and work with an accountability partner. Toggl Track suggests, "Being part of a small mastermind group can be very helpful. They can be a good sanity check and poke holes in faulty logic."

11. **Abandon what you're doing now for something new only when you have an excellent, compelling reason.** The attractiveness of a management fad or other shiny object is not a sufficient reason to abandon your current plan. Dsouza warns, "The temptation of better results from another goal can blind your judgment." Consider how far you have come with your current strategies and how far you are from the results you seek. "Take into account the price you pay for losing the progress you have made so far," Dsouza says. Can your current strategies work, if given more time and effort? If *yes*, is it best to stay the course?

12. **Revisit your mission.** Read and think about your mission word for word. Every philosophy and strategy you choose should help you to accomplish your mission. Douglas Shaw[8] suggests, "If the shiny new object doesn't fit with your mission, ignore it."

13. **Build on successes.** It's a very serious step to lead your organization away from what it does well. That's why Toggl Track suggests, "See if you can channel your desire for something new and exciting into something that will positively benefit your existing business or customer base."

14. **Play devil's advocate.** Does the management fad or other shiny object look too good to be true? Do you have enough time, resources, energy,

and money? Do you have incomplete goals or benchmarks that need to be reached before you can safely implement a new process? Try to poke holes in every argument for the shiny object. In other words, try to talk yourself out of it. S. Butcher[9] suggests, "Think about what advice you would give to a friend in the same situation."

15. **Test drive the shiny object before committing to it.** Let's say that you see the value of the new management fad or other shiny object, and you're ready to pull the trigger. Before you do, test it in a small, low-risk way. For example, run a test or pilot program with a small group. Fingerprint for Success[10] suggests, "See how they react and ask for their feedback." A pilot program can help you see if the management fad or other shiny object has the benefits you seek. However, it also can help you to identify problems, shortcomings, and costs you hadn't considered. It's worth the time, effort, and money to do a pilot test rather than to commit your organization to a new management approach that ultimately won't work.

WHAT TO DO IF YOUR BOSS OR COLLEAGUE HAS SHINY OBJECT SYNDROME

Organizations value leaders who come up with great new ideas, so having a boss or colleague who gets excited about new initiatives is not an inherently bad thing. Problems occur, however, when those new ideas come fast and furious and aren't carefully analyzed or curated. The Highlands Company[11] warns that bosses and colleagues sometimes get carried away by management fads and other shiny objects and expect them to be acted upon without doing the necessary homework. The Highland Company explains, "Each new idea will burst forth as if it were the key to the problem." The result is that you and your team may shift your time and energy aimlessly from one project to another, feel frustrated by the inability to complete anything, and become confused about your goals and priorities.

If your boss has fallen prey to shiny object syndrome, Liz Kislik[12] suggests that you and your direct reports may have thoughts such as, "Do I need to add this to my priorities? Will I still need to deliver on all my other goals too? Are there really enough resources available to get this done?" At the same time, you're in a delicate position. It won't be easy for you to rain on another person's shiny object parade, especially a gung-ho boss. But there are some things that you can do when you have a boss or colleagues who have been lured by a management fad or other shiny object.

First, be sure that you stay in regular close contact with your boss and colleagues. There are leaders who will be attracted to and excited about so many different initiatives that they forget what others are working on. Kislik warns, "It's demoralizing to complete a project, and have your boss express surprise that you've done it at all. So don't let too much time pass between check-ins."

In addition, be diligent about limiting the times that are available for discussions about a management fad or other shiny object. For example, Kislik suggests that you start all meetings with an "anchoring" statement that sets what will and won't be discussed. Kislik explains, "It can be as simple as, 'Today we're going to cover the Blue, Green, and Red initiatives. Any great ideas we have for anything else will be recorded and taken up in the appropriate staff/strategy/development meetings.'" Make sure that at least one meeting participant is responsible for recording, and at least one will be vigilant for digressions. That will keep your boss's or colleagues' enthusiasm for a management fad from derailing your meetings.

Another strategy for managing a boss or colleague who has shiny object syndrome is to agree to begin the research or development phase. Sometimes the most practical thing to do is to spend a small amount of development time and money to get to the proposal or prototype stage. Then you can determine where the initiative does and doesn't fit the current plan and commitments. Doing the initial exploration will give your boss or colleague some satisfaction, Kislik says, but still address questions such as, "If we wanted to pursue this, should it be outsourced? Is it on brand? Will it strengthen our customer relationships or attract new customers?" The work you do will slow things down so your boss's or colleague's infatuation with the fad or other shiny object will have time to weaken.

Finally, speak with your boss or colleague and communicate your concerns and difficulties directly. The Highlands Company explains, "Your boss isn't trying to confuse you. He might not even realize that he's causing confusion with his shiny object syndrome. See if you can find a way to work together to sift through his ideas to find the ones that give you a solid direction." If that doesn't work, see if you can negotiate "check in" or completion deadlines for the ideas. That will make your boss's or colleague's shiny object syndrome more manageable, The Highlands Company says.

WHAT TO DO IF YOUR EMPLOYEES HAVE SHINY OBJECT SYNDROME

Sometimes, you will manage an employee who is full of ideas and brings them to you half-baked, one by one. On the one hand, you don't want to squash your employee's innovation and enthusiasm. On the other, you can't spend a great deal of time dealing with an employee who has shiny object syndrome. Karl Sakas[13] suggests the following strategies when you manage an employee who is burying you in management fads and other bright shiny ideas:

- **Acknowledge that the employee is trying to be helpful.** Sakas says, "Remember, they're not trying to annoy you to death." Your employees may not realize that an idea that's big to them may be minor compared to your other priorities. Likewise, they may not consider that their suggestion is one of dozens of things you're considering each day. Gently help them to see the bigger picture when you can.
- **Be sure your employees know your healthcare organization's quarterly, annual, and long-term goals**. When employees know where you're going, they can help you get there faster. Having an overall strategy also makes it easier for you to reject or defer management fads or other shiny objects when they're clearly not on-strategy. Sakas suggests, "You can say, 'Bring this back in six months, after we've finished the XYZ implementation.'"
- **Keep your employees focused.** This may mean asking employees to explore management fads and other shiny objects outside of regular business hours, Sakas says. Otherwise, they may use shiny objects as an excuse for not keeping up with their workload.
- **Ask if they've spoken with other stakeholders.** If the management fad or other shiny object means more work for other people, Sakas says, the other people should be on board before the proposal reaches your desk.
- **Ask them to batch their proposals.** For instance, you can ask them to save their ideas for weekly, monthly, or quarterly meetings. Sakas suggests, "You'll be more productive because they won't be interrupting you all week long with a new idea they just heard at a professional development event."

If your employee's enthusiasm for management fads or other shiny objects persists, try to keep the problem in perspective. Remember that it's better to have employees with too much initiative than zero initiative. Sakas says, "It's easier to channel too much energy than it is to motivate the unmotivated."

—————— **CHAPTER 4 BONUS FEATURE** ——————

DO YOU HAVE SHINY OBJECT SYNDROME? TAKE THIS QUIZ

Is the new management philosophy, strategy, tool, or service attracting you the right thing for your healthcare organization? Or have you just fallen under the spell of a management fad or other shiny object? It's not always easy to tell. To help, here is a five-question quiz to help you figure this out:

1. **Do you have many unfinished projects?** Are you energized by new ideas and frequently starting new projects, but not finishing them? If so, take an honest look at the work you've done over the last year or several years. Do you see a lot of projects that you didn't complete? Did you abandon projects shortly after beginning them? Toggl Track suggests, "If you look to your history and see a long string of forgotten initiatives, that's a solid indicator that shiny object syndrome is serving as a major distraction."

2. **Do you frequently change the way you do things?** Nobody can blame you for wanting to find the most efficient, safest, or most economical way to get things done. However, frequently introducing new tools and work processes can slow you down, rather than save you time and energy. Are you constantly introducing new platforms, hacks, systems, workflows, and other methods that promise to optimize your workday? Have you rarely had a repeatable process in place to get your work done? According to Toggl Track, "If you've never had even a somewhat consistent way of getting your work accomplished, chances are good shiny object syndrome is getting in your way."

3. **Do your employees seem confused because you've made frequent changes?** Sam Sid[14] asks, "Do your teammates suddenly find their goals shifted almost unpredictably or see projects they're working on suddenly

become irrelevant when a new detail emerges?" If so, you have probably fallen under the spell of shiny objects, and your employees will find it almost impossible to keep up, Sid warns.

4. **Do you burn through cash on things you don't end up using?** For example, do you spend money on books you don't read and courses you don't take or finish? Do you set up new domain names and websites without doing anything with them? Or do you subscribe to many new technological tools and services but not use them? *Entrepreneur*[15] says, "There are hundreds of technological tools for businesses that are impressive, effective and downright fun to use." Unfortunately, if you subscribe to all those services, or you jump from platform to platform, your shiny object syndrome will cause you to burn through so much cash that these tools become incredibly cost-inefficient, *Entrepreneur* says.

5. **Do you have trouble staying focused?** Are you neglecting some of your most crucial business activities because you're enticed by shiny objects? Do you find yourself procrastinating so you can daydream and shop for new ideas and systems? If so, Toggl Track warns, "It's obvious that your shiny object syndrome is controlling you — rather than the other way around."

Managing the Isolation and Loneliness of Leadership

Is it really as lonely at the top as people say that it is? Often, yes, it is. Leadership can be isolating, making leaders feel that they're out on a limb all by themselves. Ron Edmonson[1] says, "Leadership is naturally lonely. Every leader I know struggles with it at some level." Rachel Blom[2] agrees, suggesting that loneliness ramps up with increased levels of leadership. According to Blom, "With every step in leadership we make comes the inevitable increase in loneliness. The higher we climb in leadership, the more responsibilities we get, the lonelier we become." Is it any wonder, then, that you may find that your job as a healthcare administrator, leader, or manager is a lonely one, at least some of the time? The good news is that you're probably not as alone as you think you are. Leaders in other healthcare organizations no doubt feel the same as you.

Why is leading a healthcare organization sometimes such a lonely business? There are two basic reasons. First, healthcare administrators, leaders, and managers must sometimes distance themselves from their employees simply to do their jobs well. As a leader, you can't always share what you know or how you feel with the members of your team without betraying confidence or undermining your authority. For instance, you may not be able to share with your staff the problems you're facing with one of your physicians or other employees. You may not be able to vent your frustrations to your staff, or to complain to them about how difficult your job is. According to Thinking Partners, Inc.,[3] "Exceptional leaders . . . exhibit self-control. Leaders with emotional intelligence find ways to manage disturbing emotions and impulses." Unfortunately, the self-control required of your leadership can be isolating, separating you from everyone else.

Second, the employees you lead may behave in ways that exclude you simply because you're their boss. For instance, they may leave you out of their inside jokes. They may not invite you to lunch or to their outside-of-work social events. They may even treat you more formally and carefully than they do their coworkers. That's because they may fear you, although that fear may have nothing to do with you personally or with anything you have ever said or done to them. If you were promoted from within their ranks, they may resent you for being above them now in the hierarchy. Or as Shasta Nelson[4] suggests, they may look up to you so much that they treat you as though you are "on a pedestal." In any case, your employees may keep you in the margins of their social structure. They will be unlikely to forget that you have hiring, performance and salary review, task assignment, and firing authority over them. That can make many employees feel uncomfortable when they're around you. It's no wonder, then, that they may be keeping you at arm's length.

Even if you accept that loneliness is commonplace among leaders, you may be tempted to downplay the significance of your feelings. However, chronic feelings of loneliness can lead to serious problems. Let's explore some of these and the reasons that leaders must take action to prevent and mitigate their loneliness.

DO IT FOR YOU; DO IT FOR YOUR TEAM

A healthcare leader's loneliness can have health repercussions. *Psychology Today*[5] warns that lonely individuals report higher levels of perceived stress even when they are exposed to the same stressors as non-lonely people, and even when they are relaxing. Also, loneliness in adults is a major precipitant of depression, illness, and alcoholism. *Psychology Today* warns that loneliness "increasingly appears to be the cause of a range of medical problems, some of which take decades to show up." Karen Weintraub[6] adds further evidence that being lonely can make you sick. According to Weintraub, "A lonely person's blood pressure tends to be higher and change more as they age; and they are more likely to have high levels of inflammation, which leads to even more health problems." Clearly, sustained periods of loneliness at work can affect you adversely, and the problems associated with your loneliness can spill into your well-being and personal life.

A leader's loneliness also can be a problem for those they lead and serve. Christi Hedges[7] points out, "Any leader's isolation has negative ramifications on others. And it's not just CEOs who experience this kind of loneliness. . . . In fact, anyone who finds themselves peerless can feel isolated. This isn't good for decision-making, culture, or performance." Hedges warns that because a leader's actions "reverberate," their isolation and loneliness can become a larger problem when they lead to poor decision-making, negativity, fatigue, and frustration. Hedges adds, "And who wants to work for an unhappy person?"

Although the problems associated with leadership loneliness can be serious both for leaders and for everyone else in the healthcare organization, they can be managed. Hedges suggests, "The key is to deal with this loneliness in a healthy way."

10 EFFECTIVE AND HEALTHY WAYS TO MANAGE LEADERSHIP LONELINESS

Unfortunately, A. Luna[8] suggests, chronic loneliness can lead to self-destructive behaviors such as over- or undereating, overspending, self-pity, drug and alcohol abuse, physical neglect, and sabotaging relationships. However, there are healthy and effective ways to manage the loneliness that often accompanies leadership, including these 10:

1. **Accept your loneliness.** Although most people feel lonely at times, loneliness often seems to carry a stigma. According to Karyn Hall,[9] lonely people fear being judged as "unlikeable, a loser, or weird" so they don't discuss their sense of loneliness, alienation, or exclusion. Blaming yourself, calling yourself names, and berating yourself because you are feeling lonely is not effective and not accurate, Hall says. In fact, feeling lonely in the absence of meaningful connections is normal. Therefore, a good first step in managing the loneliness that often accompanies leadership will be your own understanding and acceptance, without judgment. [See "Feeling Lonely? Acceptance is the First Step" below for more ideas on this subject.]

2. **Focus more on the needs and feelings of others.** You can spend your days in your healthcare organization dwelling on your loneliness. Or you can be grateful for the diversity of people you work with every day, silently wishing them good health and good fortune, and smiling at each person you encounter. The latter approach not only is more productive and fun, but also more likely to help you lessen the feelings of loneliness. Offer kindness and generosity of spirit to all you come into contact with for their sake, as well as for your own.

3. **Strengthen existing relationships.** Your role as a healthcare administrator, leader, or manager is only one aspect of your life. You may already have friends and acquaintances that you could get to know better, or connections with family members that could be deepened. If so, why not call your friends and family more often, go out with them more, and find other ways to enjoy your existing relationships and strengthen bonds?

4. **Become more socially active outside of work.** Taking a class is a great way to meet people who share at least one of your interests. It also can provide a sense of belonging that comes with being part of a group, and help you stave off feelings of loneliness. So, too, can volunteering for an organization or for a cause you believe in, joining a gym, and getting involved in a hobby or sport in which you interact with others.

5. **Organize social functions with your team.** Don't wait for an invitation that never comes to lunch, happy hour, or an after-work outing. Organize your own staff social events. Once the members of your team have had opportunities to interact with you outside of your healthcare organization, they may be more inclined to invite you to their own gatherings. Even if not, the staff social events you organize may make you feel less isolated, especially if you make a point of connecting with each person.

6. **Develop a professional support group.** Developing a strong professional support network can help leaders to become happier, more productive, and better prepared to face the world. According to Bill George,[10] "Authentic leaders build close relationships with people who will counsel them in times of uncertainty, be there in times of difficulty, and celebrate with them in times of success." Your support group also can help you to develop much-needed feelings of belonging. Brene Brown[11] suggests, "A deep sense of love and belonging is an irreducible need of all people. We are biologically, cognitively, physically, and spiritually wired to love, to be loved, and to belong. When those needs are not met, we don't function as we were meant to." Developing a consistent group of peers with whom you can be vulnerable, who will support you, and who will not turn away from you is extremely helpful in leadership, George says.

7. **Work with a coach or mentor.** Leaders who experience loneliness may feel less alone when they work on their personal development outside. They may be able to share their frustrations and challenges with a mentor or coach, who will provide needed support and help them develop concrete solutions. Having someone reliable in your corner can make a huge difference when you're feeling isolated and lonely. Loneliness often provides a distorted picture of reality. Lonely individuals paint on a canvas of self-pity and depression, tinting everything gray and black, bleak and hopeless. A mentor or coach can bring you back to reality and encourage you to think more accurately and positively.

8. **Join or become more involved in professional organizations.** One of the greatest benefits of joining and becoming active in a professional association is that you will have opportunities to get to know other healthcare leaders. That will help you battle feelings of isolation and loneliness, knowing that they face similar challenges. Spending time with other people who do what you do every day at conferences and other meetings is ideal. But ongoing electronic communication with other leaders also can be very helpful as you face the day-to-day challenges in your healthcare organization.

9. **Represent your healthcare organization in your community.** Chambers of Commerce and other local organizations have frequent events where you can mingle and meet business and professional people from your community. From luncheons to golf tournaments to mixers to casino nights, your Chamber of Commerce will be all about widening your network and providing opportunities to develop friendships, while promoting your healthcare organization.

10. **Become a mentor.** Mentoring a new healthcare organization leader will allow you to view your own growth, and your healthcare organization, from a completely different perspective. It will also help you feel more connected to your profession, and less lonely.

FEELING LONELY? ACCEPTANCE IS THE FIRST STEP

Feeling lonely has little to do with how many people you interact with. Some people who feel lonely interact with lots of people all the time. They constantly may be surrounded by people but not feel connected to them. In fact, chances are that as a busy healthcare leader, you interact with people all day long. That means that if you are feeling lonely, that has to do with the way you feel inside, not necessarily the way you are spending your work time. Filling your time with more of the same kinds of interactions won't necessarily make you feel any better.

Unfortunately, once you begin to feel lonely, you may come to believe that something is wrong with you. Hall suggests, "Many lonely people believe they are unique in their situation and that it's not normal to feel as lonely as they do." Yet most everyone experiences loneliness at times, especially those in isolated leadership positions.

Feeling socially different from the people around you and being unable to talk with them about your loneliness can add to the problem and lead to harsh self-judgments. Be warned, though, that judging yourself for feeling lonely will compound your problem. You will feel bad because you're lonely, and then you'll feel even worse for judging yourself for not taking action to solve the problem. This cycle of loneliness and harsh self-judgment can make it even more difficult for you to change things. And, unfortunately, loneliness left unchecked may be expressed in anger or resentment, which often results in others pulling away, making the problem even bigger, Hall warns.

Accepting that loneliness is a part of the human condition can help to keep things in perspective. So, too, will recognizing that loneliness is often part and parcel with healthcare organization leadership. Hall suggests that you can lessen the impact of leadership loneliness if you:

1. Accept your feelings.
2. Do not judge yourself or others who are lonely.
3. Seek healthy ways to make yourself feel better.

Hall adds, "There is no one idea or one path to move from loneliness to contentment, but there are general ideas that seem to work. A first step seems to be acceptance without judgment."

CONFIDANTS AND LEADERSHIP LONELINESS

Leaders in any organization need to address their personal lives, emotions, intimate fears and concerns, struggles, and failures. Ami Rokach[12] suggests that a spouse or life partner can be a natural confidant for many leaders. According to Rokach, "A good marriage, a caring partner, and open communication provide the type of setting a leader needs to unload, to share, and to hear from a supportive friend."

There are things that we discuss only with people who are very close to us, Rokach explains. These important topics may vary with the situation or the person. We may ask for help, probe for information, or just use the person as a sounding board for important decisions. Confidants influence the actions of others in a constructive and meaningful way, Rokach adds, suggesting, "Leaders need such individuals in order to function both personally and professionally at their optimal level."

Healthcare leaders must be very careful when choosing their confidants. According to Lomenick, your confidant:

- Should not be a member of your team who reports to you as a subordinate or peer.
- Should not be your boss.
- Should be someone with honesty and integrity. You must be 100% sure that this individual will not talk with anyone else about what you're sharing.
- Should be someone you can rely on, share with, lean into for tough decisions, gripe to, and receive counsel from.
- Should advise you but not make decisions for you.
- Should have nothing to gain. Brad Lomenick[13] suggests, "Make sure your confidant is not motivated one way or the other by the outcome of your decisions."
- Should do more listening than talking. Lomenick says, "Advice and counsel many times can be best given through a sounding board rather than a clanging gong."

LONELY? LEAVE YOUR OFFICE

Having an office or workspace that's separate from all or most of your staff can be helpful when you need to have sensitive conversations or uninterrupted time for your work. But it also can be physically isolating. Kevin Kearns[14] warns that too much time in a workspace apart from your staff can increase the chances that you will feel lonely. According to Kearns, "It can be easy to justify staying in your office to complete all of your important tasks. After all, you have timelines to meet and goals to accomplish." However, a negative side effect of all that focus and drive can be what Kearns describes as a "sudden feeling of doubt." You may wonder if anyone cares about your efforts or whether your team even needs you, Kearns says.

Before the doubt gives way to loneliness, Kearns suggests that you get out of your office and interact with your team. Get up and walk around. Kearns' advice: "Be interested in what they are doing. Thank them for being a part of your team. Make a connection." You can take as little as a few minutes walking around your healthcare organization. The key is to get out of your chair and interact with your staff regularly. If you do, Kearns says that you will gain a clarity that keeps you focused on what is important to you and your team. You'll also feel more connected to your employees, and less isolated and lonely.

─────────── **CHAPTER 5 BONUS FEATURE** ───────────

HELPING A LONELY MEMBER OF YOUR TEAM

Loneliness is not the exclusive domain of healthcare leaders. Any employee can feel lonely too. Phyllis Korkki[15] suggests, "It doesn't matter where a person is in the office hierarchy — employees at all levels become lonely, even when other workers are all around them." As a leader, there are a number of things you can do to help prevent and lessen employee loneliness, such as:

- **Facilitate team building activities that require employees to interact.** Even simple icebreakers at the start of meetings can make everyone feel included and help the members of your team learn more about one another. Longer retreats and workshops geared toward team building also may help lonely employees to form bonds with their coworkers.
- **Assign a "buddy" to a new staff member.** The early period in any new job can be a lonely one. Having a friend to have lunch with and who takes an interest in them can help new employees feel included from the start, even if that friend is assigned.
- **Pair or group employees to tackle projects.** Form committees and work groups that will give lonely employees opportunities to collaborate with their coworkers.

- **Create a culture of inclusion.** Explicitly teach your employees the benefits and powers of including everyone in team events. Model inclusive behaviors and reinforce them whenever you see them. Teach your staff that purposefully isolating or shunning a teammate is a silent form of bullying, and that the behavior won't be tolerated in your healthcare organization.

Developing a Thicker Skin as a Leader

D o you have an employee who frequently has their feelings hurt, who seems to take everything personally, or who is prone to tears? Do you replay scenes from work in your head at night, beating yourself up for not handling or anticipating things better, or for making an honest mistake? Or do you or your employees find yourselves feeling hurt, embarrassed, or betrayed by a careless remark, a funny look, or the least bit of criticism? If so, you would all benefit greatly from having a thicker skin.

Of course, developing a thicker skin may be easier said than done. It may be human nature to make everything about us and to take things personally. However, as Lybi Ma[1] bluntly puts it, "You are not the center of the universe." Making everything about ourselves can give us a skewed view of our world and make us overly sensitive and self-absorbed. It also can encourage us to invent stories and imagine things that aren't so. For example, Ma says, we may encounter a person who is not paying enough attention to us. We may brood and ask ourselves, "'Is Christine mad at me?' 'Did I say something wrong?'" Our gloomy thoughts can intensify, Ma says, leaving us emotionally crippled and thinking that we have ruined everything. Yet, there may be a good reason for the inattention that has nothing to do with us. Christine may not have noticed us or been distracted. But even if they are intentionally ignoring us, Ma asks, "Why are you fussing about it?"

Of course, no one enjoys being ignored, facing criticism, or dealing with social rejection. However, it may be impossible to interact with people day in and day out without an occasional brush with these challenges. This is especially the case in a busy healthcare organization, where emotions and stakes can run very high, and where there is going to be a fair amount of pressure put upon you. However, being thin-skinned will help no one. Coworkers may feel they need to tiptoe around or avoid a thin-skinned leader or colleague. And a thin-skinned healthcare leader is going to feel a great deal of pain, which is unpleasant and unproductive, of course, but which also will deplete energy and focus and diminish performance.

Fortunately, healthcare leaders are in an excellent position to develop a thicker skin and to teach their employees to do the same. Aliza Licht[2] suggests, "Learning how to be emotionless in the office is a gift and one that you have to give yourself. The thicker your skin, the less stress you will have." Of course, it can be challenging to take yourself completely out of the equation, remove your ego, and remain objective. Striving to be emotionless, as Licht suggests, may not be the best goal for a healthcare leader or employee. No one advocates that you or any member of your healthcare organization's staff become so tough that they become rigid, unfeeling, and incapable of compassion. The good news is that going to that extreme is not necessary. In this chapter, we will explore skin-thickening strategies that you and your employees can use to reduce or eliminate stress in your healthcare organization, without closing your hearts to others.

EXTERNAL VERSUS INTERNAL EXPECTATIONS

Healthcare leaders and employees have many expectations placed upon them. Some of these expectations will come from a governing board, boss, HR, employee handbook, or a professional association. Some will come from a patient, physician, or coworker. And some will come from within. One way that you can begin to develop a thicker skin is to differentiate between external and internal expectations and to assign each its proper weight. Alex J. Hughes[3] suggests that internal expectations "should always take precedence" as we try to develop a thicker skin.

Of course, you will need to fulfill the expectations of your role as a leader, and no one is suggesting otherwise. But often, we are harder on ourselves than we would be on anyone else. Unfortunately, when we place unrealistic expectations on ourselves, our skin gets thinner and thinner. For example, if we expect to be perfect, we may beat ourselves up when we goof or when someone criticizes us. If we expect that everyone is going to like us all of the time, we may become upset and worried when someone doesn't. And if we expect to be appreciated and applauded, we may feel hurt and unappreciated when no one seems to take notice. Hughes suggests, "When you prioritize the internal expectations you hold for yourself, you naturally develop the thick skin required to put yourself out there."

Begin the process of thickening your skin by examining your internal expectations. Are you being fair with yourself? Are you being reasonable? If not, write and recite affirmations that help you to develop more reasonable and healthier self-expectations. For instance:

- I listen to criticism with an open mind because it can help me to improve.
- I do my best because that matters to me, even when no one is watching.
- I make mistakes, and I learn from them.
- I like myself.
- I am worthy of respect.

Although you may not be able to change the expectations others place on you, you can weigh them differently, and you can change those you place on yourself. In time, reading or reciting your affirmations can help you to shift your self-expectations so you no longer feel crushed by external ones. Hughes suggests, "Turn your attention back to what's within your control."

15 STRATEGIES FOR DEVELOPING A THICKER SKIN

Most of us admire people who can take criticism or abrasive comments without being wounded. If you believe that you or one of your employees is too thin-skinned, here are 15 strategies that can help:

1. **Try your best.** We succumb more easily to guilt and shame when we know that we have not done things to the best of our ability. When we try our best, we can take comfort in knowing that we gave it our all, even if we fail or if others don't like the outcome. Rachel Weingarten[4] suggests, "If you try your best to do something right and you fail, at least you tried, and that is better than not trying."

2. **Reframe.** If someone says something unkind to you, Ma suggests that you reframe the comment to take the sting out of it. For instance, if an employee says that you don't care about them, possible reframes may include:
   - The employee may benefit from more of my undivided attention, more eye contact, or more TLC.
   - The employee may need my reassurance that they are going to be OK.
   - The employee may be upset, hurt, or angry at someone else and is taking it out on me.
   - The employee may feel lonely and frightened.

- The employee does not know me or know that I care.

3. **Dig for the softer emotion beneath the anger.** Angry criticism almost always means the critic feels hurt in some way. Ellen Hendrickson[5] explains, "Anger is a secondary emotion. It's a reaction to a softer primary emotion underneath like hurt, shame, guilt, or humiliation." People get hurt first, Hendrickson says, and then they get angry. But when you listen beneath the anger for the softer emotion, it's much easier to feel sympathetic toward the critic. What then? Hendrickson suggests you try to find out what button you may have inadvertently pushed. Then, "kill them with kindness," Hendrickson says.

4. **Don't retaliate.** If someone says something to you that hurts you, you may be tempted to respond in kind. However, getting along with the people you lead and being kind to them is better than saying something mean because you feel hurt. Weingarten suggests, "In life, we experience highs and lows, but the lows make us stronger and more compassionate."

5. **Stop the self-talk.** Counter self-defeating self-talk with what Ma calls "truth talk." Ma explains, "You can be your own worst enemy, so give yourself a break."

6. **Remind yourself to stay strong.** If you find yourself giving in to feeling hurt, Licht suggests practicing a mental chant. For example, Licht suggests: "I am valuable, and I will not let this break me."

7. **Remember that everyone gets rejected sometimes.** Ma suggests, "Pick yourself up, dust yourself off and move on. Don't be discouraged if it takes a few times to get it right." Successful people are rejected over and over, but never stop trying, Ma says.

8. **Encourage more rejection.** The more we put ourselves out there, the more often we will deal with rejection. According to Weingarten, that is a good thing. With more rejections, we can learn to treasure criticism that can help us improve, Weingarten says. We become better at separating useful criticism from nasty, destructive comments that serve no purpose other than to hurt us.

9. **Remain cool and collected.** Licht suggests that you validate the concerns others have and that you use language that makes others feel heard. Keep your voice even and calm, then explore other avenues. For instance, Licht suggests, you might say, "I hear what you are saying, but it would be really helpful if you could show me an example of

what you are looking for." Or say, "I might have misunderstood your directions. Let me take another stab at this."

10. **Focus on your goals and the steps you need to take to get there.** Ma says, "Don't be self-focused. If you do focus on yourself, you'll likely dwell on your shortcomings."

11. **Agree when you can.** If you're getting panned for something beyond your control, Hendrickson suggest that you agree with the critic. For instance, if test results are late getting back from the lab, agree that the delay is disappointing. Hendrickson suggests, "Redirect the anger away from you and toward the situation."

12. **Don't become defensive.** Hendrickson warns that defensive arguments don't come across as logical or reasonable, but rather "tiresome and difficult." Blaming usually is even worse. Hendrickson strongly suggests not throwing someone under the bus. "It just looks pathetic," Hendrickson says.

13. **Realize that you can reject criticism.** It is possible that the critic is wrong. Hendrickson suggests, "When it's your turn to hear criticism, remember: Just because someone says it doesn't mean it's true." You don't have to heed or accept every piece of advice or criticism you receive. Rejecting useless criticism can be very empowering, Hendrickson says. [See the bonus feature for this chapter, "10 Ways to Thicken Your Skin against Criticism," to learn additional empowering strategies.]

14. **Find thick-skinned role models.** The next time someone lobs a criticism bomb your way, think about people you admire who kept forging ahead, despite their obstacles and critics. Melissa Dinwiddie[6] suggests, "You might even want to post their picture, or quotes by them, by your workspace to inspire you to keep going." Dinwiddie's examples of famous people who overcame rejection include Dr. Seuss, Madonna, Lady Gaga, Hillary Clinton, and Gloria Steinem. Additionally, Bill Gates, Jim Carrey, Albert Einstein, Stephen King, Benjamin Franklin, Richard Branson, and Oprah Winfrey all overcame tremendous obstacles and criticism. Search for and learn about more examples of accomplished thick-skinned people to identify those who inspire you the most.

15. **Reject insults.** A catty, entitled, selfish, or demeaning remark reveals more about the person who says it than it does about you. Don't accept it. Hendrickson suggests, "The only person those remarks degrade is the critic."

WHAT TO DO WHEN YOU FEEL YOUR SKIN THINNING

Despite your best intentions to keep your skin thick, it is the rare person who never succumbs to having a bad day because they have been hurt by others. In fact, being hurt is part of the human experience. Keep in mind that you will be more likely to be hurt when you are worn out and vulnerable, when someone has found and exploited your Achilles heel, and when you are plagued with self-doubt.

You don't have to allow occasional bouts of thin skin to destroy you. On the contrary, you can look at them as opportunities to grow stronger. Scott H. Young[7] suggests, "The only way to develop thicker skin emotionally is to have some scar tissue." Look to the human body for inspiration. Our bodies have an amazing healing mechanism, Young explains. For example, when we break a bone, the refusing of bone tissue makes the point of breakage stronger than it had been before. It can be that way with your emotions, too. Young suggests that the best way to absorb and handle pain is to use it to make yourself stronger against similar attacks in the future. Think of your pain as an emotional wound that will heal and scar over. However, as you build your emotional scars throughout your life, be mindful not to overdo it. Don't scar so easily or so extensively that you close your heart completely. Remember that each scar is relatively small, just as each refused bone from a former break is in just one bone, not the entire skeletal system.

STAY TRUE TO YOUR VISION

Developing emotional scar tissue goes hand in hand with developing and staying true to your vision. Young says, "It's important to focus on your goals constantly and your vision of how you want your life to be. If you can make the picture of what you want perfectly clear and desirable, then you can take a lot more abuse before you get there." Criticism has the potential to derail leaders, Young warns, to make you focus on pleasing everyone instead of staying committed to your vision. Young says, "Whenever I face a lot of criticism, I go back to my goals and what I want." If you don't have goals that are clear and real in your mind, Young warns, "they will be outspoken by the next jerk who doesn't like your ideas." Know what you want, Young says, and keep that first and foremost as you move forward.

But what if you don't know what you want? Young suggests that you start there. Otherwise, it's going to be very easy for people to "seduce and threaten you off track," Young says. In the end, having a thick skin means that you'll be more independent. Young says, "When you don't rely on the constant approval of other people, you're free to pursue what you really want." Being able to thicken your skin, therefore, is not only liberating; it also will enable you to take more risks, accomplish great things, and inspire others.

TAKING THINGS PERSONALLY? HERE'S WHY, AND WHAT TO DO ABOUT IT

Most people who take things personally learned to do that in childhood. Gail Brenner[9] suggests, "When we are young, events happen that bring about emotional reactions in us. If you didn't have the means to experience the feelings and let them go, they leave an impression in your body and mind, creating a sensitivity to reacting the same way again and again." Decades later, Brenner explains, we experience rejection and disappointment as we did in childhood and revert to the childhood tactic of taking things personally. Then, Brenner warns, the "spinoff stories start." For example, we tell ourselves, "I'm not deserving," or "I'm inadequate." These experiences congeal into an identity in which our adult selves take everything personally. That keeps us frozen and limited.

Unfortunately, an identity in which we take most things personally can be very real to us. It can become who we are. We then go through life thin-skinned and easily hurt. However, when we step back and examine things more objectively, we can begin to see that we are creating stories. When that happens, Brenner says, "You realize that you don't have to make a big deal over something that isn't real anyway." Brenner's advice: Be like the sky. Let dark clouds and difficult thoughts and feelings move through you. Think of them as "nothing more than insubstantial wisps of energy that appear and disappear," Brenner says.

It takes time and effort to erode lifelong habits that feel so real. However, you must learn to be very kind to yourself. Brenner suggests, "When you notice that you are taking something personally, step off the habit wheel. Pause and take a breath." Consider that your thoughts and feelings don't accurately match up with reality, and that they don't define you. When you discover that everything in the world is not personal, Brenner says, you will find "the deepest peace beyond imagination."

——————— **CHAPTER 6 BONUS FEATURE** ———————

10 WAYS TO THICKEN YOUR SKIN AGAINST CRITICISM

Criticism is the fodder for a thin-skinned person's anxiety mill. If you crumble at the first sign of criticism, Ayodeji Awosika[9] suggests that you:

1. **Understand the limited mindset of others.** People who are afraid to move outside of their comfort zone will try to project their limitations onto you. Unfortunately, many of us have been raised to view life with a limited mindset. Understand how your critics see the world and you won't take offense at their comments.

2. **Understand who you seek approval from, and why.** Why do you want others' approval? How important is it that they approve? What is the worst-case scenario if they don't?

3. **Understand that haters come with the territory.** Awosika suggests, "It's impossible to be well known or recognized without having critics." You'd be hard-pressed to identify an effective leader who has not received criticism. Ask: Is this person giving me thoughtful feedback? Or is this person just trying to get under my skin and/or one-up me?

4. **Recognize that being upset is a choice.** You may not be able to control what another person says or does. But you can choose how you react to it.

5. **Don't tie your well-being and self-worth to the opinion of others.** Find your happiness and meaning in the effort you put forth and in what you produce, not on what others think of you.

6. **Don't respond to people who are trying to tear you down.** Don't feel the need to defend yourself when you're being attacked. It's a waste of your time and energy, and it probably won't do any good. Put that energy toward continuing to create something positive through your work.

7. **Google negative comments about Mother Teresa.** You will find about a half-million or more results of people bashing Mother Teresa.

Awosika suggests, "Even the most pious individuals aren't immune to criticism." Understand this fact and embrace it.

8. **Value work over criticism.** Awosika suggests, "No one ever built a statue of a critic." A critic takes a small amount of time to judge work you may have spent several hours, days, months, or even years to create. Awosika says, "It's much easier to critique other people's work than to do work of your own." Pay the closest attention to the people who walk the walk, not just talk the talk.

9. **Appreciate the people who look up to you.** There are going to be people who respect you for putting yourself out there. And there will be those who will appreciate your hard work. Awosika suggests, "Keep in mind that you're touching other people's lives with the work you do." It would be selfish to hide your gifts from a world that needs them because you are afraid of criticism.

10. **Do great work.** When you take the time to do great work, you can thwart potential criticism. You also can feel positive about the work you do even when it's criticized.

CHAPTER 7

Telling Stories to Lead, Influence, Teach, and Inspire

"The most powerful person in the world is the storyteller. The storyteller sets the vision, values, and agenda of an entire generation that is to come . . ."
– Steve Jobs, 1994

A key component of your job as a healthcare leader is to motivate your employees to strive for and reach new goals. One way to motivate them is to appeal to their intellect by sharing relevant facts, statistics, and advice from authorities. For example, you might tell your employees, "Here's our biggest challenge/opportunity/obstacle, here's what the metrics look like, here's what others advise us to do about it, so here's what we need to do." Such conventional rhetoric is very familiar and comfortable for most leaders. However, Bronwyn Fryer[1] suggests that there are two problems when a leader's rhetoric appeals only to intellect. First, your employees will bring their own authorities, statistics, and life experiences to the table. They may argue with you in their heads while you are speaking to them and share their arguments with their coworkers after you leave the room. Second, Fryer says, "People are not inspired to act by reason alone." Even if you succeed in getting your employees to accept your line of thinking, logic alone won't be sufficient to motivate change that requires difficult, distasteful, or sustained effort. We've all experienced times in our lives when we know that we "should" do something logically but don't because of inertia or because it's too hard or unpleasant to do it.

The other way to persuade people, and arguably, the more powerful way, is to unite an idea with an emotion. The best way to do that, Fryer says, is to tell a compelling story. Fryer explains, "In a story, you not only weave a lot of information into the telling but you also arouse your listener's emotions and energy." However, while any intelligent leader can build a case using logic, persuading with story is more difficult. C. Hazell[2] says, "It might seem simple to tell a great story about your organization as a leader, but it's not as easy as it sounds." That said, becoming a skilled and effective storyteller is not only doable but extremely worthwhile. In fact, despite the epigraph that begins this article, Steve Jobs was not always a great storyteller. Dave Byrne[3] says, "He made the choice to become one." You can, too. And once you add storytelling to your leadership toolkit, you will be able to get your employees to rise to their feet amid thunderous applause as Jobs did his, rather than doubting, yawning, and ignoring you.

THE POWER OF STORY

Stories are a universally appealing part of the human experience, which explains why every culture has them. We are drawn to stories regardless of our age, ethnicity, gender, wealth, or nationality, and we loved them in our ancient past just as much as we do now. The American Society of Administrative Professionals (ASAP)[4] says, "We tell them [stories] face to face and around campfires; through pictures drawn on cave walls and through song; to family and to strangers." In fact, stories have been implanted in us thousands of times since we were young children barely able to understand them. We've heard fairy tales, read books, seen movies, attended plays, and consumed story-based songs, comedy sketches, and jokes. And whether we know it or not, we continue to engage with stories every day, from those adorable animal videos on social media, to the television ads that melt our hearts, to the biographies we crave about our favorite leaders and celebrities.

Effective storytellers often describe what it's like when we must deal with difficult choices and opposing forces. For example, they may explore whether we should do what will benefit us personally or do what is right, whether to have fun now or to forego fun because of a greater need in the future, or whether to give in to laziness or to work slow and steady to win the race. Stories call upon the protagonist to dig deeper, work with scarce resources, make tough decisions, take needed action, make mistakes, and, ultimately, discover the truth. Fryer explains, "All great storytellers since the dawn of time — from the ancient Greeks through Shakespeare and up to the present day — have dealt with this fundamental conflict between subjective expectation and cruel reality.

In fact, the conflict between our expectations and reality is played out in a considerable number of our most popular stories. Taken to the extreme, this conflict threatens the protagonist's very survival. Stories of expectations versus reality typically follow a pattern. Our fairy tales and fables, for instance, begin with a protagonist's personal desire or objective — to marry a prince, to go to grandmother's house, to win the race, or to see what's at the top of the beanstalk. Fryer explains, "Desire is the blood of a story. Desire is not a shopping list but a core need that, if satisfied, would stop the story in its tracks." In "The Three Little Pigs," for example, the protagonists' core desire is to have a house to live in. However, there is an unavoidable conflict: on the one hand there's a hungry wolf out there who likes to eat pigs, but on the other, it takes a lot of time and hard work to build a strong house. It's much more fun to play. The story unfolds and the pigs face their cruel reality: the wolf is very strong, and flimsy houses do not provide adequate protection. The storyteller then leaves it to us to draw our own conclusion; put in the hard work or you may not survive. This pattern — the protagonist's desire and expectations + conflict + actions + cruel reality — is the same pattern we see in many of our classic adult stories, too, such as *Oedipus Rex, King Lear, Anna Karenina*, and even most episodes of *Seinfeld*. Leaders can follow this pattern equally well when crafting stories to share with their employees.

A good story entertains us but also helps us to connect with one another and with our shared traditions, legends, and universal truths. It can become engrained in our culture. A good story also increases our understanding and empathy, engages our emotions, and helps us to share our enthusiasm, problems, sorrows, and joys. A good story can provide the structure, order, and reassurance that employees seek in trying times by making their disconcerting ideas and experiences seem more familiar, predictable, and comfortable. It can also convince them to take action, trigger their imaginations, tap into their creativity, and help them to see and believe what is possible. As well, storytelling is a powerful leadership tool because:

- **Stories appeal to all types of learners.** In any group, roughly 40% will be predominantly visual learners who learn best from videos, diagrams, or illustrations. Another 40% will be auditory, learning best through lectures and discussions. The remaining 20% will be kinesthetic learners, who learn best by doing, experiencing, or feeling. Paul Smith[5] explains, "Storytelling has aspects that work for all three types [of learners]. Visual learners appreciate the mental pictures storytelling evokes. Auditory learners focus on the words and the storyteller's voice.

Kinesthetic learners remember the emotional connections and feelings from the story."

- **Our brains process imagined experiences as though they are real.** Neurological research indicates that our brains produce the stress hormone cortisol during tense moments in a story. Stories that make us feel care and connection can produce oxytocin, and the more oxytocin we produce, the more empathy we feel. According to Hazell, "Stories that captivate emotion and hope can literally change the way our brains process the world."

- **Stories stick.** Good stories are easy to remember. Hazell explains, "We remember rules and lessons best when we're told them in the form of a story." Research bears this out. Vanessa Boris[6] explains, "Organizational psychologist Peg Neuhauser found that learning which stems from a well-told story is remembered more accurately, and for far longer, than learning derived from facts and figures." Similarly, Smith[7] says, psychologist Jerome Bruner's research suggests that facts are 20 times more likely to be remembered if they're presented as part of a story.

- **Stories are contagious.** Smith suggests, "They can spread like wildfire without any additional effort on the part of the storyteller."

- **Stories put the listener in learning mode.** Listeners who are in a logical, critical, or evaluative mode are more likely to reject what's being said. However, storytelling recreates in us that emotional state of curiosity that is ever present in children, but that as adults we tend to lose. Once in this childlike state, we tend to be more receptive and interested in the information we receive. If you doubt this, stop speaking logically, say the words *I'd like to share a story with you*, and watch what happens. Your listeners will put down their pens, open their posture, look at you more intently, and just listen.

- **Telling stories shows respect for your listeners.** Smith suggests, "Stories get your message across without arrogantly telling listeners what to think or do." Stories give people freedom to come to their own conclusions. As a leader, telling a story can be an extremely respectful way for you to explain to your employees what you need them to do without your having to issue orders.

- **Stories connect storytellers to their audience.** Nathanael Yellis[8] suggests that stories can help listeners empathize with the storyteller. They also provide a way for storytellers to demonstrate their empathy for the listener and to build a powerful emotional connection. Yellis says, "Stories bring the teller's emotions to life for the audience."

- **Stories are disarming.** Although debate and arguments can be threatening, storytelling is not. BB & Co. Strategic Storytelling[9] suggests that telling a story is like a "momentary cease-fire" in the most contentious of discussions, giving all sides the chance to pause, take a breath, and simply listen. BB & Co. says, "In that moment, tempers can calm, and cooler heads can prevail."

Storytelling may seem like an old-fashioned tool in this era of technology. Nonetheless, it is extremely powerful. BB & Co. Strategic Storytelling suggests, "Because we learn best from stories that we relate to emotionally, the most effective leaders . . . the most effective advertising . . . the most effective art . . . even, the most effective relationships embrace stories."

WHERE TO FIND YOUR STORY

You don't have to be a superhero to tell great stories. Esther Choy[10] says, "You don't need to have scaled Kilimanjaro or invented the next Google to tell stories from your life. Somebody who's good at telling stories can make plywood or even paperclips interesting!" Material for good stories is all around you if you know where to look:

- **Paint a picture of the future.** Fryer suggests that you begin your search for a great story by analyzing your organization's past. Then, project the future as a story. As Fryer explains, "You create scenarios in your head of possible future events to try to anticipate the life of your company or your own personal life." However, while crafting your stories, don't tell a beginning-to-end tale describing how results meet expectations. That is boring, predictable, and banal, Fryer says. Instead, display the struggles that you and your organization have faced in the past between expectations and reality, as well as those you are most likely to face in the future.
- **Share a real (not imagined) failure.** It takes courage to talk openly about our failures, and some leaders are loath to do so. However, a compelling story can often be found when we are willing to speak honestly and openly about what has gone wrong. Fryer explains, "Ever since human beings sat around the fire in caves, we've told stories to help us deal with the dread of life and the struggle to survive. All great stories illuminate the dark side."

- **Share a mistake.** If you don't have a catastrophic failure or deep dark side to weave into your story, focus on the smaller mistakes you've made. Employees' ears perk up when they hear their leaders speak of their mistakes and how they overcame them. They like to see their leaders as human and flawed, and they appreciate it when their leaders are willing to admit their errors, even dumb ones. S. Thompson[11] suggests, "By sharing relevant stories about their mistakes and struggles, and how they've helped others, leaders offer evidence that we can trust them to lead us towards some objective."

- **Tell your origin story.** We all started somewhere, and how you or your healthcare organization began can serve as good material for your story. Choy suggests, "People are naturally curious about how movements, causes, or companies got started." Choy recommends that you reflect on how the past has influenced the present. For instance, Choy asks, "What has changed since the beginning, and what core values or visions have stayed the same?"

- **Share your rags-to-riches or underdog story.** This is not a story every leader can tell, because not everyone has had a rags-to-riches life. However, such stories, when true, can be very compelling. They can be especially effective to explain when you started to feel like you'd made it on your journey upward. As well, Choy suggests, "Reflect on how the 'rags' give you perspective on the 'riches.'"

- **Describe overcoming the monster.** Many organizations have had to overcome seemingly impossible obstacles. Others have powerful examples of how their employees, founders, or leaders had to look a difficult "monster" in the eye and overcome it. Choy suggests, "These organizations are sitting on a goldmine! Their stories will inspire and motivate their employees, customers, investors, or donors." Choy suggests that it is most effective to describe the setbacks and rebounds you experienced on your way to overcoming the monster. Choy suggests too that the storyteller reflect on what he and others have learned from the battle.

- **Use everyday moments.** A remark from a patient, an employee accomplishment, or even "a funny thing happened on the way to work today" can all be good material for a story. It can be especially powerful to highlight what an employee has done well, large or small, and to give credit where it is due.

WHEN TO TELL A STORY, AND WHEN NOT TO

Healthcare is not entertainment. Most of the time, employees do not need or want to hear stories from their leaders, and, in fact, telling poorly timed stories can do more harm than good. According to Randy Shattuck,[12] inopportune stories can become "a distraction and even disrupt a focused work environment." However, although there are times when stories are not going to be welcome or effective, there will be key leadership storytelling moments when they most definitely are. Great leaders seize those moments. Choy[13] cautions, "There can be harmful consequences if they [leaders] do not present a coherent narrative to their teams during these key moments."

When will your stories be most effective? It will be in the big moments in your healthcare organization, when something important is at stake. Shattuck suggests that leaders reserve their stories for these occasions so they will have the greatest impact. Times of uncertainty are arguably the biggest and best moments for leadership storytelling. Choy suggests, "When your team faces uncertainty, they need you to tell them what you think is going on." Is your healthcare organization about to go into a new market? Launch a new service? Reorganize? Merge? Be acquired? Is there going to be a change in leadership? Systems? Facilities? Has there been an unflattering story about you in the newspaper, or are you embroiled in a lawsuit that has gone public? Or is the country, city, or community going through a macroeconomic shift or battling an extraordinary health crisis? These are leadership storytelling moments when your team will crave your perspective the most. Missing the opportunity to tell a compelling story in such moments can create what Choy calls a "story vacuum." Choy explains, "When times are uncertain and those in the know are not speaking up, others will rush to fill in the gaps with their own stories. This is fertile ground for rumors! People will be constructing a narrative no matter what." It's up to you whether you intentionally contribute to that narrative through storytelling or leave your employees to their own devices, Choy says.

Times of disappointment and failure also are great opportunities for leadership storytelling. Employees will be looking to you for inspiration and reassurance when their confidence has been shaken. Sebastian Kipman[14] points out that there are many great examples of famous people who have failed on their way to success, such as Abraham Lincoln, Thomas Edison, Steven Spielberg, Walt Disney, Albert Einstein, J.K. Rowling,

Oprah Winfrey, Stephen King, Elvis Presley, and Michael Jordan. Telling their stories of failure, perseverance, and comeback, as well as your own personal stories, can inspire employees who have been beaten down by disappointment and failure.

Finally, if you find yourself stepping into a new leadership role or a higher level of leadership, that, too, is a perfect moment for you to share a story with your employees. It is natural for the new employees you manage to want to know who their new boss is. They may be nervous about how things will change, loyal to a leader who has left, or skeptical about your abilities. David Grossman[15] says, "Employees don't want to follow leaders who they don't really know and understand. You can't get anywhere with your team if they don't see you as a real person who's not perfect but who has a real vision. . . ." A sincere, heartfelt story that reveals who you are as a person and what you foresee for the future is just what is needed in such moments.

HOW TO DELIVER YOUR STORY: 10 TIPS

You don't need to be a stand-up comedian or a witty raconteur to deliver an effective story. A plain, simple, and direct style often works best. Stephen Denning[16] suggests 10 storytelling style tips:

1. **Be fully present for your employees.** Storytelling is a performance art. You must be ready to deliver your story at peak performance at the appointed day and hour. When you open your mouth to begin your story, make yourself totally available to your employees. Denning says, "If you are there for them, they will be there for you."
2. **Put nothing between you and your employees.** If there is a podium or table, come out from behind it. Don't use notes if possible. Notes are a huge distraction and will signal to your employees that this is not a conversation but a one-way rehearsed lecture. Look at the employees when you're telling them a story, not at notes or a PowerPoint slide.
3. **Tell your story as if you were talking to one person.** Your voice should be the voice of dialogue, not of a booming lecturer. Give your story the rhythm of a conversation.
4. **Show interest to all of your employees.** Don't talk to one subgroup of employees or to one side of the room. Move toward your employees and look at everyone. Maintain direct eye contact as much as possible.
5. **Be rehearsed but seem spontaneous.** Your story should not feel like a hackneyed set piece that you have labored over and delivered time

and again. Speak as though the words are just coming to you in the moment. Denning admits, "The appearance of spontaneity is of course an illusion." Nonetheless, the story should not seem overly polished and rehearsed. Denning explains, "Even if you are telling the story for the seventh time, you relive it afresh in your mind as if you are experiencing it for the first time. You feel the emotions of the original participants yet again, and the audience will also feel these emotions." Because the story is fresh each time for the storyteller, Denning says, it's fresh for the audience, too.

6. **Keep your storytelling focused, simple, and clear.** Use language that doesn't draw attention to itself and avoid unusual mannerisms and striking gestures. If anything, tell your story in an understated manner. Your goal is not to make your employees think you're a great storyteller, but to focus on the content of your story.

7. **Avoid hedges.** Avoid disclaimers that you don't have the time to tell the whole story, or phrases like "as far as I know."

8. **Present your story as something valuable.** A good story is a gift. Don't rush through it and don't apologize for taking the time to tell it. The time you spend on your story is time well spent as it may give your employees a meaning or an insight they may not have otherwise.

9. **Be lively.** Vary the pace and tone of your story to keep your employees alert. Raise and lower the volume of your voice appropriately to convey your emotions.

10. **Adjust for your employees.** If your employees laugh, dwell on the point for a moment or two longer to take advantage of their laughter. If your employees fidget or seem otherwise disengaged, move swiftly to another story element that is likely to be more appealing.

SHOW, DON'T TELL

It's easy to make statements such as, "Never underestimate the power of a caring coworker." While that statement is true, it is not gripping, exciting, entertaining, or memorable. Sarah Peck[17] says, "The point of your story isn't to beat someone over the head with the idea, but rather to SHOW it through lots of vivid detail and an example that highlights your core philosophy." For example, here is a story, adapted from Peck, that illustrates the impact of showing through story rather than telling through statement.

Notice the use of rich description, the storyteller's admission of feeling guilty, and the element of surprise:

> Do you remember when we were completing our EHR data migration a few months ago? That was a very busy time for us, wasn't it? Like many of you, I was putting in extra hours to keep up with everything. Then, at the end of a very long day, my mother called me to tell me that my grandmother had passed. You can imagine the pain of my grief. I loved my grandmother. But on top of that, I also felt tremendous guilt because I knew that my grandmother had been ill but I didn't make the time to travel back home to see her or to say my goodbyes. I also had let my mom down. I knew that she spent that last terrible day in hospice watching her mother slip away without me there to help or support her.
>
> As if things couldn't get any worse, there was a relentless foggy drizzle that night that made visibility poor, so, of course, traffic on the way home was terrible. I realized while straining to see through my windshield that I hadn't eaten lunch that day. In fact, a dull headache had already taken root. That's when I remembered that I had almost no food at home and that I had planned to go to the grocery store after work. But at that moment, I had no energy, desire, or time for that. I didn't even want to take the time to drive through a fast-food window. I just wanted to get home, eat whatever I could scrounge up, and book my airline reservations to travel home for the funeral. When I finally pulled into my driveway, I saw someone sitting on my stoop. "Probably another homeless person," I thought to myself. I approached with caution and irritation. Could there have been a worse time for this? But as I got closer, I saw that it was Andy sitting there in the damp fog, with two bags of Indian takeout food beside him. He stood to greet me and wrapped me in a big hug. "I thought that you could use this today," he said, pointing to the food. "Let's go inside and eat."

As you finish a story such as this one, you may be tempted to tell your employees the moral. In this example, it would be, "Never underestimate the power of a caring coworker." But resist this temptation if you can. Peck suggests, "Whatever your core philosophical statement, think about leaving it unsaid." It is much more powerful to leave it to your employees to draw their own conclusions about your story. Unless you're telling Aesop's fables, which include moral lessons, choose your story well, tell it effectively, and leave the moral unspoken. Your employees will come to the conclusion that you had in mind all along, Peck says and feel so much more connected to you and to your story for doing so.

--------- CHAPTER 7 BONUS FEATURE ---------

WHEN STORYTELLING GOES WRONG: 10 FATAL MISTAKES

Have you ever told a story that bombed, or that didn't get the response you were hoping for? That happens to every storyteller and is part of the learning process. However, Rob Biesenbach[18] says, "If you want to keep it from happening again, you need to diagnose what went wrong. Chances are, you made one (or more) fatal storytelling mistakes." Below, Biesenbach offers 10 mistakes novice storytellers make, and that you should avoid:

1. **Not understanding your audience:** Whether you're talking to one employee or hundreds, you must know your audience to ensure that your story is relevant. Do your homework. Who are your employees? What are their needs, concerns, doubts, and misperceptions? What angers or frightens them? As part of your research, assess your employees' mood. Are they discouraged? Frustrated? Jaded? Cynical? What's happened lately? Have they just gone through a round of layoffs? Are they feeling over-burdened and worried for their jobs? Biesenbach says, "These are important things to know before springing some rosy, feel-good story on them or reminding them of their pain points."

2. **Having bad timing:** Your employees will be most receptive to your story when they aren't distracted by other tasks. Choose a time for storytelling when your employees can give you their time and attention without feeling pulled in multiple directions.

3. **Being too generic:** Your story should be about a specific character, time, and place. This is true even if you make up a story.

4. **Cluttering your story with extraneous details:** Your employees don't need to know the name of every minor character in your story or the precise date that every event happened. Avoid tangents and meandering. Separate the "nice to know" from the "need to know." Biesenbach warns, "A perfectly good story can be ruined by too much detail."

5. **Leaving out conflict:** At the heart of good story structure is conflict, usually an obstacle that is preventing your protagonist from getting what they want. Biesenbach suggests, "That's where the drama and human interest lie. If there's no conflict, the story is flat — there's no reason for us to listen."

6. **Creating an unrelatable character:** Your employees need to be able to see something of themselves in the protagonist of your story. That character must come from your employees' world or at least share values, traits, or struggles that your employees can relate to. Your protagonist also must seem real to your employees. Biesenbach says, "That means flawed in some way. Nobody's perfect — even superheroes."

7. **Trying too hard to be funny:** The best humor arises organically from the everyday foibles and frustrations of life that we all experience. It's based on truth. Biesenbach suggests, "People are much more likely to laugh at your story about losing your luggage than at some manufactured setup and punchline."

8. **Not practicing:** Good storytelling requires practice. You need to tell your story over and over, to yourself and, preferably, to others. You need to shape it, sharpen the turning points, heighten the highs, enhance the lows, and hone it down to its most critical elements. Then, you need to internalize it so you don't stumble as you tell it. Practice will enable you to focus on your emotions in the moment, rather than on what comes next in your story.

9. **Leaving the story unresolved:** Your story must go somewhere worthwhile; it must arrive at a satisfying conclusion. Resolve the conflict or if you can't, have your protagonist learn something. "There has to be a clear lesson for the audience to take away," Biedenbach says.

10. **Telling an overused story:** Employees will be understandably tired of hearing the same old stories again and again. If you've found a story at the watercooler or circulating online, chances are that at least some of your employees have already heard it. Biesenbach urges, "Be original."

CHAPTER 8

Healthcare Leadership for Introverts

Leadership does not need to be a dramatic, fist in the air and trumpets blaring activity.

—Scott Berkun[1]

H ealthcare leaders often are described with adjectives that we associate with extroverts, such as *forceful, dynamic, outgoing, high-spirited, exuberant,* and *social.* It's no surprise, then, that many people assume that extroverts make the best leaders. This belief is reinforced by the many successful extroverted leaders we've witnessed in action, but also by a sweeping cultural shift that began in the 1920s and 1930s. Back then, Dale Carnegie's courses and his book *How to Win Friends and Influence People* soared in popularity and became a catalyst for what Susan Cain[2] has dubbed a new "Culture of Personality." Cain explains, "Americans started to focus on how others perceived them. They became captivated by people who were bold and entertaining." Americans were increasingly drawn to matinee idols, politicians, business leaders, religious leaders, friends, and neighbors who were outgoing, charismatic, and extroverted. Our love affair with extroversion flourished throughout the remainder of the 20th century and continues to thrive in our culture today.

Throughout history and even during and after our cultural shift toward extroversion, however, some of our most effective, successful, and famous leaders have been introverts. For example, Bonnie Monych[3] writes, Bill Gates, Warren Buffett, Mark Zuckerberg, Elon Musk, Abraham Lincoln, and Mahatma Gandhi are/were introverts. The Harvard Division of Continuing Education[4] adds Oprah Winfrey, Ruth Bader Ginsberg, and Michael Jordan to the list of introverted leaders. John Rampton[5] reports that Steven Spielberg, Al Gore, Hillary Clinton, and Barack Obama are introverts. And Jennifer B. Kahnweiler[6] says that Nelson Mandela, Mother Teresa, and Martin Luther King Jr. were introverts too.

Oprah and President Obama aside, most introverts choose to keep out of the limelight, and many people think that that's where they should stay. Ty Belknap[7] explains, "The world is full of loud sports events, loud parties, and loud traffic. It's full of open office layouts, big-gathering holiday parties, and more meetings than you can shake a stick at." In many healthcare organizations, group brainstorming, in-person networking, board meetings, community outreach programs, and splashy fundraisers and events for donors are the norm. Healthcare leaders often find themselves having to work a room or to perform in front of large numbers of people with all eyes upon them. It would seem that introverts would be ill-suited to these leadership tasks. But if that's the case, how can we explain why there have been so many examples of introverts who have been great leaders? Are they flukes? Are introverts better suited to the challenges of leadership than a lot of people think, and if so, how? And what exactly do effective introverted leaders do to thrive in what Belknap describes as an "extroverted world"?

WHAT IS INTROVERSION?

Imagine that you can store your energy in a rechargeable battery. Extroverts charge their batteries by being with people, whereas introverts charge their batteries by going within and taking time alone. Most people are not extreme introverts or extroverts but fall somewhere toward the middle range of the introvert/extrovert spectrum. According to Kahlweiler, quoted in Henna Inam's interview,[8] "Where you fall [on the spectrum] can often be determined by how important it is for you to have a break after being with people. If you must have a break, you may be more introverted. If taking a break from people is nice, but not necessary, you may fall on the extroverted side." Kahlweiler reports that an estimated 40% to 60% of people fall on the introverted side of the spectrum and that they share many of the same patterns of behavior. For example, Rachel Reiff Ellis[9] says that introverts:

- Need quiet to concentrate.
- Are reflective.
- Are self-aware.
- Take time making decisions.
- Feel comfortable being alone.
- Don't like group work.
- Prefer to write rather than talk.
- Feel tired after being in a crowd.

- Have few friendships but are very close with these friends.
- Daydream or use their imaginations to work out problems.
- Retreat into their own minds to rest.

Scientists don't know for sure if there's a cause for introversion or extroversion. What they do know is that the brains of the two personality types work differently from one other. Ellis reports, "Researchers have found that introverts have a higher blood flow to their frontal lobe than extroverts do. This part of the brain helps you remember things, solve problems, and plan ahead." Introvert brains also react differently to dopamine than extrovert brains do. Introverts and extroverts have the same amount of the chemical, but extrovert brains get an excited buzz from their reward center. Introverts, on the other hand, tend to feel "run-down by it," Ellis says.

Introverts often are more misunderstood and undervalued than extroverts, especially in highly extroverted workplaces and cultures. Inam explains, "Their [introverts'] lack of seeking attention is often misconstrued as lack of ambition, lack of ability to connect with people, or lack of being able to influence and lead others." Often, introverts are more reserved and calmer than extroverts, express their thoughts after reflection, are private (especially at first), and have a low-key or neutral facial expression. They typically prefer small group or one-on-one discussions and often are humble. These characteristics are sometimes misconstrued for weakness, especially when compared with the behaviors we see in gregarious, highly social extroverts. Ellis says that other misconceptions about introverts are that they are unfriendly and hard to get to know and that they don't make good leaders. However, the opposite is often true. Being an introvert doesn't affect how friendly you may be, Ellis says, and introverts often develop very deep friendships. As well, Ellis says, "Some of their [introvert's] qualities make them effective leaders."

Another area of misunderstanding is that it is not as easy to spot an introvert as many people think. Belknap explains, "Extroverts would be surprised at how many people are introverts because we have learned to act at being extroverts." Extroversion is expected in the United States and in most of the western world, Belknap says. In fact, introverts who are attuned to this expectation and who have the desire and strength to succeed will usually develop their extroverted tendencies and bring them to the forefront when the situation calls for it. That can explain why introverts may behave in a more extroverted fashion in the workplace, at social events, and when they go on a dating app than they do in other parts of their lives.

THE ADVANTAGES OF BEING AN INTROVERTED LEADER

The job of healthcare leaders is not only to rally the troops, talk, and push their followers forward. Leaders also must be able to adjust their strategies based on new data, input, and analysis. They must be active listeners and astute observers who are able to summarize and synthesize key points for their followers. Often, leaders must recognize what others do not see and anticipate what others do not anticipate. Belknap says, "Yes, extroverts can do that, but introverts were born to do it."

Furthermore, the ability to pay careful attention to others generally goes hand in hand with introversion. Brenda Miller[10] suggests, "An extrovert will speak a lot when placed in any group, thus making them the center of attention." Introverts, on the other hand, are less often the focus of attention. Their introverted traits — listening to others, paying attention to details, quiet reflection, critical outside-the-box-thinking, and problem solving — are what often help them to excel as leaders. Monych explains, "After all, it takes a listener to gather customer feedback and employee observations, and a critical thinker to put together common elements that may result in a new business opportunity." An introverted leader is likely to listen actively and to think critically before rushing to judgment and speaking. In today's complex workplace, Monych says, a well-thought-out response may be the better option than quick action (depending upon the urgency of the circumstances, of course).

Introverts also can be excellent communicators and tend to excel particularly at writing. Kahlweiler (interviewed by Inam) says, "They prefer writing to speaking and will clarify their points through carefully thought-out emails." Introverts tend also to be very well-prepared speakers. They usually take less airtime at meetings than extroverts and let others do more of the talking. By listening and not speaking, they set the stage for people to "step into their own strengths," Kahlweiler says. When introverts do speak, people generally pay close attention precisely because they don't talk all the time. Miller explains, "There is power in silence."

Additionally, introverted leaders may have an edge over extroverts when communicating with younger employees. Monych says, "Extroverts, brace yourselves. Today's all-digital, all-the-time environment means that young people entering the workforce tend to communicate in a more introverted fashion." They're accustomed to highly individualized social interaction and communicating by text, social media, and email to access and share information, Monych says. This change, already seen in workplaces that hire millennial and Generation Z employees, points to training and development opportunities for extroverted employees so they can learn how to succeed in today's more introverted work environments. Introverts probably will find it easy to adjust to this workplace culture shift, Monych suggests.

Finally, introverts tend to be humble, and it is their quiet humility that has pushed many of them up the chain of authority. Miller says, "They [introverts] don't boast about their accomplishments" and are quick and happy to give credit to others. Introverts usually acknowledge their mistakes and accept their limitations. Being naturally and genuinely humble, introverts welcome new ideas and suggestions without feeling threatened. "It is this trait [humility] that makes introverts quietly confident," Miller says.

THE CHALLENGES OF BEING AN INTROVERTED LEADER

Any overused strength becomes a weakness, and this is as true for introverted leaders as anyone else. Introverted leaders face several challenges. For example, they may:

- **Miss opportunities to build relationships.** Kahlweiler suggests that introverted leaders can become too comfortable in their solitude and avoid building key relationships.
- **Miss opportunities for new projects and promotions.** Introverted leaders don't like to toot their own horns and, as a result, may stay under the radar and be passed over for new projects and promotions. Kahlweiler explains, "If you inform people about what you are accomplishing, they will better understand your value and consider you for opportunities."
- **Be too empathetic.** Introverted leaders are keen observers and prone to being more empathetic than extroverted leaders. Adam Wakowski[11] explains, "This trait [empathy] is not always welcome in leaders because it restricts them from being tough enough when the situation so requires."

- **Lack small talk skills.** Introverted leaders may not be the best at small talk, which Wakowski describes as "an important factor in developing relationships between colleagues."
- **Find interruptions draining.** Introverted leaders are easily distracted and challenged by external stimuli. Jason Cornes[12] says, "While they might be too nice to say anything, they get very frustrated with constant interruptions when they are trying to concentrate." Workplaces where people are constantly striking up conversations or breaking up the day with meetings make it almost impossible for introverts to engage in deep thought, Cornes says.
- **Have smaller networks.** While extroverts collect contacts easily, introverts are likely to have smaller networks. They may not have the breadth of relationships that extroverts do. Therefore, they may not know as many people who can help them or who have faced the leadership challenges they're facing.
- **Encourage others to invent things about them.** Introverts are more likely to be labeled as weird or snobbish than extroverts because they don't interact as much. Kathleen Elkins[13] explains, "In almost every real-life situation, folks are going to be suspicious of the person who keeps to themselves." Others may invent things about an introverted leader in the absence of personal experience, and they may assign a lot of negative traits to them. For example, Elkins says, others may think, "She's aloof. Snobby. Has something to hide. Strange. Selfish." Occasionally, people may invent something good about an introverted leader, but 80% of the time the introvert is going to be a "shady character," Elkins says.
- **Need time to recharge.** Introverts need time away from others to regain their energy, especially after highly social events, and there will be consequences if they don't get that time. For instance, they may become frustrated, irritable, and fatigued. They also may lose focus and experience headaches or other physical symptoms of stress. Cornes explains, "If they are forced to sacrifice this [down time], they won't be operating at full capacity until they have had a break."

10 STRATEGIES FOR INTROVERTED HEALTHCARE LEADERS

Extroverts stepping into leadership often do so with a lot of advantages. They find their energy from being with others and do not need as much time to themselves. They usually are accepted and embraced quickly by their followers because they act the way most people expect leaders to act. What you see with extroverts is typically what you get. Introverted leaders, on the other hand, often have a harder row to hoe. They may have to overcome strong misconceptions and cultural biases against them. Zachary Crockett,[14] citing various research studies, reports several concerning findings for introverted leaders. For example, Crockett says:

- 96% of high-level executives self-identify as extroverts.
- There is a strong, scientifically proven bias against leadership candidates who fall on the introverted end of the spectrum.
- Extroversion is consistently ranked by research participants as the most important trait a leader can have.
- 65% of senior executives see introversion as a "barrier to leadership."
- Only 6% of research participants think introverts have the people skills required to oversee a successful team.
- 71% of research participants said that they believed that there was a stigma against hiring introverts into a leadership role.

Many businesses have a singular vision for what a good leader should be — outgoing, gregarious, and an expert networker. They write off introversion as a form of "social pathology," Crockett says. Nonetheless, introverts can, do, and must overcome the misconceptions and biases against them when they aspire to leadership. Here are 10 strategies that will help introverted healthcare leaders thrive in an extroverted, often biased world:

1. **Describe yourself in positive terms.** Don't label yourself as an introvert. Cha Tekeli[15] warns that labeling is "dangerous territory" and brings with it a lot of baggage that isn't necessarily your truth. Focus instead on describing your introverted characteristics and tendencies as strengths. For example, are you detail-oriented, analytical, and a quick study with strong strategic skills? Are you an astute observer, an active listener, and a reflective and thoughtful speaker? These positive traits are less likely to elicit bias than the label "introvert" will.

2. **Actionize your observations.** Introverted leaders usually are keen observers who notice things that others miss. However, your observations alone may leave others in a quandary about what you want or expect them to do. Crockett says, "Turn all your listening and observing into actionable suggestions."

3. **Be brave and push yourself.** Miller suggests, "We all must learn to push ourselves if we want to grow personally and professionally." That means that introverted leaders may at times have to push themselves into conversations and into social situations where they feel vulnerable. Keep in mind, though, that there is a big difference between needing time alone and hiding from challenges. Do not use your preference for solitude to shrink from challenges, avoid risk, or miss difficult conversations that you should be part of.

4. **Be genuine.** An introverted leader does not need to play act at being highly extroverted to be successful. Therefore, don't force yourself to be the bubbly, back-slapping, joke-telling life of the party. Push yourself, yes, but only within reason. Crockett says, "Be unapologetically genuine."

5. **Communicate what you are thinking.** Introverts can be hard to read, which sometimes leaves others feeling uncertain and uncomfortable. They will fill in any blanks that you leave for them. Therefore, clearly describe what is in your head so people can stop guessing or jumping to the wrong conclusions. Tekeli suggests, "Provide your team with information in multiple ways. Make them feel in the loop and watch productivity soar."

6. **Schedule and prioritize alone time.** Time to oneself is a key to success for introverts. Carve time for yourself away from draining stimuli, both at work and at home. For example, Tekeli says that introverts may find that being alone for the first hour of the day can be very helpful and worthwhile, even if that means that they must wake up an hour earlier. Crockett suggests, "The most successful introverted leaders find ways to carve 10- or 15-minute intervals out of the workday for quiet decompression time to recharge their empty "social/people tank." In addition, they leave one or two evenings a week free from work or social obligations to recharge. Crockett suggests that ideally, "For every 1-hour meeting, make sure to plan at least 30 minutes to yourself." While that may not always be possible, you get the point. Introverted leaders cannot go to meeting after meeting all day every day without a break, without suffering the consequences. Schedule alone time as you plan your calendar.

7. **Ask more questions.** Of course, introverted leaders can say what's on their minds whenever they choose. However, they may find it uncomfortable to speak or difficult to be heard over the most extroverted

voices in the room. Stella Ma[16] suggests, "A simple way to fix this is to ask if you can lead the agenda, which gives you the opportunity to talk first." Then, "depersonalize" your ideas, Ma says, by turning them into questions. For example, Ma suggests, ask, "Should we consider researching the topic further as the takeaway from today's meeting?"

8. **Create an introvert-friendly work environment.** Think about the work environment that would allow you to do your best work. Then create a work culture that supports that environment. For example, Ma suggests, introverted leaders will shine when they can mull things over before they must render their opinions. Therefore, create opportunities and time for research, reflection, and preparation before meetings. Joanne Markow[17] suggests, "Make one-on-one meetings part of your leadership style." Although large group meetings are inevitable, plan your meetings when you can so you can communicate individually or in smaller groups. Space your big meetings and limit your open-door office hours. Use electronic communication rather than face-to-face when you can do so without sacrificing work quality.

9. **Build a strong team.** Every leader has strengths and weaknesses, and no one person can be expected to excel in every skill area. That's why astute healthcare leaders, whether introverts or extroverts, create teams of diverse individuals who complement one another and fill in the skill gaps. For example, Steve Friedman[18] says, "For me, I wanted at least one person with team/industry experience, at least one with deep technical expertise, and most importantly, at least one extroverted 'people person' who could strike up conversations and develop connections."

10. **Step up during times of crisis.** There will be moments when everyone is going to look to you for leadership, so be sure that you give it to them. Take a strong stand, be decisive and reassuring, speak up, and put yourself front and center when that is what is best for you to do your job.

CREATE AN INTROVERT AFFINITY GROUP

Many healthcare organizations form affinity groups for their employees. Alyse Maguire[19] explains that an affinity group is "a group of people having a common interest or goal." In the workplace, an affinity group can be a sports league, book club, or club focusing on a hobby or recreational activity. However, in most organizations, the most powerful affinity groups will be those that focus on creating a diverse and inclusive workplace, Maguire says.

For example, many organizations form affinity groups for LGBTQ employees, employees with disabilities, women in leadership, Hispanic employees, and employees who are veterans. In addition, Friedman argues that employers should form affinity groups for their introverted employees. Such groups can provide a safe space for introverts to talk about their challenges at work and to learn effective coping strategies. In a much larger context, leadership's support for an introvert affinity group (or multiple groups at all levels within the organization) can become a powerful statement to all employees. Top-down support for introverts can change the culture of the organization while providing an opportunity for introverted employees to "bring voice to the table," Friedman says.

CHAPTER 8 BONUS FEATURE

INTROVERTED OR SHY? WHO MAKES THE BETTER LEADER?

Being introverted and being shy are not the same thing, even though a shared preference for alone time may look the same to a casual observer. Carol Bainbridge[20] explains, "An introvert enjoys time alone and gets emotionally drained after spending a lot of time with others. A shy person doesn't necessarily want to be alone but is afraid to interact with others." Not all introverts are shy, and many have excellent social skills. However, after engaging in social activities, introverts tend to feel emotionally drained and need time alone to recharge their emotional batteries.

Introversion is a personality type; shyness is an emotion. Bainbridge explains, "People can get therapy for shyness, but not for introversion." Introverts are not weak, damaged, or sick. Cain suggests, "Don't think of introversion as something that needs to be cured." Introverts can and often do learn how to succeed in more extroverted environments. Nonetheless, they will always be true to their stripes. Bainbridge explains, "Introverts can learn coping strategies to help them deal with social situations, but they will always be introverts." Shy people, on the other hand, can learn to overcome or at least reduce their shyness, usually with therapy and practice.

A key distinction between shy and introverted people can be found in the ways that their anxiety plays out. Melanie Curtin[21] explains, "Introverts can choose to be social and interact with others; they often just don't want to. Shy people — depending on the level of shyness — can't make that same choice without a high cost." For them, a party isn't just a drain as it can be for an introvert; it's a struggle. Ellis suggests that people who are shy tend to feel awkward or uncomfortable when they're in social situations, especially when they're around strangers. Their discomfort can manifest physically and become intense. According to Ellis, "They [shy people] may feel so nervous, they become sweaty. Their heart may beat quicker, and they may get a stomachache." Shy people may be inclined to skip social events because they don't like the negative feelings that take over their thoughts and bodies when they go to parties, big meetings, or other social activities. People who are introverted also may prefer to skip social events, but for a different reason. They probably know that they will feel more energized or comfortable doing things on their own or with one or two other people. Ellis explains, "Introverts don't choose to skip social events because they have strong negative reactions to larger gatherings the way that shy people do; they just prefer being alone or in very small groups."

Shy people will find it challenging to be thrust time and again into the social requirements of leadership. *Healthline*[22] suggests that relaxation techniques such as deep breathing can help shy people to cope with their anxiety. Group therapy also can be helpful for adults experiencing shyness. *Healthline* adds, "In rare instances, medication can provide temporary relief for shyness." But left untreated, very shy people would be unlikely to succeed in a conventional leadership role without experiencing significant anxiety that would take an enormous toll on them emotionally and physically. Introverts, on the other hand, can and often do become great leaders.

CHAPTER 9

The Pros and Cons of Transparency in Healthcare Leadership

"Trust happens when leaders are transparent."

—Jack Welch

"If a leader shares too much information with employees who do not have the ability to understand or control it, it can unnecessarily distract employees and increase their anxiety."

—Catherine Iste

Transparency is a buzzword in healthcare leadership today, and it's easy to see why. Sandy Clarke[1] suggests, "Today, people resonate with leaders who are transparent. A leader who is open and engages in honest communication is someone people can trust and get behind." Specifically, Clarke says, transparency in leadership fosters trust, builds relationships, creates cohesion within and among teams, and enables leaders to solve problems more quickly and easily. And as you'll see below, many others similarly extol the virtues of leadership transparency, including the late Jack Welch,[2] whose famous quote on this topic serves as the first epigraph for this chapter.

Does this mean that we are focusing in this chapter on the whys and the ways that you can become a more transparent leader? Yes. There are many reasons that healthcare administrators, leaders, and managers should consider being more transparent with their employees. However, as our chapter's title and dual epigraphs suggest, this chapter will not be one-sided. We also will look at the unsavory consequences when leadership transparency goes too far, and yes, Catherine Iste[3] says, there comes a point when that can happen. Julian Birkinshaw and Dan Cable[4] warn, "There is a 'dark side' to transparency. Executives sharing information creates problems of information overload and can legitimize endless debate and second-guessing of senior executive decisions."

What's a healthcare leader to do? Be more transparent? Be less transparent? The answer to this question is not simple, because it all depends on the leader and the circumstances. This chapter considers the pros and cons of leadership transparency to help you to figure out when it will pay for you to be more transparent in your leadership and when doing so may backfire. As you'll see, transparency is not a cure-all, but a leadership strategy like many others that you need to balance with your goals and other needs. Hendri Augustine Sugiarto[5] suggests, "Consider the pros and cons of bringing more transparency into your workplace before you take action."

THE PROS: FIVE REASONS TO LEAD WITH TRANSPARENCY

Transparency in leadership means keeping your employees in the loop, sharing the good and the bad with them, and welcoming their honest feedback. D. Perucci[6] explains that when leaders are transparent, "There should be no unpleasant surprises, no concerns around uncertainty, and no wishy-washy behavior that may weaken your reputation as a leader." Transparent healthcare leaders strive to practice what they preach. They set crystal-clear expectations and communicate effectively with every member of their team. That sounds great, right? That's because it is. In many cases, transparency is an excellent leadership strategy.

Furthermore, if you ask employees if they want their leaders to be transparent, almost all will say *yes*. Very few will tell you that they prefer opaque leaders who keep things from them. In fact, Sam Caucci[7] says, "Most employees rank transparency at the top of their list when it comes to what they care about most." This desire to be in the know at work is an extension of a much larger cultural shift toward more transparency. The desire and need to know what's going on and what is true is at an all-time high in our society right now. According to Glenn Liopis,[8] "There is a reason people would rather 'see' a video blog than 'read' a blog. They want access to one's facial expressions, eye contact and body language." People both inside and outside the workplace want to evaluate whether someone is acting or being genuine, and they look for greater transparency in their politicians, celebrities, influencers, friends, family members, colleagues, managers, and leaders. Simply put, people want to know what's going on, and they will become suspicious when they feel that they don't. They will naturally seek to find out what is real and true

Following are five top reasons to become a more transparent healthcare leader, gathered from several sources. Keep in mind as you read that we also will consider other sources that warn that leadership transparency can and sometimes does backfire. For now, let's begin with the pros. Transparency in leadership can:

1. **Give employees greater peace of mind.** Liopis explains that employees have grown tired of surprises. They don't want to be blindsided, especially if they have been before. They want to eliminate the unknowns that creep into their minds. They want to be a part of a workplace culture that puts a premium on delivering the truth to them. They also want their leaders to be proactive in sharing where the organization is headed. This desire for leadership transparency makes perfect sense, because self-preservation is highly motivating. Liopis explains, "They [employees] just want transparency so they can plan and protect themselves."

2. **Make leaders seem more human.** Gone are the days when employees expected their leaders to remain mysterious and hidden behind intimidating office doors in a far-away C-suite. Today, employees want to know that their leaders have experienced the same problems that they have and that they have overcome personal hardships. Liopis says, "We are living during a time when people want and expect their leaders to be more human, less perfect and at times a bit more vulnerable — regardless of hierarchy or rank." Transparent healthcare leaders who present themselves as human beings, or what Caucci describes as "just like anyone else," are more likely to receive greater support from their employees and their peers.

3. **Foster trust.** Numerous sources suggest that leaders who are transparent enjoy greater trust from their employees. For example, Tanya Ahmed[9] suggests, "The more transparent you are, the more likely you are to build trust within your team." Liopis writes, "If you are transparent, especially during the worst of times, you actually strengthen your leadership as people begin to trust you as a person and thus will respect you more as a leader." Kate Dames[10] says, "When you have a transparent leader in a team or organization, there is automatically trust." Perucci suggests

that when leaders are transparent, "Employees will give you their loyalty and trust." And Catherine Ellwood[11] says, "Increasing transparency is an accessible first step for leaders to take in order to build trust." We could go on and on. Suffice it to say that it is very easy to find sources that argue that leadership transparency fosters employee trust.

4. **Increase employee happiness.** The employee experience in your workplace hinges on many things, including leadership transparency. In fact, NeuroLeadership Institute[12] says, "Management transparency is the most significant predictor of employee happiness." Conversely, if employees feel uncertain or suspicious about what is being discussed and decided for their futures, they are likely to jump to the wrong conclusions or to feel anxious, not happy, NeuroLeadership Institute says.

5. **Improve employee performance.** The argument here is that leadership transparency leads to increased trust and a better workplace experience, which, in turn, leads to higher levels of performance. Liopis warns, "Unfortunately, the lack of transparency that still exists among leaders in the workplace…leads to less optimal levels of performance." NeuroLeadership Institute makes a convincing argument, suggesting that the transparent sharing of information is crucial for creating certainty. NeuroLeadership explains that for most people, "The brain perceives ambiguity as inherently threatening." When employees feel out of the loop, they feel threatened because they trust their leaders less and, in turn, are less likely to be motivated to perform. There is some merit in this argument. Certainly, employees who feel plagued by uncertainty and ambiguity may spend a great deal of their time and energy speculating and worrying about what's going on, rather than focusing on the task at hand. When they spend their time discussing their concerns with their coworkers, it is plausible that work output may well suffer for everyone.

THE CONS: FIVE REASONS TO BE WARY OF LEADERSHIP TRANSPARENCY

We live in a world that is clamoring for more and more transparency. There are some, however, who make a convincing case for why, perhaps, there are times when it's best for leaders to share less. For example, John Coleman[13] suggests that leaders need to be able to "exercise discretion and consider the implications of their communication" before disclosing information to their employees. Iste asks, "Does creating a transparent environment [for employees] require being a transparent leader? Not completely." Sian Harrington[14] suggests, "Smart leaders need to know when to share and when to keep things back." Harrington warns, "If you are trying to build trust through greater transparency with your employees and customers, you are going about it the wrong way." And Ethan Bernstein[15] writes, "More-transparent environments are not always better." As you can see, transparency is a double-edged sword. Healthcare leaders may want to be more transparent, but at the same time, they need to become smarter about when to share information with their employees and when not to. Following are five reasons that transparency sometimes can backfire. Transparency in leadership can:

1. **Make hard decisions even harder.** You may encounter instances when you must invest a lot of time, research, and energy before you can make a hard call. Being transparent in such moments can interfere with the work you need to do. Coleman suggests, "There's a directness that's required and a need for contemplative thought that full transparency can compromise. I find that when you have an infinite number of voices chiming in you get weak or watered-down solutions that can appease many but accomplish nothing." Difficult decisions need to be made by informed leaders in the face of ambiguity and uncertainty. At times, therefore, discretion would be the better part of valor. In fact, Coleman reports that in his own leadership, he shares information with his employees only if it is appropriate for the audience and within their ability to understand and control it. Coleman explains, "I don't believe that full disclosure is always necessary," or even desirable. The key, Iste suggests, is to maintain a balance between "full disclosure" and the appropriate amount of detail that is necessary and best.

2. **Erode trust.** Transparency and trust may not always be as interdependent as the sources cited earlier suggest. In fact, Rachel Botsman[16] argues, complete transparency eliminates the need for employees to trust their leaders at all. Do parents demonstrate trust when they insist on knowing and verifying every single thing that their teenagers do when they are out of the house? No. That is not trust. Likewise, Botsman argues, employees don't need to trust you when you show them and tell them absolutely everything. They need to trust you when you *don't*. You will know that you've taken transparency too far in your leadership

when your employees don't trust you to make good decisions unless you lay everything out on the table for them. Botsman suggests, "Trust is a confident relationship with the unknown," not the known.

3. **Create anxiety for employees.** Being transparent when things are uncertain or in a state of flux can throw gasoline onto a small fire. Coleman describes the problems he faced as a leader when he was overly transparent with his employees during an especially troubling time in his organization. Coleman says, "For many, it [transparency] was a confusing distraction as they tried to process all the information and understand the personal implications. It was also debilitating in the sense that most weren't in a position to control the outcome. And for some, it was overwhelming." Uncertainty led to heightened anxiety, Coleman says, as many employees convinced themselves that the worst-case scenario was inevitable. He adds, "I even once lost a senior creative team who overreacted to a financial situation they perceived as much worse than it actually was." Today, Coleman says, he is much more selective about sharing information with his employees. He says, "I've found this to be drastically more effective at keeping the organization motivated, challenged and constantly improving."

4. **Overwhelm employees.** Too much or too frequent communication in the interest of transparency can quickly lead to information overload. Sugiarto explains, "Some people aren't able to process so much information due to the lack of their information filtering ability. They will most likely be disturbed with too much information." Valene Jouany and Kristina Martic[17] say, "Most employees have to deal with excessive amounts of information and data every day at work." Therefore, you may want to hold back on sending out very frequent email updates to your employees or holding frequent staff meetings in the interest of being transparent. That strategy can easily overwhelm your employees with high volume and too frequent information, Jouany and Martic say.

5. **Leave your organization open to attack.** Only trusted employees who have a need to know should consume proprietary and sensitive information about your healthcare organization. There always is the possibility that something you say or write to your employees can be misunderstood, taken out of context, mistaken for a promise, or shared. Sugiarto suggests that transparency creates "an opening for crucial information to be leaked to a competitor," to news media, and to others outside of your organization. Therefore, if you would not want information about

your healthcare organization to be broadcast on the evening news or otherwise to become a PR nightmare, hold it very close. Take measures to ensure that your employees clearly understand the information you do choose to share with them. Be sure that your employees know precisely what you are saying, and what you are not saying. For example, if you would *like* to make a change that will benefit your employees, be sure that they know that you are not promising them that you will. If something *may* happen, be sure that your employees know that you are not saying that it will. Be mindful that people sometimes hear what they want to hear, not what you say, especially when they are excited, afraid, or upset. When in doubt, repeat what you tell your employees. Then, ask your employees to repeat what you have told them to make sure that they have understood you correctly.

12 WAYS TO BECOME A MORE TRANSPARENT HEALTHCARE LEADER

Leadership transparency can be a scary proposition because it puts the healthcare leader in a vulnerable position. Caucci suggests, "Many of them [leaders] fear that in being transparent they will come off as less authoritative." Although the steps to becoming more transparent are relatively straightforward, practicing them, Dames says, requires "a lot of courage." There are many reasons that leaders fear transparency. Dames suggests, "Maybe you're afraid you'll be seen as less authoritative, or maybe you're scared of criticism. Maybe you are an introvert or simply don't have enough time in the day."

Organizational transparency begins at the top. Executive Velocity[18] says, "Unless top-level executives, leaders, and board members buy in to a culture of transparency, the company cannot hope to achieve it." Therefore, do not let your fear of feeling vulnerable stop you from becoming more transparent with your employees. Strive to be more transparent as soon as you have determined that transparency is your best leadership approach. Here are 12 strategies:

1. **Walk the walk.** Saying that transparency is one of your core leadership values is a good start. However, Michelle Bennett[19] explains, "You can't just make a company-wide announcement that you're now transparent and call it a day." Look for ways to demonstrate your

leadership transparency regularly, in moments big and small. For example, Bennett says, routinely share key information, hiring plans, and progress toward your goals with your employees. Tackle difficult conversations, and don't be afraid to be transparent about your emotions. And show up as human and vulnerable when it is appropriate and helpful for you to do so.

2. **Model the transparent behaviors you want to see in others.** Your employees will look to you as a role model for many things, including your transparency. Ellwood describes a leader's transparency as "contagious." Ellwood explains, "Leaders demonstrating that expressing honest opinions and being open is acceptable and gives permission for others within their teams to do the same." Be sure that your employees both see and appreciate when you are being transparent with them. Make certain that they know when you are *choosing* to share information with them, not doing so because you must.

3. **Be honest.** When an employee asks you a question that you are not prepared to answer or can't answer, admit that you don't feel comfortable answering it. Dames says, "Don't avoid the subject, and don't ever lie about it or give half-truths intentionally."

4. **Own your mistakes and failures.** Transparent leaders don't become less trustworthy simply because they make a mistake or fail at something. In fact, they can become more trusted when they admit their shortcomings. Bennett says, "Taking responsibility for your part in a mistake will encourage others to follow suit."

5. **Be open and accessible.** Transparency means that you will open yourself to criticism, taking it on the chin when it serves the greater good. It takes courage to hear how you have fallen short or failed as a leader, However, provide opportunities for that to happen. Dames suggests, "Provide for a company-wide channel where employees are invited to express their concerns or ask questions and be sure to read it and respond in a positive and open way."

6. **Share your reasoning.** Ellwood suggests that you allow your employees to understand the thought process behind your decisions. Summarizing the factors at play will enable them to experience your transparency but also to get on board with your decision and embrace change. Of course, this doesn't mean that you need to divulge every detail of your decision-making process. The key factors may be

sufficient. Bennett suggests, "Focus on answering the 'Why is this happening? Why now?' question that is typically on everyone's mind."

7. **Ask questions and show interest.** Transparent healthcare leaders engage with their employees regularly and ask relevant and empowering questions. According to Dames, "The manager of the past was he who knew the most answers. The leaders of the future are those who ask the most powerful questions."

8. **Solicit feedback.** Encourage your employees to give you their honest feedback about your healthcare organization's policies and recent changes or announcements. For example, administer an employee satisfaction survey. As well, Advanced Resources[20] suggests, "Adopt an open-door policy and ask team members in upper management to do the same."

9. **Accept criticism gracefully.** It can be challenging enough for employees to provide you with their feedback, because they may be afraid of your power. Then, if you react defensively to their feedback, they may regret speaking up. Dave Nevogt[21] says, "Transparency can't exist without openness." Defensiveness will make your employees hide things from you and may make them assume that you are hiding things from them, too, Nevogt says. Therefore, strive to accept feedback gracefully and thank your employees for sharing their honest opinions with you.

10. **Confront difficult situations**. Most people choose to avoid conflict. However, Dames says, "The transparent leader invites conflict functionally, listening intently to opposing perspectives."

11. **Be consistent and honor your commitments.** Consistent behavior is a form of transparency, because it demonstrates for your employees that your word has value and that you do what you say you will do. Jon Youshael[22] suggests, "Consistently transparent behavior in leadership demonstrates the value of each employee so that everyone feels like they have a voice." Being consistent also will lead to greater employee satisfaction and engagement, Youshael says.

12. **Involve others in decision-making.** Many leaders make decisions alone. However, Dames says, "A transparent leader will always involve people in decision making." Be careful to be consistent and fair in how you make decisions and to what degree you involve people in the decision-making process. Be sure that everyone who should have a seat at the table has one. Bernstein warns, "The empowerment of a select few can leave the other people in the organization feeling

voiceless, especially if they aren't explicitly invited to improve systems, processes, roles, and tasks."

TO BE OR NOT TO BE TRANSPARENT? TAKE THIS QUIZ

As you can see, a healthcare leader walks the fine line between being transparent and oversharing. Granted, there always will be things that leaders cannot share with their employees, even if they want to. There will be other things that they choose not to share because doing so would needlessly heighten their employees' anxiety, make leadership decisions more difficult, or put the organization at risk. Leaders must earn employee trust by being transparent but not create the expectation that they will tell their employees everything. Bennett says, "It's all about defining boundaries with employees and managing their expectations."

Certainly, leaders who strive to be more transparent share many admirable characteristics. For example, Executive Velocity says, transparent leaders are honest, ask for and accept constructive feedback, deliver bad news with compassion, admit mistakes, and have the ability to say that they are sorry. Executive Velocity writes, "When leaders own up to their individual mistakes and take ownership of problems within their own departments, their direct reports will sit up and take notice. They, in turn, will begin to trust a little more, and they may also begin to mimic their behaviors." Clearly, no one is arguing that you should lie to your employees or that you should lack compassion for them or that you should not take responsibility for your mistakes. Quite the opposite. Every healthcare leader should strive to be honest, responsible, and compassionate.

Nonetheless, being 100% transparent with your employees may not always be possible or desirable. When it isn't, it may help you to think of leadership transparency as a spectrum. On one end is the leader who shares nothing and on the other is the leader who shares everything. Most leaders fall somewhere in the middle, at least most of the time. As the demand for transparency continues to grow within the workforce, leaders may feel pressure from their employees to adapt their policies, systems, and communications to meet that demand. Do not knuckle under to this pressure. Ultimately, it is up to you to decide where you will fall on the transparency spectrum, not only in a hypothetical sense, but for each unique leadership challenge you face.

Ask yourself the following 10 questions when you are wondering whether it is prudent for you to share particular information with your employees or whether such transparency risks too many negative consequences:

1. **Is this information proprietary or confidential?** You may not be able to share certain information with your employees, or you may take a big risk if you do. Organizations mitigate that risk by requiring key employees to sign nondisclosure agreements (NDAs). Be sure that you or your healthcare organization have taken this step to safeguard proprietary or confidential information before you share that kind of information with them. Bennett says, "Ideally, you should not be sharing your proprietary information with anybody who has not executed an NDA."

2. **Do I have all the facts?** This question has tripped up the best of leaders when they attempt to be as transparent as possible. So says Terri Klass,[23] who explains, "It's not good enough to have a 'general take' on what a situation is before explaining if things are running smoothly or at a roadblock." You need to have as many of the available facts as possible. For example, Klass suggests that you reflect on how much has been accomplished, analyze a missed target or deadline, delve into how the missteps happened and why, and gain clarity about what is happening and timeframes. Take the time you need to prepare fully before you share information with your employees, Klass says. Sketchy, partial, or premature information may alarm, confuse, misinform, or misguide them.

3. **What are the risks of sharing this information?** Will your transparency potentially hurt someone? Could it hurt your healthcare organization? Is it worth your taking that risk? If yes, what can you do to reduce that risk? For example, Klass suggests, "If you think someone may be harmed by what you are sharing, consider speaking with them ahead of time." Consider also what would be the best way and time for you to deliver the information to your employees. Choose your

words carefully. And, as much as possible, anticipate questions and pushback and plan how you will respond to them.

4. **Who would this affect the most?** Which colleagues, departments, and other stakeholders may be affected by the information? Is it necessary for you to share this information with everyone? Klass warns, "Just be inclusive enough. If in doubt, widen your net of who needs to hear the update."

5. **Do I need to make a fast decision?** There will be times when you will welcome employee feedback and input and times when transparency will make it harder for you to make a timely decision. However, do not underestimate how much your employees will look to you for information when the decision is urgent or at crisis level. Birkinshaw and Cable suggest, "Leaders should act with deliberate calm and bounded optimism. Those who can visibly demonstrate these qualities help their organizations feel a sense of purpose, giving them hope that they can face the challenges ahead." Your employees will look to you for reassurance in a crisis. Humans are biologically wired to have a stress response (i.e., fight, flight, or freeze) when confronted with volatile environments, unpredictable events, and stress. However, don't give your employees information as a knee-jerk response to appease them or because you believe that you always must be transparent. Consider whether sharing more information with your employees at this time will help them or whether doing so could make things worse.

6. **Will sharing this information heighten or assuage employee anxiety?** There are things that your employees need and deserve to know, so those are no-brainers. However, you need to consider everything else in the context of whether it will benefit your employees to know more or whether it will make them worry needlessly about things they can't control. Of course, your employees are not children, and you are not their parent. However, Coleman says, "Many people do not want to know the full details of how their firm is doing, nor do they want to be held fully responsible for its outputs. Instead, they want to know enough to do their job well and they want to have the right to know more, but for the most part they are happy for someone else to process and manage that information on their behalf." Therefore,

avoid sharing information that causes anxiety without much benefit, or "pain without much gain," Birkinshaw and Cable say.

7. **Will sharing this information build or erode trust?** Sharing necessary or beneficial information with your employees can help you to earn their trust. However, your employees do not need to know everything that you know or think. Botsman says, "One of the mistakes I hear is that the way to build more trust is through transparency. It is a common narrative. But if you need for things to be transparent, then you have practically given up on trust." Ask yourself: Will this information help your employees to trust you more? Or do you feel pressure to share it with them because they feel entitled to know everything?

8. **Will employees find out anyway?** Should your employees hear the information from you? If so, then tell them. This will be a delightful task if the news is good, but a difficult and potentially damaging one if it is bad. Kimberly Paterson[24] explains, "There is a mounting body of scientific evidence that shows we tend to take a dim view of people who bring us bad news — even when the person is an innocent messenger with no control over the situation." Paterson suggests that you can soften the blow of sharing bad news by providing advance warning when possible and by being direct, conveying that you care, dealing with the emotions first, and having a next-step plan. Or, if possible, ask someone else to be the bearer of the bad news. For example, Paterson says, ask a colleague to share the distressing information, then step in to handle your employees' reaction and explore alternatives. "Shooting the messenger" is far more than a metaphor, Paterson says; it is a known psychological phenomenon.

9. **Would I benefit from employee feedback and input at this time?** The argument for transparency lies in the wisdom-of-crowds effect. K. Super[25] explains, "By broadening the number of people involved, we will make smarter decisions and we will increase buy-in." However, there can also be problems with this approach. One that we've considered earlier is that it generally takes longer for leaders to make decisions when they get many people involved. Employees also may dislike it when they give you their opinions and you decide against them. An even larger concern is that your employees may weigh in "without relevant knowledge, or without any responsibility to see

things through," Super says. Therefore, limit the occasions when you will seek employee input to those when it is not only going to be helpful to you but also within their ability and experience to make helpful suggestions.

10. **Will sharing information stop or encourage the rumor mill?** Giving your employees partial or vague information will cause them to fill in the gaps with their own ideas. Once that happens, your organization will be abuzz with rumors. Is the information you plan to share sufficient so your employees don't have to invent the who, what, why, where, when, and how behind it? Super suggests that when you don't give your employees clarity, when you "cover up bad numbers, conceal that someone left the company, deliver confusing and inconsistent messages on organizational goals, compensate in secretive or biased ways, or fundamentally break peoples' trust," they will fill in the gaps with their own (often worse) assumptions and scenarios. You can go crazy putting to bed internal rumors about your company, Super says. Or you can be forthright with the information that will satisfy your employees. According to Super, "Being transparent not only equips your people with information that provides insight, but also saves you time from refereeing conversations throughout your company."

The Challenges of Being a Positive Role Model for Your Employees

Many leadership gurus and texts extol the virtues of becoming a positive role model. Clearly, employees will be more positively influenced by a leader who says, "Do as I do" than one who says, "Do as I say." Healthcare administrators, leaders, and managers who are positive examples for their employees command respect because they are authentically excellent. Their shining examples can and often do encourage that same excellence in others.

If role modeling is so effective, why do some leaders find it challenging to be a positive role model for their employees? Do they know what excellence looks like? Do they care? For most, the answer is *yes*. Most higher-level and experienced leaders know what excellence looks like, and they care a great deal about the behaviors they model. However, leaders face many challenges that can thwart their efforts, even when they want to model the best version of themselves for their employees.

Admittedly, the idea that leaders are role models is nothing new. Jennifer V. Miller[1] suggests, "This [role modeling] seems rather intuitive, doesn't it?" Leaders are role models for their employees because they lead by their own example. However, precisely which values, attitudes, and behaviors should healthcare leaders model for their employees? What misconceptions do leaders have about role modeling? And what are the challenges or obstacles that can get in the way of their being positive role models? As you'll see, being a positive role model for your employees may not always be as easy as it sounds.

VALUES, ATTITUDES, AND BEHAVIORS WORTH MODELING

What you do sets the standard for what you expect from others. For example, Ready Training Online[2] suggests, "If you want your employees to treat one another with respect, you must model respectful behavior yourself. If you want your employees to deliver exceptional service, you must treat customers with superior service yourself." In fact, leaders who set a high standard for their employees often set an even higher standard for themselves. As you'll see later in this chapter, it is neither realistic nor desirable for a role model to strive for perfection. However, here are some of the values, attitudes, and behaviors that are worth modeling for your employees:

- **A strong work ethic.** Your employees will notice if you come in late or leave early, or if they see you socializing with colleagues when they believe that there is work you should be doing. David Ingram[3] warns, "If an executive consistently leaves the office an hour early, for example, it is very likely that other employees will take opportunities to sneak out early, as well."
- **Pitch in.** Be willing to roll up your sleeves and jump in to help when the situation calls for it. Ready Training online says, "Effective role models work hard and pitch in when their staff needs help." You can demonstrate to your employees that you do not believe in an "it's-not-my-job" attitude when there is a need or demand and they see you stepping in to help them.
- **Honesty.** Align your words and your behaviors. If you follow ethical guidelines, fulfill your promises, and admit your mistakes, Ingram says, "Employees are more likely to do the same in response."
- **Accountability.** Keep your promises and do not candy-coat your mistakes. Ready Training Online says, "Never blame others or make excuses."
- **Refuse to play office politics.** Commit to equity. Ingram urges leaders not to play office politics so they can inspire their employees to focus on professionalism and performance rather than "political maneuvering."
- **Respect.** Respect will be especially important when you must correct employee behavior. Be mindful of your tone and words and focus on the behavior, not the person. Never criticize an employee publicly.

- **Show, don't just tell.** Don't just tell your employees how to do the things they need to do or furnish them with an instructional guide. When possible, perform or demonstrate the task or strategy for them. According to Ingram, "Modeling behavior in this way allows employees to ask questions and gain insights from those with first-hand experience."
- **Positivity.** Be realistic but look for the good wherever you can find it, especially during trying times.
- **Integrity.** Leaders with integrity have a moral compass that guides their behaviors. Don't give yourself a pass. Follow the rules and procedures you expect your staff to follow.

FOUR MISCONCEPTIONS ABOUT BEING A ROLE MODEL

Do you know what it means to be a role model for your employees? Let's check four popular misconceptions about role modeling before we go any further:

1. **I can choose to be a role model.** A leader in a healthcare organization cannot choose to be a role model. Derek Pangelinan[4] explains, "You are always leading by example whether you choose to be or not." Your colleagues and employees have been and always will be watching you with critical eyes. Some may have shared their observations about you with one another. Like it or not, what they have seen and heard has already modeled your behaviors for them.

2. **Employees will trust me when I model new behaviors for them.** If you decide to model new behaviors for your employees, perhaps as a result of reading this chapter or doing other work to develop your leadership skills, they may respond with skepticism. Your employees already have an opinion about who you are and what you do. They may not trust anything you do differently, especially at first, even if they like the changes you make. Ken Blanchard[5] warns, "People will feel awkward, ill at ease, and self-conscious." Change of almost any kind means doing something different, and, as a result, people almost always will react with some degree of discomfort. You will need to be consistent and patient. You'll also need to give your employees the time they need to catch up to the new "you," which most of them, in time, will do. However, there may be some employees who never will be completely sure that you've

changed, no matter how long you try or how consistent you are. This will be the case if they are mistrustful in general or if you've burned a bridge with them that can't be rebuilt.

3. **Role modeling will get the results I want.** Leaders sometimes put too much faith in the power of their own example. Do you assume that being a role model for your employees means that if you do your leadership job well your employees will automatically follow suit and do their jobs well too? If only it were that easy. Unfortunately, "monkey see, monkey do" is not a given when it comes to positive role modeling. Pangelinan explains that employees think, "As a start, you (leader) need to do your job well if you expect me to even consider doing my job to the same standard." Leading by example may establish the standards to which employees should work, but it doesn't mean that they will *actually* work toward those standards. In fact, Pangelinan warns, "Listen for the words 'I like to lead by example.' When you hear them, be aware that whoever said them is probably not doing enough to effectively lead others." Being a positive role model for your employees is not synonymous with good leadership. It is just one of many components of good leadership.

4. **Modeling positive behaviors makes me a positive role model.** Like beauty, role models are in the eye of the beholder. David Cancel[6] warns, "For most people, when they hear the word *role model*, they immediately conjure up images of a positive one — a successful person whose values and behavior are worthy of imitation." However, your employees will not necessarily perceive your positives as *their* positives. For example, they may see you working a lot harder and longer than they want to, and view that negatively. They may not be privy to confidential information that you can't share with them, but nonetheless judge your decisions harshly. They may lack your training, skills, and experience but think that they know better than you. They may think you're too critical of them, too demanding, or too unrealistic, especially if your predecessor was more of a laissez-faire leader than you are. In fact, some of your employees may cast you in a negative light because they think that you're too perfect a role model. They may reason, "No one is like that. It's just an act." Or they may think, "Well, that's fine for you, but I'm not like you. I'm just a mere mortal." Even excellent leaders can fall into the category of reverse role models for some of their employees — someone who models the behaviors and values they *don't* want to emulate. Cancel

explains, "Reverse role models check a lot of the same boxes as positive role models: they're successful, they've achieved something you want to achieve and they provide models of behavior you can follow to achieve the same thing. But their values are different." Reverse role models can be a huge turnoff. When employees perceive them, they may think that imitating those behaviors would not align with their values. They even may go so far as to self-sabotage just to be nothing like a role model they view so negatively.

THE CHALLENGE OF STRIKING OUT

As you can see, striving to be a positive role model won't guarantee that you will inspire every employee. Even leaders who model the highest levels of excellence won't be universally perceived as positive role models. You will have the greatest impact on willing and capable souls. Nonetheless, it can be disappointing to put your best self out there and fail to affect the change you seek in everyone.

It will be helpful to do two things when your role modeling efforts don't pay off. First, be realistic about what you can accomplish. Role modeling is not a panacea, and, as we've discussed, it is not synonymous with leadership. Think of role modeling as one tool in your leadership toolkit. If it doesn't do what you want, pull out another tool. Second, consider the intentions and capabilities of the employees you don't reach. Some of your employees may have personal issues that are distracting them or interfering with their professional development. Some may lack the self-awareness, work ethic, or skills that excellence requires. Some may have deep-rooted issues that have nothing to do with you and that they need to address outside of work with professional help. You may be able to help some who are resisting your role modeling with encouragement, one-on-one coaching, training, and follow-up. However, accept that you will employ some people who are not a good fit with your healthcare organization. Some will have to go immediately; some may have to go later. Accept that. Remember that your actions as role model alone will not inspire positive changes in every employee every time. Find productive ways to manage your disappoint-ment about those you don't reach. Alesia Latson[7] suggests, "How you handle disappointment speaks volumes of your leadership style and your credibility in your organization."

THE CHALLENGE OF HAVING ONLY REVERSE ROLE MODELS

Most of us have encountered people in our work and our lives whom we do not want to emulate. Reverse role models can motivate us, often strongly, not to behave in the negative ways we've observed. However, we need role models not only to show us what *not* to do, but also, what *to* do and how to do it. That leaves healthcare leaders who have encountered only reverse role models in a quandary. They may know what they don't want to do but have to figure out the rest on their own.

Unfortunately, many leaders, especially those who are new to their positions, may be inclined to take a page from their boss's playbook when interacting with their employees, even when that playbook includes some negative behaviors. In some circumstances, Min-Hsuan Tu *et al.*[8] found, new supervisors may feel that it is acceptable to model their boss's abusive behavior. Specifically, new supervisors who took part in Tu *et al.'s* study felt that it was acceptable to be verbally abusive to their direct reports when they observed or experienced the same type of behavior from the manager they reported to (if that manager's department was performing up to expectations). The researchers' working hypothesis is that the new managers felt that the toxic behavior was acceptable because the means seemed to justify the ends. Tu *et al.* conclude, "The stronger an individual identifies with the leader, the more impact we would expect his or her leadership self-concept to have on behavior."

Negative language is particularly insidious and potent when modeled by those who are in positions of authority. You may have had a boss who didn't abuse others verbally but who frequently shared negative thoughts with you. Such a boss may have normalized a gloom-and-doom lens through which to see the world. They may have complained incessantly or peppered conversations with negative hyperbole, describing small challenges as "devastating," "awful," "unfair," and "terrible." Be on high alert if your most influential role models spewed such negativity and if they looked for (and no doubt found) the bad in every person and situation. Consider carefully what you are thinking and what you are saying as a result of that modeling. Christine Porath and Mike Porath[9] suggest, "Yes, those around you influence you and your mood, but we have more control over our thoughts and feelings than anyone else. And what we say out loud also carries significant weight." Actively choose to walk away from your role model's negativity and walk toward positivity, Porath and Porath say. Think twice about how you frame things for your employees. If you tell them that the sky is falling, they will very likely believe you. Your negative spin will be both accepted and contagious.

Of course, verbally abusing employees or casting everything as negative for them is the opposite of being a positive leadership role model. Miller warns, "If you're a newly promoted supervisor and your boss is a jerk, you're more likely to act like one too." Be on guard when the negative behaviors modeled for you by others begin to feel normalized or justified, Miller says. Actively seek positive role models when you are lacking them. If you can't find any, Porath and Porath suggest, "You may not be able to stop the flow of negativity in your life, especially right now, but you can resist its toxic effects by making smart choices about who and what you surround yourself with, the mindset you adapt, and the information you consume." Surround yourself with and spend more time with *energizers* — the people in your life who make you smile and laugh and lift your spirits. Increase your resilience in the face of negativity by exercising, eating well, and getting enough sleep. These are the "things we know we're supposed to do," Porath and Porath say, but we often fail to when we're bombarded with negativity. If you are lacking positive role models, cling to these basics until you find at least one person you can learn from.

THE CHALLENGE OF BEING A ROLE MODEL WHEN YOU SCREW UP

You may have every intention to model excellence for your employees. However, you are human, and at one time or another, you may do or say something that you regret. Unfortunately, Joseph Folkman[10] says, "When a leader sets a bad example, they are more like an onstage actor with a spotlight shining directly on them. The vast majority of direct reports notice the bad behavior." The rest will probably learn about it from their colleagues, Folkman says, who will be happy to describe the error of your ways, sometimes in great detail. When leaders set a bad example, they encourage others to feel justified in the same behaviors such as breaking the same rule, not following a specific standard process, or losing their cool. A negative behavior modeled by someone in authority is like a crooked picture on a wall, Folkman says. It will be difficult if not impossible not to notice it. Sometimes you may regret doing little things that probably would not make a huge difference if you weren't in a leadership position. However, in Folkman's research, the impact of a leader's negative behavior is substantial. Being a poor role model, even momentarily, "permits others to act in the same way," Folkman says.

Left unchecked, your negative behaviors can become contagious and spread like a virus that infects your organization. Fortunately, you can do some damage control if you act quickly and take the following steps:

1. **Acknowledge.** Begin by acknowledging that you are not perfect, that you made a mistake or spoke or acted out of turn, and that you regret your behavior. As well, acknowledge your omissions — what you should have done or said but didn't.
2. **Express your regret.** Tell those involved that you regret what you did.
3. **Apologize.** Say that you are sorry for the results of your behavior, such as wasted resources, extra work, misunderstandings, stress, embarrassment, or hurt feelings. Be specific.
4. **Ask for forgiveness.** State it simply: "Please forgive me."
5. **Ask for feedback.** Ask those involved to tell you how they feel and what they would like you to do differently.
6. **Explain how you will use the feedback.** Timea Csizik[11] warns, "One of the most disappointing features of a leader is when they ask and even seem to accept feedback, but then they're reluctant to use it for their development." Commit to using the feedback you receive and dedicate the time and effort you will need to improve.
7. **Promise only what you can deliver.** Do not say, "I will never do that again," unless you can make good on that promise.
8. **Forgive yourself.** It will not help anyone if you continue to beat yourself up over the behavior you regret. If you can't forgive yourself, try talking to someone you trust to help you get to a place of acceptance.

THE CHALLENGE OF COMING ACROSS AS TOO PERFECT

You walk a fine line as a role model for your employees. You want to model excellence. However, you won't want to come across as perfect because that can be a huge turnoff. Keith Krach[12] says, "The most inspirational people out there understand that being authentic and real — and yes, flawed — is one of the most important elements of leadership." Krach explains that the best leaders share a common and underappreciated "superpower." It isn't being the smartest person in the room and it definitely isn't magically having all the answers. It is that they are willing to poke fun at themselves to disarm, build trust, and create a safe environment for their followers. Krach says, "They are unashamed to admit that they, too, have flaws and make mistakes." In short, their leadership philosophy is "never to look too good or to talk too smart," Krach says.

Krach makes an important distinction about flaws in leadership. He says, "I'm not talking about pretending to have flaws to manipulate people and make yourself more likable. Believe me, we all have plenty of genuine imperfections. I'm talking about being willing to be honest about your true shortcomings." There is no need for you to pretend, because the truth will come out and may be out already. Krach adds, "The real key to building a high-performance team is to establish the kind of safe environment where everyone is willing to admit their flaws and even have some fun with it."

Having fun with your flaws would be a tall order for most of us. In fact, walking the fine line between your own excellence and flaws is not something that most of us enjoy doing. However, we don't have to hate our flaws. Krach says, "Great leadership is grounded in the idea that people need to be inspired, not driven to attain perfection." What should you do if see your flaws and shortcomings only as overly negative? Work on that by yourself or with someone else who can help you. Krach suggests: "A self-deprecating sense of humor is a superpower and a key to being an authentic leader." [See Chapter 15: "Discovering Your Leadership Superpowers and Origin Story" for more information on leadership superpowers.]

THE CHALLENGE OF ALWAYS BEING ON STAGE

Being a healthcare executive is not solitary work that you can do closeted away in an office behind a closed door. Jeb Blount[13] suggests that as a leader, "You are always on stage." Some healthcare leaders won't mind being under constant scrutiny as much as others. More extroverted ones may be more comfortable with the attention than those who are more introverted. However, there will come a time when almost every health-care leader will want to get out of the spotlight, if only for a little while.

According to Blount, "The higher your level on the org chart, the more a misspoken word, display of raw emotion, or slip of the tongue can hurt you and your people…Everything you say or don't say, do or don't do, your facial expressions, tone of voice, and body language can and will have an impact on your people and productivity."

Feeling that you are on stage all day every day at work can be exhausting. D. Lykken[14] says, "The hustle and bustle of activity as you try to lead your organization through countless hurdles toward success can really start to weigh down on you." Therefore, be sure to build time away from the spotlight into your schedule, in two ways:

- **Establish daily quiet time.** Block out time in your daily schedule when you will not be interrupted or under scrutiny. If possible, schedule a quiet hour or even half hour when it will do you the most good. Some leaders take their quiet time first thing in the morning, even if that means that they must come to work early. Some make it their practice not to socialize over lunch. And some find that an afternoon break works best. Just knowing that the time is yours and that no one can interrupt you or observe you can help you to get the break from the spotlight you need, even if you are at your desk and working.
- **Take your vacation days:** Taking vacation time off will be beneficial for you and for your employees. It will give you a break from the pressures of your work and from your employees' watchful eyes. It also will be a positive behavior to model for your employees, because taking time off is necessary for everyone so they can reflect and recharge. Camille Preston[15] suggests, "Block off time when you're not only not at work, but also unavailable." This is bound to be challenging for some leaders, because being fully unplugged requires a high level of trust in their employees, established systems, and structures. However, it is the best way for leaders to feel that they are away from the expectations and scrutiny of others, Preston says.

WHAT TO DO WHEN YOU CAN'T FIND LEADERSHIP ROLE MODELS WHO LOOK LIKE YOU: FIVE STRATEGIES

Marian Wright Edelman[16] famously said, "You can't be what you can't see." The importance of seeing role models who share our personal identities starts at a young age. However, Rebekah Bastian[17] warns, "Biases about what people in leadership roles look like don't end at childhood." People who hold identities that aren't represented in positions of leadership may have a more difficult time climbing corporate ladders, Bastian says. There are several possible explanations for this. Bastian suggests that a lack of representation in leadership can stem from "the mental cost of assimilation when someone feels like an only, the toll that microaggressions can take on performance, and a lack of confidence that it's possible to rise higher, when others that share someone's identities aren't there to inspire them."

The focus of this chapter has been on your position as a role model for your employees. In addition, it's very important that you find role models with whom *you* can identify. That may be a challenge for you if you are a trailblazer because of your gender identity, sexual orientation, race, color, ethnicity, national origin, cultural background, or disability. Nonetheless, it will be beneficial for you to find role models who are like you and who can inspire your continued growth and professional development. Here are five strategies:

1. **Look outside your work organization.** Being active in local, state, regional, or national professional organizations can widen your network for finding positive role models who look like you.
2. **Have multiple role models.** Choose a different role model for each of the specific situations you find yourself in. For example, find a role model for handling conflict, for being a team leader, or for speaking at a meeting. May Busch[18] suggests, "Taken together, these situation-specific role models can act as a combined or composite role model."
3. **Seek role models outside of the professional arena.** Look for leadership role models in your family, volunteer and social organizations, and in the community where you live. Laura Hills[19] describes a female

African American senior-level leader in her research study who found her best role models not in the workplace, but among the women in her community. According to Hills, "This very senior level and highly accomplished leader told me that the African American women whose leadership she admired most were homemakers or had jobs cleaning houses during the week. However, they modeled extraordinary leadership for her through their voluntary leadership roles in their church."

4. **Choose a role model you don't know.** A famous or fictional leader can serve as an excellent role model. Many leaders study famous leaders such as Abraham Lincoln, Ruth Bader Ginsburg, or Nelson Mandela and consider them to be their role models. Busch writes that one of her favorite role models for maintaining composure under pressure was the fictional character Diane in the television show *The Good Wife*. Busch writes, "As head of a highly political law firm, Diane encounters serious challenges in every episode and somehow retains her poise and professionalism. I channel her whenever I need that kind of backbone and self-assured confidence."

5. **Imagine a role model.** Create an imagined role model who embodies the leadership qualities you most admire. Give this imaginary leader a name and think of them whenever you need to make a hard decision or you need inspiration. You even may imagine your future self as that composite role model, occupying a higher-level leadership position than you do now. Says Hills, "If you can imagine yourself as a role model, you may just become that person."

Leading Your Healthcare Organization with Charisma

The reason we're successful, darling? My overall charisma, of course.
—Freddy Mercury

Although the epigraph to this chapter may suggest to some that Freddy Mercury was pretty full of himself, most people would point out that he was probably right. One of the things that set Queen apart from other rock bands was their stage presence, led by charismatic lead vocalist Freddy Mercury. For Mercury, as for other successful entertainers, charisma was that intangible "it" factor that people often say that you either have or you don't.

Is leadership charisma an "it" factor too? Are charismatic leaders born with their charisma, a result of excellent genetics, dumb luck, or divine intervention? Do you either have charisma, or you don't? Many people think so. However, current leadership research and coaching practices suggest that charisma is neither an inborn trait like blue or brown eyes nor a personality type à la Myers-Briggs. Rather, charisma is a learned set of behaviors and tactics. For example, John Antonakis, Marika Finley, and Sue Licht[1] say, "Charisma is not all innate; it's a learnable skill or, rather, a set of skills that have been practiced since antiquity." Marianna Pogosyan[2] suggests that although some people may have an "innate ability to be more charismatic," charisma can be taught. Pogosyan explains, "Some people have learned [charismatic] tactics through experiences and role models and use them without even realizing it. Others need more practice." Either way, charisma is not inborn, Pogosyan says, but can be broken down into behaviors that are teachable and learnable. Similarly, John Mattone[3] argues that any leader can develop their charisma. According to Mattone, "You do not have to innately have great 'people skills,' a strong personality, or

Hollywood good looks to have charisma." In fact, charisma can be learned and developed like any other skill, Mattone says, adding, "But first, you must believe that you are capable of being charismatic and deserving of the rewards it can bring."

So, if leadership charisma is learnable, what exactly do you need to learn to become a more charismatic leader? And what are the rewards that your charisma will bring both to you personally as a leader and to your healthcare organization? This chapter answers these questions. First, let's explore what leadership charisma is in theory and what it looks like in practice.

WHAT IS CHARISMA IN LEADERSHIP?

In the study of leadership, charisma is a special quality of leaders whose purposes, powers, behaviors, and extraordinary determination differentiate them from others. In general, to be a charismatic leader means to possess a charming, likeable, pleasing, and colorful personality. The many and various definitions of charisma in leadership have a unifying theme: charisma is a positive and compelling quality that makes others want to be led by a person who has it.

What are the specific qualities of a charismatic leader? Alexander Lyon[4] suggests that charismatic leadership embodies three basic characteristics. Lyon says, "It [charisma] means, Number 1, *appeal.* Charismatic people have an attractiveness, charm, a special kind of magnetism." Second, charismatic leaders possess a gift, or at least seem to. Lyon says, "We think of charisma as a divine, magical, or supernatural gift and power that sets charismatic people apart from ordinary people." What's important here is that the divine characteristic of charisma is in people's perceptions; it is not a fact nor is it a quality that can be quantified or measured. Third, Lyon says, "Charismatic leaders have loyal followers." They inspire and excite an enthusiastic and loyal crowd and have an influence over a group of followers. Most importantly, Lyon stresses, "There's something about charismatic leaders and their mission that goes above and beyond what we're used to seeing." Charismatic leaders, in short, are not garden-variety leaders. There is something different about them. It may be hard to pin down precisely what that difference is. Yet, like pornography, we recognize charisma when we see it. Carlin Flora[5] suggests, "Charisma is, in fact, just short of magic. It's a rare quality but common in figures who inspire devotion."

There are many flavors of charisma and, arguably, each charismatic leader is unique. However, Peter G. Northouse[6] says that we can see five commonalities or typical behaviors in charismatic leaders. They are:

1. **Role models.** Charismatic leaders walk their own talk, or at least appear to do so. They model the beliefs and values they want their followers to adopt. For example, Mahatma Gandhi was a great role model for the nonviolent civil disobedience for which he was advocating.

2. **Competent.** Charismatic leaders know what they are doing, or at least seem to. They demonstrate their competence to their followers not only through their words, but through their actions.

3. **Good communicators who have clear goals.** Charismatic leaders' goals usually are driven by a clear ideology or moral position. Dr. Martin Luther King Jr., for example, drove his message to his followers brilliantly with a clear, consistent, and moral message and an engaging oratorical style.

4. **Aspirational.** Charismatic leaders show a strong desire to rise above the status quo. They communicate very high expectations for their followers and believe in their followers' ability to meet those expectations. They ask a lot and, in turn, their followers gain confidence in their own capabilities and their ability to succeed.

5. **Empathetic.** Charismatic leaders understand what makes their followers tick. They correctly identify and address the motives of their followers. We can see this in John F. Kennedy's famous quotation, "Ask not what your country can do for you; ask what you can do for your country." Kennedy recognized and aroused the motive of service in his followers and encouraged them to translate that motive into action.

As you can see, a charismatic leader cannot exist in a vacuum. A theme that runs through Northouse's five behaviors of charismatic leaders is the way they engage their followers. Lyon explains, "If they [leaders] don't get their followers engaged, excited, and motivated in a special way, then leaders may not qualify as charismatic." Therefore, who the followers are and what they do in response to their leader is an essential ingredient in a leader's charisma.

Another ingredient in charismatic leadership is the context. Charismatic leaders are more likely to find a place and time to lead effectively when the situation or the context is putting pressure or stress on their followers in some way. Lyon says, "Sometimes there is a felt need and exigence for a powerful leader to come in and show followers the way. There are some problems, some unmet needs in the followers' lives and the charismatic leader comes along and offers a compelling solution." Certainly, we see this charismatic leadership strategy at play in political debates and advertisements where candidates paint an alarming picture of what's wrong and explain what they will do to fix the terrible problem looming over their constituents.

Sometimes, manipulative leaders create an urgent context for their followers where there isn't one. They point to problems that are minor or that don't exist. Then, they stir up their followers' fears and biases and offer them a solution to the problem they just exaggerated or invented. That strategy, in fact, is the premise of the Broadway musical "The Music Man." Traveling salesman Harold Hill comes to River City, Iowa, and says that the new pool hall in town is causing the folks there "trouble with a capital T." He says that it will corrupt the boys in the community and lead them into a downward behavioral spiral. The solution? He organizes a boys' band to "keep the young ones moral after school." In reality, there is no problem with the pool hall. However, Hill stirred up that trouble so he could sell the good people of River City band instruments, instruction books, and uniforms for their children. By doing this, he earned the huge sales commission he was after all along. The stakes were relatively low for the hoodwinked citizens of River City, Iowa. However, the stakes are much higher and far less charming in real life when an evil leader uses this same tactic to whip a real or imagined problem to a frenzy and stir up hatred toward others. Adolf Hitler comes to mind.

Charisma in the right hands can help a leader to effect positive change that leads followers into good. However, there also is a potentially dark side to charisma that we know all too well. Throughout history, there have been infamous leaders like Adolf Hitler, Charles Manson, and Osama bin Laden who have used their charismatic influence for their own benefit or to further hateful goals. Some have had a very destructive influence on society and on their followers for the sake of power, greed, and personal gain. Lyon warns, "Charisma and ethics do not come in a package."

Finally, charisma is not one and the same with leadership, and charisma alone does not make a great leader. In fact, it is not necessary to have charisma to be an effective leader. Lyon warns, "Some people turn up the volume on their charisma to cover over a lack of actual leadership skills." For example, some leaders may light up a room and command attention, Lyon says, but then have trouble meeting simple deadlines, analyzing important data, or making sound, informed decisions. Not everyone who has that special spark of charisma can back it up with leadership competence. Unfortunately, incompetent individuals may be given too much leadership too quickly simply because they are charismatic. However, their lack of competence eventually will be exposed and they will fail, Lyon says. Antonakis *et al.* explain, "Leaders need technical expertise to win the trust of followers, manage operations, and set strategy; they also benefit from the ability to punish and reward." In the end, the most effective leaders will be those who layer charismatic leadership on top of well-developed leadership skills, Antonakis *et al.* say.

There are many ways to be an effective leader that have nothing to do with charisma. In fact, many leaders have accomplished incredible things, and we would not describe them as charismatic. Lyon points to the example of Bill Belichick, former head coach of the New England Patriots. Belichick holds numerous coaching records, including winning a record six Super Bowls as the head coach of the Patriots, and two more as defensive coordinator for the New York Giants. Says Lyon of Belichick, "He's incredibly effective at getting results. But few people would describe him as having charisma. He's almost completely unlikeable, even among his own players."

In short, having charisma does not guarantee that leaders are effective. It doesn't guarantee that they are good and moral, or that they are capable. In the wrong hands, charisma can be destructive and devastating. Charismatic leadership is in the eye of the beholder. What is charismatic for one group of followers may not be charismatic for another. Also, charisma is not a precondition for successful leadership. Nevertheless, charisma can be very helpful to achieving one's leadership goals and can give good, ethical, and capable leaders an edge. It can offer healthcare leaders many benefits.

THE BENEFITS OF CHARISMATIC LEADERSHIP

Charismatic leaders often operate on the courage of their convictions and stand up for what they believe in. Some of the benefits of charismatic leadership include:

- **More engaged employees.** Charismatic leaders are adept at motivating and inspiring their employees. Status Net[7] suggests, "Employee engagement will increase."
- **Stronger teams.** Charismatic leaders have inspired connections with their followers. They also foster teamwork. Western Governors University[8] suggests that they place "an emphasis on collaboration and team-oriented support to meet the needs of a project or mission."
- **Leader creation.** Charismatic leaders can spur up-and-coming employees to become leaders. By modeling charisma, their own charismatic behaviors can become a part of an employee's eventual leadership style.
- **Higher productivity.** Charismatic leaders are exceptionally skilled at gaining trust and respect. As a result, employees are more likely to adhere to the high expectations of their charismatic leaders. Status Net suggests, "The effects of this have a high probability of spurring increased productivity and better-quality work."
- **A move toward innovation.** Charismatic leaders are driven toward change and innovation. They will seek opportunities to better the organization and improve processes.
- **More inspired employees.** Charismatic leaders are able to inspire an element of belief. Keith Miller[9] suggests, "Their goal is to make employees feel that their work and talents matter" and that they can do and be more than they may have thought possible. In some instance, Miller says, "They [inspired employees] can even begin to think of bigger dreams and plans that are achievable."
- **A learning culture.** Charismatic leaders typically focus on improvement and growth more than on punishment. Under their leadership, mistakes usually are treated as learning opportunities. Status Net says, "Employees are encouraged to find another solution to problems when the original plan did not work." Charismatic leaders typically create a setting where employees feel more comfortable taking risks and finding better solutions, Status Net says.
- **Higher loyalty and lower turnover.** Employees often feel connected and loyal to a charismatic leader, more so than to the organization that employs them. According to Miller, "Employers often seek out charismatic leaders when they are struggling with high attrition rates." Status Net agrees, suggesting that charismatic leaders can and often do lower employee turnover.

DEVELOPING YOUR CHARISMA: 12 CHARISMATIC LEADERSHIP TACTICS

Charismatic leadership depends on the individual's ability to influence, to appear to be trustworthy, and to have a "leaderlike" style in front of others. Antonakis *et al.* have identified 12 charismatic leadership tactics (CLTs) that they believe will have the greatest effect on leadership charisma. Their empirical study suggests that these 12 CLTs will have a larger positive impact than other leadership tactics, such as strong overall presentation skills and speech structure. Antonakis *et al.* also report that leaders who practiced and used these 12 CLTs saw the leadership scores that their followers gave them skyrocket by 60%. They add that in eight of the last 10 U.S. presidential races, the candidate who deployed these 12 CLTs more often won. Antonakis *et al.* say, "The aim [for leaders] is to use the CLTs not only in public speaking but also in everyday conversations — to be more charismatic all the time." Antonakis *et al.*'s top 12 CLTs are discussed in the following sections. Let's begin with the first nine, each of which has to do with the style leaders use when they speak:

1. **Use metaphors, similes, and analogies.** Charismatic leaders help their followers to understand, relate to, and remember their messages. A powerful way to do this is by using metaphors, similes, and analogies. King used metaphors masterfully. In his "I Have a Dream" speech, for example, he likened the U.S. Constitution to "a promissory note" guaranteeing the unalienable rights of life, liberty, and the pursuit of happiness to all people, but noted that America had instead given its black citizens "a bad check," one that had come back marked "insufficient funds." Antonakis *et al.* point out that King's banking metaphors made his message "crystal clear and easy to retain."

2. **Tell stories and anecdotes.** "I'd like to share a story" are magical words that immediately grab attention. According to Laura Hills,[10] "Stories are a universally appealing part of the human experience, which explains why every culture has them. We are drawn to stories regardless of our age, ethnicity, gender, wealth, or nationality, and we loved them in our ancient past just as much as we do now." Pogosyan suggests that we imbue leaders with charisma if they are good storytellers, especially when their stories help us to understand something abstract or to take action that will solve a problem. Pogosyan says, "We assume

they [storytelling leaders] have unique abilities to see the future and know how to handle things." Fortunately, even leaders who aren't born raconteurs can learn how to tell a good story and employ storytelling skills in a compelling way, Hills says. [See Chapter 7: "Telling Stories to Lead, Teach, Influence, and Inspire" for more information on becoming a good storyteller.]

3. **Use contrasts.** Contrasts are effective because they combine reason and passion. They can help leaders to clarify their positions by pitting them against the opposite, often to dramatic effect. For example, a healthcare leader can use contrast to motivate employees by saying, "I could ask you to take this on because it would be great for our healthcare organization. I'm asking you to take this on so we can save more lives."

4. **Ask rhetorical questions.** Antonakis *et al.* readily admit that rhetorical questions may seem "hackneyed." However, their research suggests that charismatic leaders use them often to encourage engagement. A good example of a rhetorical question: "So, where do you want to go from here? Will it be back to your office feeling sorry for yourself? Or do you want to show what you are capable of achieving?"

5. **Use three-part lists.** Using groups of three is an old rhetorical strategy that works extremely well, because three-part lists distill complex messages into only three key takeaways. Why three? Antonakis *et al.* explain, "Most people can remember three things; three is sufficient to provide proof of a pattern, and three gives an impression of completeness." Charismatic leaders can announce their three-part lists when issuing directives. For example, they can say, "There are three things we will need to do." Or charismatic leaders can and often do unveil a three-part strategy. For example, "First, we need to look back and see what we did right. Second, we need to see where we went wrong. And third, we need to come up with a plan that will convince the board to give us the resources to get it right the next time."

6. **Express moral conviction.** Sharing what you are committed to will establish your credibility and reveal the quality of your character. This will be true even when your sentiments are negative. For example, you can motivate employees to keep going after a major screw-up by saying, "Who do you think will pay for our mistake? It is not our donors who will feel it, but the patients we serve. Apart from wasting money, this is not right. But we can do better. We must. And I have a plan."

7. **Make statements that reflect the sentiment of the group.** Charismatic leaders have their finger on the pulse of the people they lead. They help their followers to align themselves both with their leader and with one another. Antonakis *et al.* suggest that Winston Churchill was masterful at doing this, citing his famous words:

> "This is your hour. This is not victory of a party or of any class. It's a victory of the great British nation as a whole. We were the first, in this ancient island, to draw the sword against tyranny….There we stood, alone. The lights went out and the bombs came down. But every man, woman, and child in the country had no thought of quitting the struggle….Now we have emerged from one deadly struggle — a terrible foe has been cast on the ground and awaits our judgment and our mercy."

8. **Set high goals.** For example, on August 8, 1942, Mahatma Gandhi set the almost impossible goal of liberating India from British rule without using violence, as laid out in his famous "Quit India" speech. And on May 25, 1961, Kennedy announced before a special joint session of Congress the dramatic and ambitious goal of sending an American safely to the moon before the end of the decade. Both of these goals seemed impossible to many people at the time, but they were achieved.

9. **Convey confidence that goals can be achieved.** A leader's goal may be ambitious, but their followers must believe that it is possible. Therefore, charismatic leaders emphasize not only the *what* and the *why*, but also the *how*.

The last three of the top 12 CLTs are nonverbal tactics that Antonakis *et al.* say are key to a leaders' charisma. These may not come naturally to everyone, Antonakis *et al.* admit, but they can be studied and mastered. Additionally, charismatic leaders must be aware of culturally sensitive nonverbal tactics. Antonakis *et al.* say, "What's perceived as too much passion in certain Asian contexts might be perceived as too muted in southern European ones. But they are nonetheless important to learn and practice because they are easier for your followers to process than the verbal CLTs, and they help you hold people's attention by punctuating your speech." Antonakis *et al.'s* three remaining top 12 CLT's are:

10. **Use voice modulation.** A leader who drones in a monotone will not be perceived as charismatic. It is important, therefore, to modulate your voice to express your passion and enthusiasm. Hrideep Barot[11] explains, "Voice modulation is basically how you adjust your voice while speaking. Fast or slow, high pitched or low pitched, taking the right pauses, stressing on words, etc." Leaders who speak with a well-modulated voice will be very effective at engaging their employees. Leaders who speak without much modulation can work with voice teachers to add more liveliness to their speech. Teachers of English to speakers of other languages can be especially helpful for non-native speakers of English whose voice modulation is not the same as that of a typical speaker of North American English.

11. **Use strong, genuine facial expressions.** A leader with a deadpan face will not seem charismatic. However, charismatic leaders do not fake their facial expressions. Amy JC Cuddy, Matthew Kohut, and John Neffinger[12] warn, "Efforts to appear warm and trustworthy by consciously controlling your nonverbal signals can backfire: All too often, you'll come off as wooden and inauthentic instead." What is the right way to use your facial expressions? Cuddy *et al.* suggest, "Warmth is not easy to fake, of course, and a polite smile fools no one. To project warmth, you have to genuinely feel it. A natural smile, for instance, involves not only the muscles around the mouth but also those around the eyes — the crow's feet." Their advice? "Find some reason to feel happy wherever you may be, even if you have to resort to laughing at your predicament." Cuddy *et al.* add that introverted leaders can single out one person to focus on. They suggest, "This can help you channel the sense of comfort you feel with close friends or family," which can lead to warmer facial expressions.

12. **Use positive body language.** It is hard to overstate the importance of good posture in projecting authority and an intention to be taken seriously. Charismatic leaders do not slump. However, good posture does not mean the exaggerated chest-out pose known in the military as standing at attention or raising one's chin up high. It means simply reaching your full height, using your muscles to straighten the S-curve in your spine rather than slouching. Cuddy *et al.* suggest, "It sounds trivial, but maximizing the physical space your body takes up makes a substantial difference in how your audience reacts to you, regardless of your height." Also, gesturing naturally will engage your employees

and make you seem more sincere. Be mindful, however, not to overdo or overstudy your gestures. Cuddy *et al.* suggest, "Twitching, fidgeting, or other visual static sends the signal that you're not in control." Charismatic leaders are calm and unruffled, punctuating what they say with natural hand gestures. In particular, Laura Hills[13] suggests, "Gesture with your palms up, not down." Open palms usually have a positive effect on others. Hills says, "Combined with outstretched arms, they communicate acceptance, trustworthiness, and openness." "Palms down" gestures, on the other hand, generally convey rigidity and authority, even dominance and defiance. As well, show your hands whenever you can. Hills explains, "Concealing your hands (for example, under a desk or table, behind your back, or in your pockets) makes it harder for people to trust you." Therefore, don't hide your hands when you're trying to build rapport with your employees.

Antonakis *et al.* add that there are many other CLTs that leaders can use, such as creating a sense of urgency, invoking history, using repetition, talking about sacrifice, and using humor. However, the 12 CLTs described here are the ones that will have the greatest effect and that can work in almost any context.

Would you like to seem more charismatic to your employees? Antonakis *et al.* suggest that leaders who wish to be more charismatic can begin to incorporate the 12 CLTs they have identified and rehearse them, for example, when preparing to give a speech. They also encourage leaders to think about them before one-on-one conversations or team meetings, especially when they need to be persuasive. Antonakis *et al.* say, "The idea is to arm yourself with a few key CLTs that feel comfortable to you and therefore will come out spontaneously — or at least look as if they did." The goal isn't to employ all the tactics in every conversation, but to use a balanced combination. "With time and practice," Antonakis *et al.* say, "they will start to come out on the fly" and your charisma will soar.

——————— **CHAPTER 11 BONUS FEATURE** ———————

MISTAKES TO AVOID IN THE PURSUIT OF CHARISMA

Becoming a more charismatic leader in your healthcare organization will provide many benefits. However, this leadership strategy also has some potential pitfalls. A trusted colleague or advisor who is familiar with your leadership style can provide you with valuable unbiased feedback. You will need that to help you to keep your efforts to be more charismatic from veering off track or backfiring. Here are the most common mistakes charismatic leaders make:

- **Wrong focus.** Charismatic leaders can become too focused on their own personality and belief system to the detriment of what is best for their followers and their organization. Status Net warns, "Their power to influence others could drive them to become arrogant and shun humility or compassion."
- **The creation of "yes men."** Charismatic leaders can turn their followers into admirers or even worshippers who accept and agree with everything they say. As a result, Status Net says, the ideas of a charismatic leader can go unchallenged, leading to the implementation of plans that are "less than favorable." Charismatic leaders must be mindful that while they want to influence their followers, they want them also to follow their own minds and hearts. They must not expect or want those they lead to follow them blindly.
- **The organization will suffer when they leave.** A good leader must not be indispensable. Unfortunately, very charismatic leaders can easily become just that — the indispensable backbone of their organizations. Their tenacity, drive, and inspiring leadership may cause their followers to depend too much on their abilities, without developing their own. Followers also may reject other leaders who attempt to take the place of charismatic leaders who leave their organizations. As a result, Status Net warns, a charismatic leader's departure can leave a gaping hole that "no one has been trained to fill." Therefore, a very important responsibility of charismatic leadership is to create and develop new leaders, ones who followers will accept and respect. Charismatic leaders also

must be mindful to help every follower to develop their knowledge, skills, and abilities.

- **A lack of clarity.** With a little success under your belt, it can be tempting to rely on your charismatic abilities and forget to employ the leadership tactics that also are necessary for your success. Status Net urges charismatic leaders not to forget "consulting the team, looking at previous performance data, and remembering the mission and vision of the company." These and other basic leadership skills will still be needed for you to succeed.

When we think of what can go wrong with charismatic leadership, Adam Robert Graham[14] urges us to remember the extreme and infamous example of Jim Jones, who deceived and abused his trusting followers right up until their mass suicide in 1978. Graham argues that we can easily make the connection between Jones' charismatic leadership style and the decision of his followers to commit suicide by cyanide poisoning upon his order, resulting in the death of more than 900 men, women, and children in an isolated compound in Guyana. He says, "They [Jones' followers] had complete faith in him, and for the most part, saw no reason to question his demands." What is even more sobering is that Jones began his preaching career with some very noble intentions. For example, Graham says, "He promoted racial equality in his church at a time when that wasn't widely common, and he had this vision of a peaceful utopia." However, when narcissistic traits began to slip through the cracks in Jones' leadership, we can see where things got off track. Graham explains, "As Jones' narcissism began to prevail, it's easy to see how a leader's self-confidence can become overwhelming. The self-absorption and need for admiration can transform their [leader's] previous good intentions into the concern for oneself as opposed to the group." Such a high sense of self-belief can lead some, like Jones, to feel infallible, and, in turn, they can lead their followers down a dangerous road. While the Jonestown massacre is an extreme example of what can happen when charismatic leadership goes wrong, Graham suggests it to us as a reminder that charismatic leaders bear a huge responsibility — to keep themselves from believing that they are infallible or abusing their influence and power.

Fortunately, the vast majority of charismatic leaders are nothing like Jim Jones, and they do not fall prey to these mistakes. In fact, most develop and use their charisma to improve their organizations and to better people's lives. You can too. Just be mindful that you must never use your charisma to seem to be something that you are not or to serve your own needs above the needs of others. Remain humble, stay on course with excellent leadership skills, respect your followers, and your charisma can help you to achieve great things in your healthcare organization.

Why and How to Become a More Resilient Leader

If we've learned anything in recent years, it is that we need to be resilient. Of course, a leader's resilience helps a lot when facing a challenge as staggering as the global pandemic public health crisis we faced in the early 2020s. However, there are many other times in healthcare organizations that may involve unpredictability, change, and stress. When you face big challenges in your role as a healthcare leader, your resilience, or lack of it, will determine how well you fare. It also will determine how well your employees cope, perform, and recover. Brent Gleeson[1] explains, "You can't build resilient teams without resilient leaders." Your employees will be looking to you as a role model of how to handle themselves during times of turbulence, uncertainty, and change. Those who see you behaving calmly and with positive focus while under pressure will feel reassured and will most likely try to emulate you. However, leaders who react emotionally and become visibly overwhelmed when under stress will undermine their employees' confidence, in both their leadership and in the organization. Janice Gair[2] calls this a "ripple effect" and warns that modeling fear, doubt, and anxiety, especially in tough times, can negatively affect productivity and hurt your employees' overall sense of well-being.

It is relatively easy to captain a ship in calm waters. Keeping the ship stable, afloat, and on course in a storm is far more challenging. Yet, the storm is exactly where the true mettle of a leader is tested. Your personal resilience is vital to your ability to guide your employees through the dark times, and research bears this out. For example, Joseph Folkman's[3] leadership competency study found that when looking at ratings of leaders' overall leadership effectiveness by their managers, peers, and direct reports, "It is obvious that the most resilient leaders are viewed as the most effective leaders as well." Frederick S. Southwick *et al.*'s[4] research suggests that one of the reasons that resilient leaders are so effective is that they understand the importance of facing fear, particularly the fear of change. Southwick *et al.* found that leader resilience is "a facilitator of change, along with a means of quick recovery."

It is easy to see that leaders need to become as resilient as possible so they are ready and able to meet the challenge of whatever lies ahead. This chapter explores specifically how you can become a more resilient leader. It warns you of the obstacles you may encounter when trying to do so and also suggests how you can build more resilient healthcare organizations and teams. We begin by determining precisely what it means to be a resilient leader. As you'll see, it is far more than appearing to remain unruffled while under pressure.

WHAT IS A RESILIENT LEADER?

The American Psychological Association[5] defines resilience as "the process and outcome of successfully adapting to difficult or challenging life experiences, especially through mental, emotional, and behavioral flexibility and adjustment to external and internal demands." Resilience in leadership is the capacity not only to endure the great challenges your healthcare organization faces, but also to get stronger in the midst of them. Southwick *et al.* say, "Resilience can be defined as the ability to regain balance following exposure to an adverse event," and to lead others forward successfully.

Notably, a leader's resilience is not an end state of being, as many people think. Rather, it is a process of adaptation and growth within a risky landscape. A leader's resilience will be tested anew by each challenge, and they will adapt their resilience strategically to whatever will be most effective in that particular moment. Resilient leaders, therefore, accurately assess both the challenge and the appropriate response. They are able to adapt to stressors, recover from setbacks, maintain a relatively stable trajectory of healthy functioning, harness resources to maintain well-being, and find personal growth as a healthy adaptation to each unique stressor. Folkman suggests that when faced with ambiguity during a challenge, a resilient leader "finds ways to move forward and avoids getting stuck." A leader's positive attitude while facing a stressor, or lack of one, also is a measure of their resilience.

Leader resilience is not simply a matter of toughing it out or keeping a stiff upper lip when one is needed. We often think of resilient leaders as bold, unflappable, and not easily affected by stress, failure, or setbacks. Although resilient leaders handle challenges with grace, most feel the impact of the challenges they face, even if they don't share everything they feel with their employees. They may appear to be unruffled swans that glide effortlessly and gracefully on the water, yet they may be paddling like crazy below the surface. How leaders look, what they say, and how they behave while under pressure is only one part of what it takes to be resilient; it's what's below the surface that matters too. Gleeson suggests that a leader's resilience is the product of a "broad perspective," including how to act while under pressure, but also being attentive to knowledge and care of oneself before, during, and after a challenge. Gleeson explains, "Resilience taps into your ability to adapt but also relies on your own knowledge about yourself — your values, confidence, and optimism."

Resilient leaders know who they are and stay true to themselves even in the toughest of circumstances. They have defined and live their core leadership values and are guided by them through the stressful times. They overcome major difficulties without engaging in what George Kohlreiser et al.[6] call "dysfunctional behaviors" that harm themselves and others. They check in with themselves frequently while facing challenges to see what they need and what would help them most, be it food, exercise, rest, talking out their concerns, self-care, or asking for support. Kohlreiser et al. say that resilient leaders identify healthy coping mechanisms that will best allow them to relieve their tension and regain their positive energy. Resilient leaders know that they must be ready to jump into action quickly at any time. Therefore, they invest in their own physical and psychological health as a way of life, knowing that both will be needed when facing unforeseen leadership challenges. Moreover, resilient leaders do not hold their stress inward, at least not indefinitely, or take their stress out on others at work or at home. They recognize when and how to relieve their stress and/or know when to ask for help, and from whom.

Resilient leaders are not all cut from the same cloth, and they probably will not behave the same way in every situation. However, Gleeson suggests that they generally tend to do the following:

- Maintain emotional equilibrium and composure under stress.
- When upset, avoid agitating others by spreading tension and anxiety.

- Tolerate ambiguity or uncertainty and adapt readily to new situations.
- Handle mistakes or setbacks with poise and grace.
- Put stressful experiences into perspective and avoid dwelling on them.
- Invest in their own physical and psychological health.
- Communicate confidence and steadiness during difficult times.
- Have the support necessary to cope with emotional overload.

25 WAYS TO BECOME A MORE RESILIENT LEADER

There are many strategies that you can use to develop your resilience as a leader. Choosing to work on even one or just a few of the 25 strategies below can help you both to become more resilient and to appear to be resilient to others:

1. **Become more self-aware.** The body is very smart and often knows how we are feeling before we do. Pay closer attention to your body's response to stress and don't discount or dismiss how you are feeling. Gleeson asks, "Do you feel your heart rate going up? Do you get hot? Do you clench your jaw?" The sooner you recognize that your body is going into stress, the sooner you can do something to manage it.

2. **Define your core leadership values.** Resilient leaders believe in a core set of moral and ethical principles that help guide them and give them strength during times of uncertainty and stress. Christopher Peterson and Martin E.P. Seligman[7] identify six virtues as signature resources that leaders can draw from to increase their performance during challenging times, as well as good times: wisdom, courage, humanity, justice, temperance, and transcendence. According to Southwick *et al.*, "Taken together, these signature characteristics are powerful components for both personal resilience and by extension, leadership resilience." [See Chapter 13: "Developing and Using Your Core Leadership Values" for more information on this topic.]

3. **Learn to be more flexible.** Resilience has been associated with multiple expressions of flexibility. According to Southwick *et al.*, these include "knowing how to accept situations that cannot be changed, having the capacity to switch between different modes of thought and coping mechanisms, learning from failure, and finding meaning, opportunity, and the potential for growth in the context of adversity."

4. **Cultivate more and better relationships.** Trusted friends and colleagues can be a source from whom leaders can draw strength and

guidance, especially when facing seemingly insurmountable crises. According to Matt Gavin,[8] "A robust professional network can provide access to people with different perspectives and skills, along with resources that can be leveraged to build high-performing teams and drive key projects forward." Strong personal bonds give us the confidence to take risks, stretch, and aim for high goals. They also are vital in supporting us as we recover from failure and disappointment. Growing your network and learning from peers with diverse backgrounds and talents are two resilience strategies that will help you to overcome your leadership challenges, Gavin says.

5. **Become more focused, organized, and disciplined.** Look for ways to organize and streamline your work when a task is causing you stress. Gleeson suggests that effective strategies include defining roles, clarifying expectations, managing a project schedule, and completing tasks ahead of deadline. Gleeson says, "Gaining focus may reduce stress."

6. **Become better at asking for support.** Resilient leaders have at least one trusted person with whom they can let down their hair and ask for support. However, they do not share their stress with people who are not trustworthy or who may be hurt by it. Gair says, "It may be tempting to vent to colleagues about a stressful situation or bad news, but remember that as a leader, you help set the tone for the organization. Find healthy ways to vent that frustration to people who don't work with you, like a family member or a friend." A coach also can provide needed support and useful feedback in trying times.

7. **Regularly reflect and assess.** Self-reflection and feedback from trusted peers and others can help leaders to identify their strengths, weaknesses, and motivational drivers, and approach challenges with what Gavin calls "a keen sense of emotional intelligence." Assess your leadership effectiveness regularly. In so doing, Gavin says, "You can adapt your leadership style to tackle complex business problems and steer your team through turbulent situations."

8. **Develop wellness rituals.** A fitness ritual, good sleeping habits, maintaining excellent hydration, and even getting some fresh air can help you to manage challenges more effectively. Gleeson suggests that taking short breaks won't significantly eat into your work time but will be well worth it to help you manage the pressure you're under.

9. **Become a better communicator.** The most resilient leaders are effective at communicating their intentions to others. Folkman says, "They

are willing to help others understand a new strategy or direction." They don't assume that everyone knows the rationale behind their decisions. Rather, they share their strategy with them clearly and in as much detail as is needed so that everyone can be on the same page.

10. **Seek to improve your organization.** Resilient leaders are not satisfied with the status quo and continually ask, "How can we improve?" Innovation requires leaders to be good observers and diagnosticians. They must be able to interpret performance data and be able to encourage adaptive change. Southwick *et al.* suggest, "Modern leaders, particularly those in fields that are rapidly evolving, must know how to foster innovative change."

11. **Gain a broader perspective.** It's easy to hyperfocus on the problem right in front of you and to lose sight of the larger picture. When that happens, resilient leaders take a deep breath and put the problem into its larger context. By doing so, they often find that their challenges are not as bad and insurmountable as they originally thought. Also, resilient leaders do not inflate, dwell on, or run away from their mistakes and failures. Gleeson suggests, "Strive to get beyond the pain and disappointment and refocus on what you can learn from the experience and apply to future circumstances." Keep in mind that your leadership challenges present opportunities for you to learn more about yourself and to bolster your resolve to overcome hardship. Gavin says, "Approaching challenges with a positive outlook allows resilient leaders to bounce back from adversity and come out stronger on the other side."

12. **Create an executable plan.** Gleeson suggests that leaders develop personalized resilience development plans with the help of a coach, mentor, or trusted peer. Start by identifying any obstacles to your resilience. Ultimately, with that experience under your belt, you can develop a team resilience plan to help those you lead. (See "12 Ways to Build More Resilient Healthcare Teams," the bonus feature at the end of this chapter, for more information on this topic.)

13. **Become more receptive to feedback.** Resilient leaders are open to feedback and often ask others for it. Then, they listen, even if they don't like what they hear, and demonstrate a sincere effort to improve. Resilient leaders are both humble and coachable. Folkman warns, "As we look at this skill [receptivity to feedback] we see that younger employees are often coachable, but many people become less coachable

as they age." The most resilient leaders continue to ask for and are receptive to feedback throughout their careers.

14. **Become more realistically optimistic.** Resilient leaders are optimistic about their organizations. They believe that the future will be bright, that setbacks can be overcome, and that there is light at the end of dark tunnels. However, it is important to accept that resilient leaders also are realistic about their optimism. According to Southwick *et al.*, "Realistically optimistic leaders do not prematurely sound alarms, nor do they engage in confirmation biases or immediately discount information that does not fit with the expected business plan." Resilient leaders are neither overly nor inadequately optimistic. They base their optimism on accurate risk appraisals and pay close attention to areas of potential threat and vulnerability, giving them their proper due.

15. **Establish and maintain boundaries.** When facing big challenges, leaders often feel compelled to work long hours and drive themselves to the point of exhaustion. Unfortunately, extreme overwork is directly related to lack of effectiveness and poor decision-making. James Spillane[9] says, "When leaders don't set boundaries for themselves, they run the risk of burnout. Even worse, they set an example for their teams that can leave employees feeling worn out, undervalued, and disengaged." For these reasons, resilient leaders say *no* to overwork when it threatens their effectiveness and resilience.

16. **Focus on more delegation and less multitasking.** Resilience sometimes requires letting go of the way we do things. Gleeson warns, "You may believe that your stamina is boundless, but it is not." Resilient leaders know this and free themselves of the tasks that they can. They let go of unimportant, nonurgent work or delegate those tasks to others. In place of that work, they do something that inspires and rejuvenates them. They tackle their most important and complex work in the most productive part of their day. Then, they build time into their schedules to recharge.

17. **Become more comfortable with risk.** Resilient leaders are willing to take risks, try new ideas, and make bold changes. It is easy for leaders to become stuck in a rut in which they continue to conduct work in the same way from year to year. Folkman warns, "That approach works well until the world changes, requiring organizations to change or die." Big challenges sometimes require big responses that are different from the ones that leaders have used before.

18. **Redefine work–life balance.** The balance among the various parts of your life is complicated. Gleeson explains, "Demands and interests change over time, and what feels like balance at one point quickly becomes outdated." If your life revolves around who you are and what you value, you will feel balanced, even when you must temporarily prioritize one part of your life over other parts, Gleeson says.

19. **Learn how to face your fears.** The ability to face fear dramatically broadens the range of possibilities and choices available to a leader, while avoidance of fear is highly constricting. One of the most common fears that leaders must face is fear of change. Southwick *et al.* say, "Unfortunately, change within an organizational structure is often experienced as frightening and not all team members respond to change in a resilient manner." Resilient leaders will be aware of fear within themselves and others and work to mitigate and manage it.

20. **Develop others.** Resilient leaders are interested in their own development and also are concerned with the development of others. Folkman says, "Resiliency is needed when we encounter failure. Developing others helps everyone learn from their mistakes."

21. **Become a more curious learner.** Resilient leaders listen to podcasts. They read, take courses, learn new skills, and gain new understandings, and apply those lessons during times of stress and change. They don't resist trying new approaches to their work when under pressure. Gleeson warns, "Don't be that person [who isn't curious]. It only leads to failure."

22. **Learn to respond, not react.** Reacting is an automatic, emotional, knee-jerk reflex caused by a stressor, while responding is much more objective, thoughtful, and strategic. In most cases, modeling a response rather than a reaction for your employees will mean keeping negative emotional reactions to yourself. Gair suggests, "Acknowledging what you have heard in the moment and then sharing your thoughts once you've had a chance to process them models self-restraint and maturity," and is a hallmark of resilience.

23. **Become more purpose driven.** Resilient leaders do not lose sight of who they are, what is true, their values, and their purpose, even when they feel pressure to do otherwise. Staying true helps them to be more resilient and to lead more authentically, Gavin says, and to "rally employees around a mission when a challenge arises." In fact, resilient

organizations have leaders who demonstrate continual, unwavering support of their missions. According to Southwick *et al.*, "Through their words and action they [purpose-driven leaders] are able to visualize a positive mission charter for the organization, effectively communicate the plan to others, and encourage strong commitment to the course of action." A full "reservoir of commitment" encourages a higher tolerance for uncertainty and perseverance in the face of threat, Southwick *et al.* say.

24. **Practice being accountable.** When challenges arise, employees will need to know that they can count on their leaders to provide them with the support, resources, and guidance they need. Spillane says, "The time to start building that track record for accountability is long before a situation that calls for resilience." Resilient leaders demonstrate their accountability when the stakes are low so their employees will trust that they have stable, resilient leadership behind them. That will help them to get back on track when they face bigger challenges and when they must overcome disappointments and failures.

25. **Become more decisive.** The most resilient leaders do not get bogged down in decision-making. They are effective at making timely decisions and moving forward. Folkman adds, "If they make the wrong decision, they are quick to make a different decision and move in another direction."

OBSTACLES TO LEADER RESILIENCE

Several psychosocial, neurobiological, developmental, and environmental factors can support or interfere with a leader's ability to remain resilient in the face of challenges. Southwick *et al.* say that psychosocial resilience factors supported by scientific literature include:

- The capacity to face fear and regulate emotions.
- Optimism and positive emotions.
- Active as opposed to passive problem-focused coping.
- Adherence to a valued set of ethical and moral principles.
- Disciplined focus on skill development.
- Altruism.
- Attention to physical health and fitness.
- A strong social support network.
- Cognitive flexibility.

- The ability to reframe adversity in a more positive light.
- Commitment to a mission or cause that is meaningful and highly valued.

Southwick *et al.* explain, "In many cases it is not known whether these factors promote resilience or simply are associated with it." Nonetheless, a lack of these psychosocial factors may be a huge obstacle to a leader's resilience. Fortunately, leaders who find themselves lacking one or more of these resilience factors can seek help to learn to develop them.

Similarly, Gleeson describes a short list of emotional and behavioral "blockages" to a leader's resilience. Gleeson suggests that the following characteristics may make a leader slower to recover after a setback or cause a leader's mental health, productivity, and relationships to suffer. According to Gleeson, you may be undermining your resilience if you:

- Have a difficult time saying *no* to requests.
- Struggle to prioritize.
- Ruminate after difficult conversations and conflicts (which prolongs a stressed state).
- Lose track of just how overcommitted you've become.
- Work in a highly competitive culture and sacrifice periodic reflection for constant action.
- Have little control over your work or what assignments you take on.
- Sacrifice empathy for toughness.
- Rely upon existing strengths, failing to develop new skills.
- Are so self-reliant that you can't trust others.
- Seem so positive that your optimism seems unrealistic to others.

Feedback and introspection can help you to identify whether you have any of these blockages. As with the psychosocial factors described by Southwick *et al.*, it is possible to improve in each of these areas through learning and practice.

The neurobiology of resilience is a relatively new and interesting area of investigation and may give us a clue as to why some leaders are more naturally resilient than others. A variety of neurochemicals have been shown to mediate resilience via the body's response to stress. According to Southwick *et al.*, some of these include adrenalin, noradrenalin, cortisol, dopamine, and neuropeptide Y (NPY). Southwick *et al.* say, "Research shows that individuals with higher levels of oxytocin, dehydroepiandrosterone (DHEA), and NPY may be more psychologically hardy and resistant to high-pressure situations." These neurohormones regulate the stress response in areas of the nervous system and brain known to be activated during fear and autonomic arousal. Additionally, Southwick *et al.* say, social bonding and interpersonal relations, important in teamwork, are mediated by oxytocin and vasopressin, while learning and critical thinking are mediated by glutamate and brain-derived neurotrophic factor. They explain, "Specific brain regions involved in these processes include the amygdala (i.e., processes emotions such as fear and threat appraisal), the prefrontal cortex and anterior cingulate cortex (i.e., make rational decisions and regulate emotions), the hippocampus (i.e., learning and memory), and the nucleus accumbens (i.e., reward)." More research will help us to understand if and how individual neurobiological differences in leaders cause or influence their resilience, or a lack of it, and even whether illness or neurochemical imbalances may be obstacles to their resilience.

Certain developmental factors may be obstacles to a leader's resilience. Southwick *et al.* explain, "The type and amount of stress that one experiences in childhood can have a marked impact on how one handles stress as an adult." Research in both animals and humans has shown that repeated stress that is overwhelming, unmanageable, and perceived as out of one's sense of control can lead to exaggerated emotional, behavioral, nervous system, and neuroendocrine responses to future stressors. In contrast, exposing children or young animals to repeated stressors that they can control or master, particularly during key developmental periods, tends to have an "inoculating" or "stealing" effect, Southwick *et al.* say, so that as adults they can better modulate neurobiological, behavioral, and emotional responses to future stressors. Southwick *et al.* add, "It is also likely that the mastery of substantial challenges early in the life has a stress inoculating effect, leaving the individual stronger and better prepared to deal with future challenges." Leaders who believe that childhood challenges and traumas may be lowering their resilience may want to seek help to address these issues. Those who lacked manageable challenges in early life to help them develop their resilience may similarly be helped with self-work.

Finally, environmental factors can be obstacles to leader resilience. For example, Jacqueline Dohaney *et al.'s*[10] study found that support, leadership, and planning are critical in building and inhibiting resilience, and that a lack of these factors can threaten a leader's resilience. They suggest also that the organization itself can foster or thwart resilience to major disruptions and challenges. Frequently mentioned organizational barriers to leader and team resilience among their study participants include:

- Lack of staff time and resourcefulness.
- Lack of institutional mandate, buy-in, and acknowledgment.
- Limited or weak existing systems.
- Employee unwillingness to change, adapt, and be flexible.
- Lack of planning for improving resilience and responding to disruption.

The most common barrier to resilience mentioned in Dohaney *et al.'s* study was employees feeling "overworked with fewer resources and sustaining high workloads." They suggest that leaders will require ongoing support and incentives to ensure that resilience-building initiatives are undertaken or maintained in their organizations.

As you can see, some of the obstacles to leader resilience are within your control, while others are not. Either way, it is important for you to recognize and assess the obstacles you encounter so you fully understand the complexity and depth of the challenge you are facing. As well, focusing and working on the obstacles you *can* improve will help you to increase your resilience, even if you are not fully successful. Small improvements can help, and taking action will help you to feel more in control as you face future leadership challenges.

HOW TO BUILD A RESILIENT HEALTHCARE ORGANIZATION

Stressors as enormous as those we have faced in recent years are harbingers of the extraordinary challenges we are likely to face in the years to come. Fernando F. Suarez and Juan S. Montes[11] warn that in addition to health crises, "Climate change, massive migration flows, and technological advances will all dramatically reshape the social and economic landscape in ways we can't fully anticipate." However, healthcare organizations aren't helpless. They can and must prepare themselves to cope with novel and uncertain situations. Fortunately, just as leaders and employees can be resilient, so, too, can healthcare organizations.

Southwick *et al.* say: "A resilient organization not only survives, but also thrives in an environment of change and uncertainty." An organization's "reservoir of commitment" encourages a higher tolerance for uncertainty and perseverance in the face of threat, they say. Resilient healthcare organizations also have sound, well-established routines for getting things done. Suarez and Montes say, "The task at hand may be as lofty as acquiring a competitor or as prosaic as filling out a time sheet, but if you look closely, you'll find a reliable process to guide you through it." Routines often are taken for granted in stable periods but become invaluable when an organization faces new challenges. Knowing what to do and how to do it provides a foundation of resilience. Therefore, before the next challenge or crisis hits, Suarez and Montes suggest, "It's wise to spend time thinking systematically about the granular nuts-and-bolts processes you use — and to experiment with alternatives."

Keep in mind that every routine and process you use in your healthcare organization is based on a significant number of assumptions. Therefore, devote some time to figuring out what those assumptions are, especially for your key routines. Then think about how you'd operate if those assumptions did not hold. Suarez and Montes suggest using the following four questions to assess the assumptions behind your routines:

1. Which types of decisions do you assume must be made by high-level managers? How do you envision those decisions being made in a crisis?
2. Do you assume (or do you know) that your existing processes have been revised and perfected over time? Are they optimal? Will they hold up in times of duress?
3. Where in the flow of work do problems consistently arise? Is there an argument for reshaping that segment of the process or allocating more resources to it? What would happen if you suddenly had to get that chunk of work done much faster or with fewer resources?
4. Do you assume that organizational resources are allocated well to your routines? Would you reapportion them if you suddenly had to respond to a major disruption? What would happen then?

In addition to routines, resilient organizations also develop simple rules that will guide them both when things are stable and when they are not. Suarez and Montes say, "Rules of thumb help you speed up processes and decision-making and prioritize the use of resources in less-predictable contexts." Furthermore, resilient organizations are good at improvisation, what Suarez and Montes define as "spontaneous, creative efforts to address a problem or opportunity." Role plays and simulations can be excellent training tools to help your employees to improve their improvisation skills.

These strategies — leader commitment, routines, rules, and improvisation — are all necessary for organizations to be resilient, and any organization will fare better if it can move easily among them. In fact, all four strategies are interdependent. Suarez and Montes explain, "People can improvise in the face of a crazy-seeming, unexpected situation, learn from the improvisation, and eventually develop a simple rule based on what they've discovered. Or they can revise an organizational routine after experimenting with new approaches to a particular task." Fluency in leader commitment, routine building, rule building, and improvisation can improve performance and enhance resilience under any circumstances, including those when an organization faces extreme uncertainty or stress. Suarez and Montes add, "In fact, we believe that the ease with which teams refashion how specific tasks get done — whatever the level of turbulence — is the defining capability of a resilient organization."

CHAPTER 12 BONUS FEATURE

12 WAYS TO BUILD RESILIENT HEALTHCARE TEAMS

Resilient leaders have a social and moral responsibility to foster resilience in their employees and to build resilient teams. Kohlreiser *et al.* suggest, "They must become attuned to the people around them and learn to recognize when a colleague [or team] is under a lot of stress." Resilient teams have a foundation of meaningful core values that all members believe in deeply and a sense of unity beyond what you find in many teams. Not coincidentally, Gleeson adds, "They also have a tendency to show consistent and better-than-average profitability year after year." Here are 12 strategies to help you build more resilient teams:

1. **Recruit effective team members.** Assembling a resilient team requires careful selection of individuals with diverse backgrounds and complementary expertise. Southwick *et al.* suggest, "Certain personality characteristics and traits are particularly helpful when working in teams. Two of the most important character traits are industriousness and enthusiasm."

2. **Practice doing more with less.** Suarez and Montes say, "It's hard for us to think of any actual crisis that doesn't involve resource scarcity of

some kind." Challenge your team by asking it to achieve an ambitious goal with significantly fewer resources than normal. Or ask your team to brainstorm about how it would respond if a key resource suddenly became scarce.

3. **Reach out to team members who seem stressed.** Engage in an honest discussion about how the team member feels and why. Kohlreiser *et al.* suggest that sometimes the best way to initiate the conversation is to ask questions, such as, "Is everything all right? It appears you may be under a lot of stress. Is there anything I can do to help you?" Your questions should be gentle and respectful, not threatening, Kohlreiser *et al.* say, and lead to a definite plan for reducing or managing the team member's stress.

4. **Help employees to understand how their work fits into the whole.** Organizations tend to ask employees to departmentalize and specialize, sticking to narrow tasks or activities. This structure is efficient and supports organizational routines. In uncertain times, however, deeper knowledge of how other areas function, perhaps gained through cross-training, makes a team more resilient. Suarez and Montes explain, "Team members develop a better idea of how their work depends on others' work, and vice versa." As a result, the team's work is less likely to be disrupted when a routine is changed or resources become limited.

5. **Talk less, listen more.** The single most useful skill for building resilience in a team is for you to listen to your team members. Stephanie Overby[12] warns that too many leaders "try to talk their employees out of what they're feeling in challenging situations," reassure them prematurely, or tell them that things are actually good and that they shouldn't be upset. According to Overby, "This approach backfires, making team members feel misunderstood, condescended to, or resentful." To build more resilient teams, never brush off a concern, Overby says, even if it seems unimportant to you.

6. **Identify individual employee strengths.** A leader who wishes to build team resilience concentrates on identifying and developing the individual strengths of each member of the team, then assigns work accordingly. Southwick *et al.* suggest, "Meet with team members separately to discuss their unique competencies; outline a plan to integrate these competencies into roles within the team."

7. **Invest in building your team's expertise.** New team routines, rules, and improvisations may appear to be spontaneous, but in reality, they rest upon a foundation of knowledge and training. Suarez and Montes suggest that knowing more prepares teams to make sound decisions and to create new ways of doing things when they need to.

8. **Promote psychological safety.** You can encourage team resilience when you make your team a safe place to take risks, share different perspectives, and ask questions. Overby explains that teams can more effectively tackle challenges and rebound from setbacks when they feel safe and supported. Protect your teams. Overby says, "Unnecessary and overly frequent change, unnecessary blindsiding or obfuscation, and even unrealistic positivity can sap otherwise resilient folks of energy and engagement." Be honest about new or difficult situations and avoid unnecessary turmoil to protect your team members and their energy. Keith Ferrazzi et al.[13] suggest, "When it feels like there's an elephant in the room, leaders of resilient teams create what we call 'candor breaks' to encourage team members to share their thoughts and feelings."

9. **Identify your team's priorities.** When a crisis is unfolding, red lights and alarms go off everywhere, and managerial attention becomes a very scarce resource. In such situations, leaders need to hyperfocus on the metrics that are central to moving the organization through the turmoil. By doing so, Suarez and Montes say, "They can help everyone tackle the most-pressing problems and concentrate on the activities that are essential to avoiding a collapse; everything else will simply have to wait." Prioritizing often requires tough trade-offs. The metrics won't be the same in every situation, so it's useful to imagine a variety of scenarios for your team and to think through what they may specifically require, Suarez and Montes say.

10. **Encourage commitment to building one another's resilience.** Ferrazzi et al. call this resilience-building strategy "co-elevation" and say that it is essential to establish clear and unambiguous expectations around team unity and peer-to-peer support. They say, "Any hesitation or reluctance to help a struggling colleague is a sign that deeper interventions may be needed."

11. **Learn to give up control.** Resilient teams have a high leadership quotient. That means that many, if not all team members feel empowered

to make suggestions and take on leadership roles in their areas of expertise. Southwick *et al.* explain, "Empowering teams serves to increase leadership capabilities within the organization and prepares others to assume a lead role when an unexpected challenge arises." In fact, organizations that have survived dangerous times often have developed the ability to delegate authority and decision-making swiftly to people with expertise "on the front lines," Suarez and Montes say.

12. **Build team resilience again and again.** Ferrazzi *et al.* suggest that team resilience is similar to a battery. They say, "It needs to be restored and recharged regularly." Do not assume that a resilient team will stay resilient without some care and feeding, especially in the face of large challenges or changes in personnel. Make resilience building an ongoing effort that you and your team treasure and continually renew.

Developing and Using Your Core Leadership Values

We can easily find impressive lists of core leadership values. Just do an Internet search or scan the leadership books at your library, and you'll find many reputable resources that list the 5, 8, 10, 14, even the 50 essential core values of leaders. When you read these lists, you will find yourself nodding along with every value listed, and with good reason. It's hard to argue against being respectful or building trust or having integrity, courage, passion, empathy, patience, humility, excellent communication, authenticity, gratitude, or dedication. But is nodding along enough? What does it mean to have core values? And even more importantly, what does it look like when leaders use their core values to guide their leadership, not just in the big moments, but every day? That's what we're going to explore in this deep dive into values-based leadership and core leadership values. By the end of this chapter, you will find that developing and using your core leadership values requires a lot more than listing and sharing your values.

To begin, your employees will not be positively changed because you define your values for them. What you describe may sound good, but they will not likely be moved to do anything because you say that you value honesty and creativity. They also may not believe you. Furthermore, they are likely to bristle if they are jaded or if what you say sounds to them like a lot of hooey. Worse, they will lose respect for you if they later find that your actions don't match your stated values. That's when the real trouble starts. Curt Steinhorst[1] suggests, "Values are an investment, not a platitude." If lists of core values sound "hollow, corrupted, misguided, and pretentious" to your employees, Steinhorst warns, they carry with them a falseness that can make them backfire against you and divide your organization. However, well-developed, truthful core leadership values can have the "strength of steel," Steinhorst says, when they are drawn from and are representative of the community you serve. So, here's the spoiler alert for this chapter: You are not going to finish reading this and develop your core leadership values alone at your desk. We'll get into a much better strategy later. For now, let's define what we mean by values-based leadership and consider the benefits and challenges of this leadership approach.

WHAT IS VALUES-BASED LEADERSHIP?

Values-based leadership is both a philosophy and a leadership style that builds on the assumption that people live and work mostly by their values and that our values are our best motivators. It tends to be selfless in nature. Maria Gamb[2] suggests that a values-based leader "creates the expectation that the leader always operates for the greater good of all." Values-based leadership suggests an ideal way to go about things based on goodness, fairness, honesty, and integrity. That is why so many people find it to be an appealing style of leadership.

Values-based leadership is rooted in emotional intelligence and is based on the belief that leaders and their employees can become their best selves. Paul Falcone[3] explains, "Self-reflection, a balanced perspective and genuine humility, among other attributes, make people stronger." Values-based leadership assumes that positive shared values will enable employees to experience greater alignment. As a result, they will be more likely to remain loyal to their organizations and to produce better work. Brent Gleeson[4] explains, "Knowing that a leader or manager has similar beliefs often encourages employees to follow their instruction, increasing the chance of success with every goal. This enhances engagement, performance, and even retention — all of which foster growth and profitability." Values-based leadership also is built on the assumption that employees who share values will be less likely to fall prey to ethical breeches. Their values will help them resist temptations to cut corners, lie, embezzle, cheat, bully, goof off, or otherwise compromise or harm the organization and one another. Values-based leaders also are more likely to stay on the straight and narrow when tested, which has become increasingly important to the public in recent years. Harry M. Jansen Kraemer Jr.[5] explains, "Breaches of ethics, betrayal of public trust, and violations of fiduciary responsibility — from the financial crisis to political leaders who have fallen from grace due to scandals in their private lives — illustrate the need for strong commitment to fundamental principles of leadership" and to leaders' personal values.

Values-based leadership suggests that a leader's values are unchanging, regardless of the circumstances. That means that a values-based leader has the same core values at home and at work, with family and with colleagues, with one employee and with the next, and yesterday, today, and tomorrow. James M. Kouzes and Barry Z. Posner[6] say that a values-based leader has a "unifying set of values that guide choices of action regardless of the situation" and that those values constitute a leader's personal "bottom line." Kouzes and Posner further suggest that leaders' values influence their moral judgments and relationships. Their values guide them when they make difficult decisions — for instance, when they choose whether to invest in and trust other people or to walk away.

Values-based leadership is mostly a late 20th- and early 21st-century concept that is believed to have evolved as a byproduct of our time and culture. The emergence of the 21st century was plagued with extensive, evasive, and disheartening ethical leadership failures. Neither the public nor private sector remained immune as many leaders were exposed for immoral or unethical behaviors. Mary Kay Copeland[7] paints a disturbing picture. Copeland says, "Financial greed and corruption, corporate meltdowns, and spiraling unethical practices were revealed as financial scandals surfaced at prominent companies." In the decades preceding, charismatic, transformational leadership was promoted, encouraged, and developed as a strategy for increasing the effectiveness of leaders and organizations. However, moral and ethical deficiencies became prevalent in many of the charismatic, dynamic, and seemingly transformational leaders who had risen to prominence. That is when scholars, practitioners, and the general public began to challenge the qualities needed for exemplary leaders. Copeland says, "It became clear that in order to restore hope, confidence, integrity, and honor to leaders and organizations, leadership theorists argued that entities needed to look beyond the persuasive lure of a charismatic, ostensibly transformational leader and ensure that leaders also possessed a strong set of values, morals, and ethics." The result was an increased focus on the concept of values-based leadership. Today, core leadership values and values-based leadership have become ubiquitous in scholarly and popular management and leadership literature and, to some extent, in practice. Viinamäki Olli-Pekka[8] adds that values-based leadership is not purely an alternative approach, but that it is "complementary to other leadership efforts." In fact, Olli-Pekka says, the value-based and ethics-based conduct of values-based leadership is thought to be "essential" to charismatic, transformational, and transactional leadership.

Most savvy leaders at least give lip service to upholding a set of values. Values-based leaders not only articulate their values clearly and consistently, both inside and outside the organization, but they live those values. Androscoggin Bank[9] says, "They use those values to build relationships and guide important decisions." Thus, it is hard to know if leaders are truly values-based without looking at their track records or at least until some time has passed. Values-based leaders talk the talk like everyone else, but what sets them apart is that they also walk the walk.

THE BENEFITS AND CHALLENGES OF VALUES-BASED LEADERSHIP

There are many potential benefits of values-based leadership. We've already alluded to some, such as helping leaders to make ethical decisions, unifying the team, and building trust. Here are some additional benefits that come from values-based leadership:

- **Clear messaging.** It's going to be easier for you to convey your values to your employees, partners, patients, and other stakeholders when you state those values clearly. Clear messaging will help you to attract people who understand and appreciate your values. Androscoggin Bank says, "When customers recognize their own values in a company they trust, they're more likely to stay loyal over time."
- **Attracting top talent.** Good employees want to work for leaders and organizations that share their values and that will challenge them to be their best. Ralph Phillip[10] says, "Organizations with strong cultures that are aligned with their values tend to attract top talent."
- **Alignment with self.** Leaders who choose values-based leadership typically have values that mean a lot to them. Bringing those personal values into their leadership will enable them to be authentic and to live their values through their work.
- **Recognizing who doesn't fit.** Values-based leaders strive to create a culture of shared values among their employees. They can use those values as a yardstick for sizing up job candidates and potential partners, and for identifying members of the team whose values do not align with those of the organization.

- **Empowering employees.** Employees will work with greater confidence when their work fits with the shared values of the team. They will not have to wonder whether they are doing the right thing or come to you for guidance about every hard decision they make. The team's values will empower its members to function more independently.
- **Differentiation.** Values also provide an opportunity to set your health-care organization apart from your competition. According to Wambi,[11] "Sixty-three percent of consumers want goods and services from companies with a purpose and values that resonate with their values and belief systems." Therefore, when patients decide where to seek treatment, the majority will want to find a healthcare organization that aligns with their values and avoid the ones that don't, Wambi says.

Of course, no philosophy or style of leadership comes without potential challenges, and values-based leadership is no exception. As we have mentioned, it will take significant time and effort to build trust with your employees. You may have some employees who are a poor fit to your values or who do not buy into a values-based way of thinking. Wambi warns that misidentified values will breed mistrust and make employees feel that they are working for an organization that is not "genuine." As well, values-based leaders may face some of these additional challenges:

- **A mismatch between values and policy or behavior.** Imagine that one of your values is work–life balance but that your healthcare organization does not have many policies to support that. Or imagine that one of your values is transparency but that there are many things that you cannot share with your employees. Or imagine that you value creativity and innovation but that you inherit managers who have been in your organization much longer than you and who actively discourage creative thinking. Aligning your values with the policies and behaviors of others can be a huge challenge. However, it is a necessary one to work through, not only for the values-based leader's sake personally, but also for the sake of the employees they lead.
- **Conflicting values.** A values conflict occurs when leaders have two values that are equally important to them that conflict with one another. For instance, imagine that you value humility but that you also value recognition for work well done. It can be challenging to foster humility in your employees when you give them a public hip-hip-hooray for a noteworthy achievement. Or imagine that you value loyalty but that you

also value personal growth. What will you do when the best way you can help employees to grow is to counsel them to leave your organization? Values-based leaders must feel their way through these challenges to decide which value has priority.

- **Living our values can be hard.** Leaders face moments when applying their values will be very costly. For instance, imagine that your boss forced a decision against your better judgment that your employees are going to hate. On the one hand, you value truthfulness and honesty. So, when you share the news with your employees and they ask you who made the terrible decision, you will want to tell them that it was your boss and perhaps add that you are opposed to it. That's the truth. On the other hand, telling your employees that it was your boss may escalate their anger toward him and toward you for your inability to protect them. Telling your employees the truth also may make your boss furious if he doesn't want that known. It can be hard to live your values when the cost is very high.

HOW TO DEVELOP YOUR CORE VALUES

Historically, a code of values or an ethical code in most organizations was developed by management, sometimes with the help of outside consultants. Olli-Pekka says, "There are a lot of critics in the leadership literature against this straightforward top-down procedure." Most of the critics argue that stakeholders should participate in formulation and articulation of values. Otherwise, they will consider values as simply "a new set of rules," Olli-Pekka says. Furthermore, trust, respect, and reactivity of and in the organization can be displaced and misused when values are handed down from on high.

Steinhorst suggests that it can be challenging to reflect a truth that is shared throughout the organization, particularly one that crosses every classic organizing force used for any group of people in history from geography to socioeconomics, religious ideology, race, gender, and education. Steinhorst adds that core values must not be a corporate declaration, rather, a "community standard," one reached through participation and collaboration. In any community, values are extracted, lived, and felt, not scripted. Values must come from what is shared and must create identity and belonging; they also must act as a compass to point the way. Steinhorst says that although values may be aspirational, "They don't start from a list of sanitized terms or hipster buzzwords."

An evident challenge is how to engage employees and other stakeholders with values and values-based leadership. It's not always easy to develop shared values by using a participative process. Kouzes and Posner urge leaders to establish credibility and trust with their employees before, during, and after the participative process. This step will become part of the shift away from the concept of the leader as the primary or sole creator of an organization's values, Kouzes and Posner say.

A participative process will be time-consuming because employees must have the opportunity to reflect and formulate values on their own. To support this effort, Olli-Pekka suggests establishing a basis or platform on which stakeholders can communicate and collaborate. In large organizations, the fact that staff and leaders may have to work through several layers of bureaucracy, rules, roles, and professional groups to implement actions, strategies, and values should be regarded as an advantage, Olli-Pekka says. They all represent stakeholders who can be included in formulating values and groups that implement values. Steinhorst adds, "Leaders who fail to understand this create 'core values' that provoke reactions ranging from open skepticism to inward indifference." They fall short of the culture of momentum, purpose, and professional kinship that most leaders seek.

Where will your core values come from? New organizations may have to invent some initially, then revisit and amend them as their culture develops. However, organizations that are well-established already have values firmly in place. Elizabeth Baskin[12] says, "Defining corporate values is more about archaeology than architecture." The task is not to pull values from thin air but to unearth the values that are already there. It is to identify the values that are currently being used across your organization to guide employee actions and decisions every day.

A typical but relatively ineffective approach to defining values is to get a group of executive leaders in a room and have them come up with a list of values. Baskin warns, "This approach often results in a long list of generic values in an attempt not to leave anything out." To get to the values that drive *your* culture, you must involve employees at all levels in your organization from the start and be willing to delete values that would apply to any healthcare organization or that may otherwise cloud the picture, even if they are perfectly good ones. Be sure to involve the employees who live and breathe your culture every day, because they will provide a rich source of intelligence on what values are being used daily in your organization. Baskin says, "Including a representative spectrum of employees in the process of defining the values also raises the employees' stake in putting those values to use."

Your first goal will be to come up with a handful of principles that are both prevalent in your culture and, ideally, specific to your organization. Here are three methods that Baskin uses successfully when involving employees in discussions of core values:

1. **Index cards or sticky notes in small groups.** Administer a survey to ask your employees to suggest values that matter to them. Then write each potential value on an index card or sticky note. Conduct a series of small group meetings with 10 to 12 employees per group. Ask them to arrange the index cards or sticky notes in order of importance on a table or wall. Instruct them to work collaboratively to move the must-have values to the top. Turn cards over to the blank side or remove them as your employees eliminate them. Baskin suggests, "We find it helpful to make this a physical session, with employees moving around the room and passing the cards back and forth as they arrange them. Somehow it engages them more fully in the discussion — which often results in a spirited debate." After 10 or 15 minutes, employees generally narrow the list to four or five values, Baskin says. Often, they'll find that there's overlap or duplication in concepts so that several potential values can be summed up in one word or phrase. Baskin adds, "When we look at those short lists across several groups, there's usually a fairly consistent set that appears across the organization." Take those values back to your leadership team, who may tweak the list a bit before arriving at a final collection of values.

2. **Employee video interviews.** The easiest way to collect video interviews is at a large event or another occasion when you will have access to a broad spectrum of people to contribute. Your camera operator and interviewer can roam the crowd and invite people to participate, one or two at a time. Ask your employees to talk about values indirectly. For example, Baskin says, "The interviewer may ask the employees to describe what the people at this company are like or to talk about the culture and how people treat each other, their clients or customers, and their vendors. We might ask what they appreciate most about the management style of leadership or the working relationships with their

peers." The results will provide clues to what the true values of your organization are. Baskin adds, "We sometimes edit this footage to be shown later at the values launch to demonstrate how the values sprang from what employees told us is true about the culture."

3. **Guided visualization.** In guided visualization, a facilitator leads groups of employees and executive leadership of 20 to 100 people per session in a guided meditation. Although Baskin admits that not every culture will be game for group meditation, they have used this approach with success. Baskin describes telling a "hero's journey" story in which the hero is the brand name of the organization. Baskin explains, "As he [the brand] armed himself, as he battled dragons and as he returned victorious with a pile of gold, we asked employees to imagine what each of these metaphors symbolized for the brand. At the end of the meditation, we asked them to picture this hero's story being passed down from generation to generation. What, we asked, is the moral of this story?" In one organization, one phrase recurred repeatedly and in every single group: This hero "does the right thing," everyone said. Baskin asked what that meant in terms of their brand, and employees from the CEO down gave example after example from the company's history and present-day business. Baskin says, "This was a remarkable instance of a culture being aligned around one powerful value."

HOW TO WRITE YOUR CORE VALUES STATEMENT

A values statement will articulate your values clearly to your existing and new employees. A well-written statement is clear, concise, and brief. Heyden Enochson[13] suggests that you keep your list to five, six, or seven values, although you can find examples of values statements that are slightly shorter or longer. Enochson also suggests describing values in brief bulleted points. Enochson says, "Concise statements are better than lengthy descriptions of desired behaviors." Most importantly, Enochson stresses that it is essential to write values that are specific enough to be actionable. For example, one of Boston Medical Center's[14] values is "move mountains." Stating that alone may not explain what mountains their employees are supposed to move. Therefore, the value is described more specifically so that it can inform employees' decisions and behaviors: "Impossibility doesn't live here. Instead, we're motivated by what can be — and we'll move mountains to make it happen." [See the bonus feature at the end of this chapter to see Boston Medical Center's complete values statement and six other examples of values statements used in healthcare organizations.]

Indeed Editorial Team[15] suggests using the following template to create your own values statement:

- Encourage [value] in [a workplace example].
- Put [value] above all else.
- [Organization] helps [persons or entity] by focusing on [value].
- [Organization] works hard to demonstrate [value] in all aspects.
- [Value] is the foundation of our purpose.

The result will be a statement that looks like this:

- Encourage inclusiveness in every step.
- Put honesty above all else.
- Springfield Health helps patients by focusing on transparency.
- Springfield Health works hard to demonstrate commitment in all aspects.
- Communication is the foundation of our purpose.

Indeed Editorial Team adds that there are three kinds of values that you can include in your values statement. *Core* values are the fundamental values of an organization and its employees. Indeed Editorial Team says that examples of core values are "creativity, empathy or responsibility." *Aspirational* values are values that an organization aims to improve but doesn't necessarily meet yet. They may include "diligence, sustainability or eco-friendliness," Indeed Editorial Team says. *Accidental* values are those you didn't plan for but that have become a part of your organization. These may include "a customer-first mentality or diversity," Indeed Editorial Team says. Enochson suggests a fourth kind of value. Enochson says that *behavioral* values usually are not given much attention because they tend to be the same across industries and organizations. Nonetheless, they can become dynamic when they differentiate your organization or when the behavior is extremely important in your culture. For example, Under Armour[16] has a value of "celebrate the wins" and defines what that means behaviorally: "We take time to have fun."

Enochson offers one more important piece of advice about writing your values statement. Enochson says," If it's in your mission, don't repeat it." There may be some overlap in language but try not to repeat content unnecessarily. Enochson says, "Each of these foundational elements must be unique to be effective and appreciated."

VALUES-BASED LEADERSHIP IN PRACTICE

It stands to reason that employees who share similar values and philosophies will work together more harmoniously. Admittedly, values-based leadership is simple in theory. But what does it feel and look like in practice and how can you introduce this idea to your team without them rolling their eyes? David R. Graber and Anne Osborne Kilpatrick[13] warn, "Implementing value systems is almost always much more difficult than processing them."

Rolling out values-based leadership will look different for your current team than it does for new hires. Falcone suggests that you approach the two groups separately and differently:

- **Your current team.** Your existing employees may meet a sudden shift to values-based leadership with skepticism. Falcone says, "It may feel awkward to suddenly call a meeting to express your leadership values with your current team, especially if you've been working together for years." Therefore, don't come into the meeting with a list of your values and read them aloud. Instead, explain that you are about to introduce a new idea, one that you've considered carefully. Then explain that you are introducing a concept called *values-based leadership* and that you want and need them all to be a part of it. Stress that this is something that you will be adding in addition to the leadership already in place. Explain briefly what values-based leadership is and that you will be soliciting their input about your organization's values in the coming days and weeks. Tell them only a little about how they will be involved and why their involvement is so important, and that more details will be provided as a follow-up to your meeting. Do not dwell on the specifics of meetings and schedules or specific values at this point. Instead, tell your employees that the task before them will be to help you create a values statement (or revise an existing values statement) that reflects the true culture of your organization. Stress that it will serve as a guide for decision-making from this point forward. Describe the benefits of articulating and living shared values and why you think it is so important. Illustrate your point with a hypothetical or real quandary that comes up in your healthcare organization when values can make it easier to know what to do. Help your employees to see that a set of shared values will be more than words on a wall or a website. They will become a guide that you and they can use every day to make hard decisions easier. Then open the floor for questions and discussion. Follow up after your meeting with a brief summary of what you discussed and next steps for involving them in the process.

- **New hires.** Consider your values statement in your hiring process and decisions. Ask questions at your job interviews that will help you to determine whether applicants are a good fit with your values. Set aside time with each new hire cohort on the first day to get to know them personally. Read and discuss your values statement and give your new employees examples of your values in action. Present them with hypothetical challenges that they may encounter and ask them to work collaboratively to apply your values to their decisions and behaviors. Then discuss what they come up with. Explain that each new hire will be accountable for perpetuating your values because they are now part of a culture that holds those values dear. Hold a follow-up meeting with new hires who are in formal leadership positions. Be more specific about your expectations. Tell your new managers that your values must now be their values, both for themselves and for the employees they manage. Address the potential negative consequences for not meeting these expectations. Stress that the management team in your organization is held to an even higher standard of accountability.

Finally, with your values statement firmly in place, teach everyone in your organization to apply your shared values in practice by asking and answering questions whenever they are faced with a tough decision. Harry M. Jansen Kraemer Jr.[18] suggests that you ask, "What is most important? What should we be doing now?" Enochson suggests that you ask, "What key non-negotiables are critical to the success of your organization? What values are you willing to stand by, even if it costs clients or revenue?" Bradley Hook[19] suggests that when faced with a values conflict you ask questions to help you establish a hierarchy of values. Hook says, "A clear hierarchy will reduce ambiguity and enable intensely focused work." In times of values conflicts, teach your employees to ask, "Which value is the most important one in this situation?" Sometimes they will answer this question alone, sometimes collaboratively, and in very tough cases they may need help from their managers or from you.

The community you serve can be very impressed by a well-written values statement. However, the most significant benefit of values-based leadership will be its use every day by the people who work in your healthcare organization. Your values statement must become a living, breathing, and accurate description of who you are, not a relic that collects dust and serves as a testament to your good intentions. Your values will be useful only if they become a guide for what to think, say, and do for every member of your organization. Mary Patry[20] says, "The North Star has been used for navigation for centuries. Acting as a guiding light, people use its brightness and prominence in the sky to ensure they are traveling in the right direction." Just as the North Star guided explorers for centuries, use the values you share with your employees to guide your behaviors, decisions, and actions every day, and for years and years to come.

——————— **CHAPTER 13 BONUS FEATURE** ———————

CORE VALUES STATEMENTS IN HEALTHCARE ORGANIZATIONS: 7 EXAMPLES

Every healthcare organization needs to develop its own core values statement. However, it can be helpful to look at examples from other organizations. Typically, a good values statement is clear, concise, and includes only a few points. Here are seven examples from healthcare organizations. Although you'll see some similarity from one organization's values to the next, you'll also see that values vary and that there is more than one way to write a values statement.

1. **Mayo Clinic.**[21] These values, which guide the Mayo Clinic's mission to this day, are an expression of the vision and intent of our founders, the original Mayo physicians and the Sisters of Saint Francis:
   - **Respect.** Treat everyone in our diverse community, including patients, their families, and colleagues, with dignity.
   - **Integrity.** Adhere to the highest standards of professionalism, ethics, and personal responsibility, worthy of the trust our patients place in us.

- **Compassion.** Provide the best care, treating patients and family members with sensitivity and empathy.
- **Healing.** Inspire hope and nurture the well-being of the whole person, respecting physical, emotional, and spiritual needs.
- **Teamwork.** Value the contributions of all, blending the skills of individual staff members in unsurpassed collaboration.
- **Innovation.** Infuse and energize the organization, enhancing the lives of those we serve, through the creative ideas and unique talents of each employee.
- **Excellence.** Deliver the best outcomes and highest-quality service through the dedicated effort of every team member.
- **Stewardship.** Sustain and reinvest in our mission and extended communities by wisely managing our human, natural, and material resources.

2. **Johns Hopkins Medicine.**[22] Our core values:
   - **Excellence & discovery.** *Be the best.* Commit to exceptional quality and service by encouraging curiosity, seeking information, and creating innovative solutions.
   - **Leadership & integrity.** *Be a role model.* Inspire others to achieve their best and have the courage to do the right thing.
   - **Diversity & inclusion.** *Be open.* Embrace and value different backgrounds, opinions and experiences.
   - **Respect & collegiality.** *Be kind.* Listen to understand and embrace others' unique skills and knowledge.

3. **Cleveland Clinic.**[23] Values:
   - **Quality & safety.** We ensure the highest standards and excellent outcomes through effective interactions, decision-making, and actions.
   - **Empathy.** We imagine what another person is going through, work to alleviate suffering, and create joy whenever possible.
   - **Inclusion.** We intentionally create an environment of compassionate belonging where all are valued and respected.
   - **Integrity.** We adhere to high moral principles and professional standards by a commitment to honesty, confidentiality, trust, respect, and transparency.
   - **Teamwork.** We work together to ensure the best possible care, safety, and well-being of our patients and fellow caregivers.

- **Innovation.** We drive small and large changes to transform healthcare everywhere.
4. **Northwestern Medicine.**[24] Values:
- **Patients first.** Putting patients first in all that we do.
- **Integrity.** Adhering to an uncompromising code of ethics that emphasizes complete honesty and sincerity.
- **Teamwork.** Team success over personal success.
5. **Ascension Medical Group.**[25] We share a common vision and are called to act upon the following ideas and beliefs:
- **Service of the poor.** Generosity of spirit, especially for persons most in need.
- **Reverence.** Respect and compassion for the dignity and diversity of life.
- **Integrity**. Inspiring trust through personal leadership.
- **Wisdom.** Integrating excellence and stewardship.
- **Creativity.** Courageous innovation.
- **Dedication.** Affirming the hope and joy of our ministry
6. **Seattle Children's Hospital.**[26] Our six values stand together — one cannot be practiced without the others. As an organization committed to health equity and anti-racism, we will practice these values through an anti-racism lens to foster a culture of respect and inclusion throughout the Seattle Children's community.
- **Compassion.** Empathy for patients, their families, and staff is ingrained in our history and inspires our future. We do more than treat the child; we practice family-centered care as the cornerstone of compassion.
- **Excellence.** Our promise to treat, prevent, and cure pediatric disease is an enormous responsibility. We follow the highest standards of quality and safety and expect accountability from each other.
- **Integrity.** At all times, we approach our work with openness, transparency, decency, and humility. It is our responsibility to use resources wisely to sustain Seattle Children's for generations to come.
- **Collaboration.** We work in partnership with patients, their families, staff, providers, volunteers, and donors. This spirit of respectful cooperation extends beyond our walls to our business partners and the community.

- **Equity.** We champion anti-racism and find strength in the diversity of our patients, their families, staff, and community. We believe all children deserve exceptional care, the best outcomes, respect, and a safe environment. To achieve this, we work to eliminate health inequities and address any form of systemic racism in our organization.
- **Innovation.** We aspire to be an innovative leader in pediatric healthcare, research and philanthropy. We continually seek new and better solutions. Because innovation springs from knowledge, we foster learning in all disciplines.

7. **Boston Medical Center.**[15] Values:

- **Built on respect, powered by empathy.** We care about our patients, employees, and community — and we're committed to doing right by them each and every day.
- **Move mountains.** Impossibility doesn't exist here. Instead, we're motivated by what can be — and we'll move mountains to make it happen.
- **Many faces create our greatness.** Diversity is our heart and soul — and when it comes to inclusion, we're all in.

CHAPTER 14

Overcoming Impostor Syndrome in Healthcare Leadership

"Whenever I feel afraid, I hold my head erect,
And whistle a happy tune, so no one will suspect I'm afraid."

Oscar Hammerstein, Lyricist
"I Whistle a Happy Tune" from The King and I

Are we rewarded when we stuff our feelings, as suggested in the song above? Arguably, yes. "Fake it till you make it" has become a commonly accepted narrative in our culture. In fact, some very successful people have suggested that we should fake our confidence when it fails us. The megastar, singer, and businesswoman Rihanna,[1] for example, suggests that when we lack confidence, we fake it. She says, "Pretend…I mean why not? It's either that or I cry myself to sleep, and who wants to do that? You wake up with puffy eyes the next day. That's a waste of tears." Many of us assume the guise of confidence to help us overcome our stage fright, ace a job interview, meet our in-laws for the first time, or tackle a daunting work project or task. As Oscar Hammerstein suggests in his lyrics, we whistle a happy tune at one time or another in our lives and hope that, as the song later suggests, "The result of this deception is very strange to tell, for when I fool the people I fear, I fool myself as well." A charming sentiment, yes. But is that true? And is this sound advice?

Almost all of us doubt our abilities and feel fear at some time in our lives and careers. We may fake our confidence, passion, or drive, not for nefarious purposes or because we enjoy deceiving others, but because we want to propel ourselves over the daunting hurdles we face. The deception seems harmless enough, and it can work. However, there are concerning long-term implications of regularly pretending to be what we are not. Alan Ibbotson[2] refers to the "fake it till you make it" narrative as "literally the birthplace of impostor syndrome." Ibbotson says, "The advice is to fake it until you're successful. A fake is a phony, a counterfeit, a sham, a fraud, a hoax. And this is advice? Be a phony until you're successful? Really?" Ibbotson and many others believe that by normalizing false confidence and abilities, "the deception" in Hammerstein's lyrics, we begin to descend a dangerously slippery slope. If you fake it often enough, Ibbotson says, part of you comes to believe that you are indeed a fake, someone not fit for the role you are about to step into or already hold.

Impostor syndrome is loosely defined as the internal experience some of us have of believing that we are not as competent as others perceive us to be. It is a psychological phenomenon in which individuals doubt their skills, talents, accomplishments, or fitness for a position or role they play, and have a persistent, nagging internalized fear of being exposed as a fraud. Unfortunately, the problem is widespread. In fact, A. White[3] suggests that impostor syndrome has become the "new normal." According to *Psychology Today*,[4] "Around 25 to 30 percent of high achievers may suffer from impostor syndrome. And around 70 percent of adults may experience impostorism at least once in their lifetime."

Impostor syndrome affects people in all stages of their education and careers. However, Manfred F.R. Kets de Vries[5] observes that the problem runs rampant in C-suite, managerial, and leadership positions. He distinguishes fleeting impostoristic feelings from what he calls *neurotic impostorism*. Kets de Vries explains, "To some extent, of course, we are all impostors. We play roles on the stage of life, presenting a public self that differs from the private self we share with intimates…." Displaying a facade is, in fact, part and parcel of the human condition, Kets de Vries says, and a likely reason that the feeling of being an impostor is so common. We are taught to stifle our feelings and to act in ways we don't want to, starting at a very young age. For example, we are urged to kiss our Aunt Peggy, who scares the bejeebers out of us, to share toys and treats we'd rather keep for ourselves, and to pretend that we like a birthday gift we received, when, in fact, we don't like it or want it.

Usually, our occasional, momentary feelings of being an impostor are not debilitating. They may be, in fact, the price we must pay for taking part in a civilized society, and necessary so we get along with one another. Neurotic impostorism, on the other hand, occurs when phoniness becomes normalized for individuals who believe that there is tremendous, relentless pressure on them to fake it. A steady diet of faking it leaves them feeling fraudulent, ashamed, and alone. Kets de Vries says, "Because they view themselves as charlatans, their success is worse than meaningless: It is a burden." Neurotic impostors believe that they are bluffing their way through their lives and their careers, and they are haunted by the constant fear of exposure. With every success, they think, "I was lucky this time, fooling everyone, but will my luck hold? When will people discover that I'm not up to the job?" Neurotic impostors will feel this way even when they are doing an objectively good job, are highly qualified, and are deserving of the recognition, praise, and rewards they receive. They brush off their accomplishments as flukes or mistakes and feel undeserving of the accolades, rewards, and opportunities heaped upon them.

Some self-doubt is normal and, in fact, prevents us from being narcissistically delusional about our capabilities and achievements. You won't need to do much or anything if you experience doubts that are short-lived and rare, as long as they don't stop you from doing what you need and want to do. However, you will need to take quick action if you are plagued by strong, frequent doubts about your abilities, especially if you have a nagging fear that you will be found out as a fraud. This is especially true if such thoughts cause you anguish, keep you up at night, hold you back, or undermine your leadership. You won't be able to live a happy and productive life, let alone lead others in your healthcare organization to the best of your abilities, if you feel that you are a fraud who is minutes away from being caught.

Impostor syndrome is not a hopeless and incurable condition, but it can cause immense distress and deserves our attention. In the following sections we will learn more about impostor syndrome and identify which healthcare leaders may be more vulnerable to it than others. We will explore when impostorism has the potential to interfere with or sabotage leadership. We will consider, too, what healthcare leaders can do to prevent impostoristic thinking and nip negative thoughts in the bud. Fortunately, leaders who feel like impostors can do quite a lot to gain or regain their confidence. To start, let's understand more about impostor syndrome.

WHAT IS IMPOSTOR SYNDROME?

Pauline Rose Clance and Suzanne Ament Imes[6] first coined the term *impostor phenomenon* in an article published in 1978. They defined impostor phenomenon as "an internal experience of intellectual phoniness" and initially focused their research on women in higher education and professional industries. Clance and Imes posited that the impostor phenomenon was less prevalent in men. However, later research found that the impostor phenomenon is spread equally among men and women. For example, Joe Langford and Pauline Rose Clance[7] report in 1993 that surveys of several populations found "no differences between the sexes in the degree in which they experience impostor feelings." Furthermore, later studies of college students, college professors, and successful professionals failed to reveal any gender differences in impostor feelings, suggesting that males, at least in these populations, are just as likely as females to experience impostorism. However, Rebecca L. Badawy, *et al.*[8] suggest that men may be more likely than women to have severe reactions to the impostor phenomenon. The researchers report that the men in their study reacted "significantly more negatively under conditions of negative feedback and high accountability" than their female participants did.

Impostor syndrome is not a diagnosable psychiatric illness (although it can be addressed with many kinds of psychotherapy). Rather, impostor syndrome is defined by Cleveland Clinic[9] as "a pattern of thinking that can lead to self-doubt, negative self-talk and missed opportunities." It is identified by the symptoms the individual experiences, identifies, and reports. Cleveland Clinic says that these may include crediting luck or other reasons for success, fear of being regarded as a failure, feeling that overworking is the only way to meet expectations, feeling unworthy of attention or affection, downplaying accomplishments, and holding back from reaching attainable goals. Kimberly Charleson[10] suggests also that there are external signs of impostor syndrome that others may notice, including minimizing or deflecting positive feedback, overpreparing, not trying for fear of failure, and distrust of others.

THE HIGH COST OF IMPOSTOR SYNDROME

Strong feelings of self-doubt can be costly to the individual even beyond the unpleasantness of fear, anxiety, and stress. They also can be financially costly. Mint[11] says, "Impostor syndrome is an extreme case of self-doubt that impacts your performance and success — which, in turn, can hinder your earning potential." Individuals who experience impostor syndrome may avoid taking on projects and reasonable risks or believe that they don't deserve a salary increase. Mint reports that the estimated costs in the following list represent missed opportunities and increased health costs for the average American who experiences impostor syndrome:

- **Burnout and stress.** $988/year
- **Work tension.** $2,244/year
- **Lack of sleep**. $2,569/year
- **Lost productivity**. $3,400/year
- **Not negotiating pay**. $7,528/year
- **Unnecessary purchases**. $1,800/year that could have been saved or put toward another good use.

Impostor syndrome robs even the highest achievers of their motivation each year, Mint says. Motivation is hard to quantify, but, nonetheless, is related to one's lifetime earning potential. The costs of impostor syndrome extend beyond the individual. Leaders who suffer from impostor syndrome ultimately can do great harm to their organizations. Alexandra Friedman[12] says, "The procrastination, perfectionism, over-preparation, self-sabotage and self-censoring that characterize impostor syndrome can deplete time and resources, and, most adversely, employee morale." Moreover, faking it can subtly and negatively permeate the work culture and become a prevalent strategy within an organization, especially when leaders model or encourage the tactic. Organizations that have leaders and employees who grapple with impostor syndrome can suffer from a lack of transparency and authentic communication. Critical feedback may be withheld and opportunities for growth missed. Judith Belton[13] warns, "Employees may feel pressured to present themselves as infallible, hindering open communication and vulnerability." The veneer of perfection that impostoristic leaders model can stifle innovation, impede authentic connections, and perpetuate a culture of pretense, Belton says.

WHO IS MOST LIKELY TO EXPERIENCE IMPOSTOR SYNDROME?

There are several potential causes of impostor syndrome, and some may surprise you. For example, *Psychology Today* says, "Calling attention to one's success, ironically, can unleash feelings of impostor syndrome." Some people begin to experience impostor syndrome when their successes are broadcast publicly, and they become the object of profuse praise, attention, and applause. For example, they may feel undeserving and doubt their abilities when they win a prestigious award, are promoted to a prominent position, or have a flattering article written about them.

Fortunately, most people handle positive recognition well and enjoy the limelight without suffering negative consequences. However, career success is not the only potential trigger of impostor syndrome. Several other experiences and conditions also can begin the spiral of self-doubt. For example:

- **Communities that have low representation or are marginalized.** Individuals who are put in positions where they do not see others like themselves may be more vulnerable to impostor syndrome. A. Benisek[14] explains, "Studies show that those who are different from most of their peers, such as women in high-tech careers or first-generation college students, are more likely to have impostor syndrome." Research also has found that impostor syndrome is common in Black American, Asian American, and Latinx college students in the United States, Benisek says. Charleson explains, "The lack of role models can lead to low confidence, a lack of peer support, and a feeling of not belonging — all of these factors can contribute to impostor syndrome." Keep in mind, however, that feeling like an outsider is not necessarily a result of impostor syndrome. In some cases, it can occur because of actual discrimination or exclusion due to systemic bias. Arlin Cuncic[15] explains this important distinction. Benisek says, "With impostor syndrome, the feeling of being an outsider is caused by internal beliefs. With discrimination, the feeling is caused by the actions of others."
- **Negative stereotyping.** Negative stereotypes may fuel impostor syndrome, even when they are not overtly expressed. For example, Lizzie Duszynski-Goodman[16] says, "Research points to the way society defines leadership qualities with masculine traits as a potential trigger for impostor syndrome in women seeking leadership roles."
- **A stressful upbringing.** The seeds for impostor syndrome can be sown in childhood. Benisek says, "Many people who have impostor syndrome grew up in families that stressed achievement and success. If your parents went back and forth between overpraise and criticism, you may be more likely to have feelings of being a fraud later in life." Cuncic suggests that

parenting styles characterized by being controlling and overprotective may contribute to the development of impostor syndrome in children. Cuncic adds, "Studies also suggest that people who come from families that experienced high levels of conflict with low amounts of support may be more likely to experience impostor syndrome."

- **High-pressure communities.** Society's pressures to achieve also can contribute to impostor syndrome. Benisek warns, "It's easy to measure your self-worth by what you've accomplished," which, in turn, can encourage impostoristic behaviors and feelings, especially for those who believe that they can't keep up. Individuals who are members of extended families, communities, academic institutions, organizations, workplaces, or professional societies that heap a lot of pressure on their members to succeed may be more susceptible to impostor syndrome.

- **Transitions.** Impostor syndrome appears to be more common when we are going through transitions and trying new things. Cuncic explains, "The pressure to achieve and succeed, combined with a lack of experience, can trigger feelings of inadequacy in these new roles and settings." That inadequacy, when taken too far, can make us believe that we are undeserving fakes who eventually will be found out.

- **A failure after a string of successes.** *Psychology Today* says that even one setback can shake one's self-confidence and "make us critique and question our overall aptitude." Two or more failures following success may undermine our confidence even more and make us feel that we fooled people but finally have been found out.

- **High-risk personality traits.** Cuncic says that certain personality traits have been linked to a higher risk of experiencing impostor syndrome. These include low self-efficacy (i.e., your belief in your ability to succeed in any given situation); perfectionism (i.e., the belief that you cannot risk ever saying or doing the wrong thing); and neuroticism (i.e., higher levels of anxiety, insecurity, tension, and guilt).

- **Social anxiety.** People with social anxiety disorder may feel as though they don't belong in social or performance situations. Cuncic says, "You might be in a conversation with someone and feel as though they are going to discover your social incompetence. Or you may be delivering a presentation and feel as though you just need to get through it before anyone realizes you really don't belong there." Keep in mind, however, that while the symptoms of social anxiety can fuel impostor syndrome, that does not mean that everyone who experiences impostor syndrome has social anxiety, or vice versa, Cuncic says.

- **Depression.** Depression has many ripple effects, and the crippling self-doubt of impostor syndrome is potentially one of them. Mahevash Shaikh[17] says, of her own depression, "While one does not need to have depression to feel like an impostor, I sometimes feel like one when my depression intensifies." Depression can make us believe that we do not have and never can achieve the level of competence that we think you should have. Therefore, Elisha Lee[18] says, nothing we do is ever going to be "good enough" and can make us feel that others have incorrectly placed their confidence and trust in us. The result is that we feel like undeserving impostors.
- **Unfavorable comparison.** Playing the comparison game can lead to feeling down or inadequate if we are not achieving our goals at the same rate as others. That, in turn, can make us feel like frauds who are faking it.

IMPOSTOR SYNDROME IN HEALTHCARE

Several sources suggest that impostor syndrome occurs in new healthcare practitioners with greater frequency than it does in many other populations. For example, Michael Gottlieb, *et al.*[19] say, "Impostor syndrome (IS) is increasingly recognised as a condition among physicians and physicians in training." Shermel Edwards-Maddox,[20] who conducted a literature review of studies of nursing students and clinical nurse specialists, found that impostoristic feelings among study participants ranged from 36% to a whopping 75%. Edwards-Maddox explains, "Due to changes in nursing education resulting from COVID-19, self-doubt and uncertainty among new nurses are expected to be heightened," leading to burnout and impostor syndrome. That said, Aimee Aubeeluck, Gemma Stacey, and Edward JN Stupple,[21] who reviewed studies of nursing students pre-COVID, similarly found, "Graduate nursing students may be particularly susceptible to 'Impostor Syndrome.'"

It is not surprising that impostor syndrome would be higher in students and new practitioners, as it usually is associated with high-achieving individuals and those who are just getting started in their careers. However, several sources suggest that senior healthcare practitioners are not immune to it either. For example, Kori A. LaDonna, Shiphra Ginsburg, and Christopher Watling[22] found that even physicians at advanced career stages question the validity of their achievements and can identify as impostors. Melissa J. Armstrong and Lisa M. Shulman[23] suggest that the impostor phenomenon could be one of the reasons that female neurologists at all career points still lag behind men in publications and job promotions. And Emily Moskal[24] reports that Stanford Medicine's study of about 3,000 practicing physicians in various stages of their careers found that impostor syndrome is "more prevalent in physicians than in other U.S. workers."

Why is impostor syndrome so common among healthcare professionals? Windy Watt[25] suggests, "Students embarking on a career in the healthcare profession quickly learn that they have entered a culture that expects perfection. There is little room for error, and 'high achiever' is the predominant personality type." Therefore, the seeds for physician impostor syndrome often are planted at the student level. Watt explains, "Students attribute their success to luck, good timing, or someone else's recommendation rather than their own hard work. This leads them to believe that they are undeserving of their role and don't belong." However, even beyond training, Michelle Davis[26] says, impostor syndrome does not go away and continues to be underacknowledged in the healthcare community. Davis warns, "Individuals who experience it rarely talk about it. Left unaddressed, impostorism can lead to inaccurate self-assessment, affecting professional identity and fulfillment of potential."

IMPOSTOR SYNDROME IN LEADERSHIP

Are leaders, like healthcare professionals, more prone to impostor syndrome than other populations? Yes. In fact, John Mattone[27] describes impostor syndrome as "the bane of leaders everywhere" and warns that it sabotages the work of many talented executives. Leaders are seen as exemplars of competence and confidence, and they often strive to model those attributes for their followers. The pressure they feel to maintain this façade creates the perfect breeding ground for impostor syndrome. That can explain why, Heather Cherry[28] says, "Many leaders experience impostor syndrome, and its effects can have far-reaching consequences."

Of course, leaders may not always feel free to reveal the full extent of their doubts and fears to their followers. They know that others look to them for optimism, strength, and confidence, especially during trying times, and most feel pressure to be a positive role model. The ancient Chinese Taoist philosopher Laozi[29] famously said, "Leadership is your ability to hide your panic from others." Whether you agree with Laozi or not, Dina Denham Smith and Alicia A. Grandey[30] refer to this as the "emotional labor" of being a leader. They say, "Effective leaders have long managed the emotions they display at work. They project optimism and confidence when team members feel thwarted and discouraged. Or notwithstanding their skepticism about the company's strategic direction, they carry the company flag and work to rally the troops." The emotional labor leaders bear can make them feel that they are straddling the fine line between authentically sharing how they feel and presenting more confidence and optimism than they have. On top of that, many leaders also strive to appear unruffled to their followers, no matter what happens. Belton explains, "Leaders may feel compelled to project an image of infallibility, fearing that any admission of self-doubt or vulnerability will diminish their authority." This paradox — the expectation of unwavering confidence and the internal struggle of impostor syndrome — can be a "lonely and debilitating journey" for those in leadership positions, Belton says.

Impostor syndrome can occur at any point in a leader's career, and even the most seasoned leaders can fall prey to it. However, new leaders seem to be especially susceptible to it. Several sources suggest that those first steps into leadership occur in an especially tender moment in a leader's career. For example, Vistage[31] says that impostor syndrome can be "especially tough for new CEOs, who have put in years of work and now sit at the top, which can be a very lonely place indeed." Friedman suggests that emerging leaders often believe that "they don't deserve their success." As well, Von Born[32] says that it is common for first-time leaders to feel self-doubt and that impostor syndrome can lead them to "unhelpful attitudes of perfection-seeking, rigidness and overwhelm." Clearly, leaders who are new in their roles, especially their first roles, seem to be at greater risk for impostor syndrome.

25 STRATEGIES FOR PREVENTING, MANAGING, AND OVERCOMING IMPOSTOR SYNDROME

As we've seen, impostor syndrome is common among high-achieving individuals, healthcare professionals, and leaders — creating a perfect storm for high-achieving leaders in a healthcare organization. Fortunately, there are many things that healthcare administrators, leaders, and managers can do to prevent, manage, or overcome impostor syndrome in themselves and in their employees. Here are 25 strategies:

1. **Assess whether you have impostor syndrome.** Self-doubt does not necessarily mean that you have impostor syndrome. Pauline Rose Clance[33] offers a free online impostor phenomenon assessment test that consists of 20 multiple-choice questions and is self-scored. You, your employees, and your mentees can take it anytime to determine whether you have impostor phenomenon characteristics and if so, to what extent you are suffering from them. Clance's test is available at https://paulineroseclance.com/pdf/IPTestandscoring.pdf.

2. **Understand the syndrome.** Keep in mind that actual frauds don't have impostor syndrome. Benisek says, "The very fact that you have impostor syndrome shows that you're not an impostor."

3. **Stop dismissing your feelings.** Don't try to ignore, disregard, or dismiss your feelings of impostorism. Cuncic says, "Instead, try to lean into them and accept them." It's only when you acknowledge these feelings that you can start to unravel the core beliefs that are holding you back, Cuncic says.

4. **Don't expect too much from yourself.** First-time leaders and those who are new to their positions are especially prone to impostor syndrome. Vivian Manning-Schaffel[34] says, "Give yourself the grace of building up the confidence you need in the role and allow yourself to sit back and learn from those around you."

5. **Separate feelings from facts.** Be on guard against impostoristic feelings, identify them, and be ready with a response. Cleveland Clinic recommends, "If your mind says, 'I don't know what I'm talking about,' remind yourself that you know more than you think you do and are capable of learning." Whenever you feel like an impostor, grab a pen and paper, draw a line down the middle, and jot down your feelings on one side and facts on the other. Benisek says, "Realize that they [your feelings] are just emotions. Remind yourself that you are capable of success." Ibbotson, who uses a similar pen-and-paper exercise with his coaching clients, says that it can help you get out of the "emotional tsunami" that is your fear.

6. **Distinguish inexperience from inability.** Duszynski-Goodman says, "An important step to dismantling impostor syndrome is to first

distinguish feeling inexperienced from feeling like you are undeserving." Just because you are doing something for the first time does not mean that you don't belong there or that you are incapable of learning, Duszynski-Goodman says.

7. **Welcome more questions.** Leaders must put down their defenses and learn how to become comfortable answering questions with "I don't know." Friedman says, "Leaders must create a culture of learning, where asking questions is the norm, where a gap in knowledge invites collaboration and sharing — rather than withdrawal and shame." How can leaders do this? "Conclude meetings with a mandatory round of questions from all attendees," Friedman says. Also, thank employees who are willing to ask you the most pressing and challenging questions. Mattone says, "Turn questions into tools that help you solve issues."

8. **Say your name aloud.** Jessica Bennett[35] suggests that the simple act of adding our name to a positive affirmation (for example, "Jessica is awesome") and speaking it aloud can help us to manage our impostoristic feelings. "And before you get bashful, Bennett says, "LeBron James does it." According to Bennett, James said "'I wanted to do what was best for LeBron James'" when he explained his decision to leave the Cleveland Cavaliers for the Miami Heat in 2010. Bennett also says that the Nobel laureate Malala Yousafzai used the strategy when she wrestled with her decision to speak out against the Taliban. According to Bennett, Yousafzai asked herself, "If he comes, what would you do, Malala?" Then, she replied to herself, "Malala, just take a shoe and hit him." Bennett suggests that if the strategy of saying our own name aloud is good enough for a top athlete and a Nobel Peace Prize winner, "I'm pretty sure it's good enough for the rest of us."

9. **Stop comparing.** Comparing yourself with others is an unnecessary distraction that will keep you from embracing your own capabilities. Instead, focus on measuring your own achievements. Cleveland Clinic says, "Turn impostor syndrome on its head: Remember that smart, high-achieving people most often deal with impostor syndrome." Ironically, the people you compare yourself with and admire may be experiencing impostor syndrome too.

10. **Note your strengths and accomplishments.** It's likely that your classmates, peers, colleagues, managers, and employees, and even strangers have pointed out your skills. Mint says, "Revisit all these compliments when you may be feeling discouraged." Keep tangible reminders of

your success in a place where you can see them when doubts start to creep in. Cleveland Clinic suggests, "When your manager sends you an email recognizing your excellent work on a project, save that email in a special folder." Hang your diplomas and awards and display cards of appreciation that you receive, too.

11. **Embrace and model authenticity.** Leaders who seek to break the cycle of "faking it" in their organizations must prioritize authenticity. That means that they must create a culture where vulnerability is not viewed as weakness but as a strength. Leaders can set the tone by openly discussing their own challenges and doubts, and by fostering a safe space for others to do the same. Belton says, "In this environment, impostor syndrome loses its power, as individuals realize that they are not alone in their struggles." Leaders who embrace their authentic selves, acknowledge their limitations, and openly share their journeys empower others to do the same. This authentic form of leadership fosters trust, encourages open communication, and paves the way for more inclusive decision-making processes, Belton says.

12. **Get out of your head.** Amal Saymeh[36] suggests that rumination, a pattern of circling thoughts, goes hand in hand with impostor syndrome. Saymeh suggests that impostoristic feelings will become less powerful when "they aren't circling." Do whatever you need to do to stop unproductive rumination. For example, write down your thoughts, go for a walk, engage in an engrossing activity, or practice mindfulness.

13. **Define what success looks like.** Impostor syndrome means that success is important to you. While doubting your abilities can be harmful, self-awareness is positive. Vistage says, "Use self-awareness to your advantage by asking yourself what, exactly, success looks like. Are there benchmarks for success? How can you ensure that each day, week, month, and quarter are successes? What should success feel like? How will you celebrate success with your team?" Most importantly, how can you achieve the success you've defined authentically, without having to fake your way to it?

14. **Escape the "I must know everything" trap.** Leaders with impostor syndrome often feel that people around them expect them to know more than they do. However, Mattone says, "Admitting that you don't know everything can be liberating and empowering." Stop trying to act like an omniscient higher entity. Mattone says, "Being vulnerable and susceptible to making mistakes is profoundly human. Intelligent

leadership is not about avoiding failure. It's about dealing with it constructively and moving towards success."

15. **Assess the evidence.** Our self-doubts may not be grounded in reality. To find out, Saymeh suggests that you make a simple two-column list. On one side, list "Evidence that I am inadequate" and on the other side, list "Evidence that I am competent." Saymeh says, "This list enables you to combat impostor syndrome by collecting, acknowledging, and reflecting on proof of your competency."

16. **Stop the negative self-talk.** Shift your negative thoughts when you start telling yourself that you are a fraud. Manning-Schaffel suggests, "We have to interrupt the cycle and replace those maladaptive thoughts with adaptive thoughts and positive messages that make sense for us." For example, you can tell yourself, "I am confident. I'm doing the best I can. I deserve to be here," Manning-Schaffel says.

17. **Give yourself permission to fail.** Accept failure as a natural part of the growth process. Learn from failures what doesn't work and focus more on what does. Mint says, "Pick yourself up and work harder to reach your career and financial goals."

18. **Use social media cautiously.** Overuse and misuse of social media may be related to feelings of inferiority. Cuncic warns, "If you try to portray an image on social media that doesn't match who you really are or that is impossible to achieve, it will only make your feelings of being a fraud worse."

19. **Note when you're *not* feeling like a fake.** There will be times when you feel that you do know what you're doing and that you are being authentic in your role. Take note of these moments. Manning-Schaffel says, "Own the expertise you've picked up and lead with it on future goals and projects."

20. **Embrace resilience.** A resilient mindset can help you overcome impostoristic feelings. Von Born says, "Resilience is adapting and recovering from setbacks while remaining optimistic instead of letting inexperience or mistakes overwhelm you. It keeps you focused on your goals and potential instead of adversity." Von Born adds that you will strengthen your resilience by prioritizing your self-care, getting enough rest, exercising, and enjoying activities that bring you fulfillment.

21. **Say *yes* to new opportunities.** Leaders with impostor syndrome may avoid new challenges for fear of being found out to be a fraud. Watt

says, "Don't let fear of failure stop you from trying something new. In permitting yourself to fail, you may find new skills."

22. **Don't fake it, wing it.** Reframe the way you describe moments when you must do something when your confidence is not fully there. Ibbotson says, "There's only so much preparation that you can do for anything. Winging it is a skill set that refers to the ability to assess your situation and judge it accurately." Winging it also is about being open to *learning how* instead of *pretending to be.* Ibbotson says, "It's about how creatively, on the fly, you're able to pull your resources together to find a solution to something or improvise." Reframing faking as winging it will help you develop the confidence you need to trust all you've learned over the years, step into the unknown, and believe that everything will work out. Unlike pretending to be what you're not, winging it is a truthful and healthy way to frame the way you face your challenges.

23. **Adopt a growth mindset.** A growth mindset offsets self-doubt because it focuses on what you can learn to be an effective leader instead of what you don't know. Von Born says, "It acknowledges that abilities and intelligence can be developed over time with focus and dedication." When you believe that you can grow, each day is a chance to work hard, gain new knowledge, and make your mark. Vistage says, "If you felt like an impostor yesterday, that leaves today, tomorrow and the rest of time to prove that you belong" because of your curiosity, drive, and work ethic. "People who adopt a growth mindset see obstacles — like the feeling of being an impostor — as temporary, as things that can be overcome," Vistage says.

24. **Change your culture.** Moskal suggests that healthcare organizations can mitigate impostor syndrome by fostering a culture that allows physicians to express vulnerability and to share personal stories in small group discussions. Particularly, Moskal says, experienced physicians, who often appear to have it all together, can describe their own "failure resumes" for junior colleagues to demonstrate that their role models also have difficulties. Moskal adds, "De-stigmatizing and normalizing help-seeking could also contribute to more professional fulfillment."

25. **Talk to someone.** Our irrational beliefs tend to fester when we keep them to ourselves. Therefore, talk to trusted friends or family members who can help normalize your feelings and remind you that your fears aren't based in reality. Speak to your mentor or a trusted colleague. Or, Benisek suggests, "See a therapist, who can help you develop tactics to

overcome impostor syndrome." A therapist can help you to validate the feelings, fears, and isolation that come with feeling like an impostor. They also can challenge your negative cognitions of self and help you replace them with positive, affirming statements. Therapy may be especially helpful if your impostor syndrome is causing you anxiety and/or you have long-held beliefs about your incompetence in social and performance situations.

─────── CHAPTER 14 BONUS FEATURE ───────

12 FAMOUS PEOPLE WHO HAVE EXPERIENCED IMPOSTOR SYNDROME

Healthcare leaders and employees who experience impostor syndrome are in excellent company. Self-doubt and the feeling of inadequacy affect many high-achieving individuals who don't believe that they deserve the praise, recognition, and opportunities they've been given. Many also believe that they are fooling everyone and fear that they will be found out as frauds. Here are 12 famous examples:

"I have written 11 books, but each time I think, 'Uh oh, they're going to find out now. I've run a game on everybody, and they're going to find me out.'"[36]

Maya Angelou, memoirist, poet, civil rights activist
Recipient of the National Medal of Arts
and the Presidential Medal of Freedom

"I still have impostor syndrome...It doesn't go away, that feeling that you shouldn't take me that seriously. What do I know?"[37]

Michelle Obama, attorney, author
First lady of the United States from 2009–2016

"No matter what we've done, there comes a point where you think, 'How did I get here? When are they going to discover that I am, in fact, a fraud and take everything away from me?'"[38]

Tom Hanks, actor, filmmaker, Hollywood legend
Two-time Academy Award winner
Recipient of the Presidential Medal of Freedom

"Who doesn't suffer from impostor syndrome? Even when I sold my business for $66 million, I felt like an absolute fraud."[39]

Barbara Corcoran, founder of The Corcoran Group
Syndicated columnist, television personality, investor

"The beauty of the impostor syndrome is you vacillate between extreme egomania and a complete feeling of: 'I'm a fraud! Oh God, they're on to me! I'm a fraud!'"[40]

Tina Fey, comedian, actress, author
Primetime Emmy Award winner
Youngest-ever recipient of the Mark Twain Prize for American Humor

"I am not a writer. I've been fooling myself and other people."[41]

John Steinbeck, novelist
Author of *The Grapes of Wrath*
Winner of the 1962 Nobel Prize in Literature

"Very few people, whether you've been in that job before or not, get into the seat and believe today that they are now qualified to be the CEO. They're not going to tell you that, but it's true."[42]

Howard Schutz, businessman, author
Former Chairman and CEO of Starbucks

"I'm always looking over my shoulder, wondering if I measure up."[43]

Sonia Sotomayor, attorney, jurist
Associate Justice of the Supreme Court of the United States

"You think, 'Why would anyone want to see me again in a movie? And I don't know how to act anyway, so why am I doing this?'"[44]

Meryl Streep, actress
Three-time Academy Award winner
Often described as the best actress of her generation

"At any time, I still expect that the no-talent police will come and arrest me."[45]

Mike Myers, comedy legend
Actor, screenwriter, producer, director
Winner of seven MTV awards and a Primetime Emmy Award

"The exaggerated esteem in which my lifework is held makes me very ill at ease. I feel compelled to think of myself as an involuntary swindler."[46]

Albert Einstein, theoretical physicist
Winner of the 1921 Nobel Prize in Physics
One of the greatest and most influential scientists of all time

"Sometimes I wake up in the morning before going off to a shoot, and I think, 'I can't do this. I'm a fraud.'"[47]

Kate Winslet, actress
Winner of an Academy Award, Grammy Award
and a Primetime Emmy Award

Discovering Your Leadership Superpowers and Origin Story

Every superhero has an origin story. For example, Superman came from the planet Krypton, where gravity is much higher than on earth, allowing him to fly here. Spider-Man was bitten by a radioactive spider, giving him heightened senses and the ability to walk on walls and swing from building to building on wrist-mounted web shooters. And Batman witnessed his parents being killed in a mugging, which turned him into a vigilante with fantastic determination, fighting skills, intellect, and wealth.

Healthcare administrators, leaders, and managers have superpowers and origin stories too. Like all superheroes, their defining moments helped them to develop their superpowers and become who they are. Your origin story, for example, could be that you overcame great adversity, learned from a mentor, identified an acute need, witnessed something that went terribly wrong, or coped with tragedy. And whether you recognize your origin story or not, you do have one and it has foregrounded your leadership.

J. Bryan Bennett[1] shares the inspiring leadership origin story of Chris Van Gorder, president and CEO of Scripps Health, whose story began many years ago when he was working as the security guard at a hospital. One day, Van Gorder saw the hospital's CEO walking toward him, so he stood and got ready to say "hello" and shake the man's hand. However, the CEO walked past Van Gorder as though he wasn't there. As Bennett tells the story, "Van Gorder decided that if he ever rose to a leadership position that he would treat his people differently, and he has lived up to that pledge." Van Gorder's superpower, or at least one of them, is that he treats every employee at Scripps Health with the care, courtesy, and respect they deserve.

Like Van Gorder, discovering your superpowers and sharing your leadership origin story will help you to clarify and promote your leadership identity, values, and purpose. As you'll see, a good origin story also can humanize you and help your employees to become more receptive to you.

WHAT MAKES A COMPELLING LEADERSHIP ORIGIN STORY?

People of every culture love origin stories because we crave narratives and are naturally curious. We have shared stories in caves, huddled around campfires, across the dinner table, or in the late hours when the party has wound down. Mihirini De Zoysa[2] says, "Origin stories hold us enthralled because as human beings, we are storied beings. We are drawn to mysteries and meaning-making…and underdogs who rose above their circumstances and challenges and changed the world." Compelling origin stories can inspire us to imagine that we, too, can make a difference. Add to that that the people you lead every day want to be able to relate to you, and it becomes easy to see why your well-crafted leadership origin story will appeal to them.

Before turning your attention to crafting your leadership origin story, Shannon Emmerson[3] suggests once again that you take a lesson from superheroes. She says, "Most of us come from humble beginnings, and we love it when successful people…reveal theirs, too. It makes us feel a little bit better that Superman was raised by two normal parents on a farm, and that Clark Kent is treated like a bit of a geek." Like Superman before he was Superman, we know what it's like to have felt that there's something more in store for us in life, even if we were not yet sure what that was. Perhaps that's why we grin when we see a photo of Jeff Bezos sitting at his desk years ago in his modest start-up office beneath a hand-written paper banner that says amazon.com, or that we get a kick out of imagining Steve Wozniak and Steve Jobs starting their business in a garage. We love stories of humble beginnings and how others overcame and grew from them.

Don't despair if your beginnings were not quite so humble or if the adversity you overcame wasn't equivalent to a superhero's. You can make your leadership origin story as compelling as that of a superhero if you consider what makes *any* origin story compelling. Typically, Emmerson says, compelling origin stories reveal some or all of the following four things about the leader:

- **Obstacles.** No doubt, you have had to overcome or currently are facing obstacles in your life. De Zoysa says, "Maybe you experienced an unexpected life interruption, trauma, or crisis that changed the course of your life or your perspective on life." Most of the time, people will want to hear about such obstacles, perhaps not in excruciating technical detail, but told simply and in a way that stimulates their empathy and tugs on their heartstrings.

- **Humanity.** Superheroes respond to their new superpowers as any human would. For example, they demonstrate frailty, crushed egos, error, awe, or clumsiness, especially when they are trying to get the hang of things. Like superheroes, you had to cut your teeth somewhere, and you probably made some bad choices and mistakes. Sharing these challenges in your leadership origin story can make you seem human and relatable.

- **Heroism.** Maybe you were just happily going about your life and something completely out of the blue came along and pulled you into an adventure or exploration. Perhaps that led you down a path you would have never taken, but that eventually transformed you into who you are today. De Zoysa suggests that this usually is seen as the hero's journey, described by mythologist Joseph Campbell, and popularized by many novels and Hollywood films. If you have a heroic story to tell, keep in mind that superheroes' origin stories demonstrate why they are heroes, and it is *not* always because of their superpowers. Their character, altruism, and pureness of heart make them worthy of their powers and our admiration. These are the same characteristics that made *you* worthy of your leadership. Robin Rosenberg[4] observes that superhero origin stories tend to show us *not* how to become super, but, through challenges, "how to be heroes." For example, superheroes often choose to do right and good over stroking their egos, impressing others, or acquiring wealth, fame, admiration, or power. Those choices have nothing to do with their ability to leap tall buildings or read minds, Rosenberg suggests, but with their best human qualities. You can weave your best human qualities into your leadership origin story, too. When you do, you'll want to emphasize your basic goodness and humanity in your story, rather than your superpowers such as your extraordinary analytical knowledge, skills, technical abilities, or fluency in several languages.

- **Balance.** We especially like superheroes who are multidimensional, like us, and who balance the different sides of their personalities. For example, origin stories cue us to take superheroes seriously, yet superheroes aren't serious all the time. We are delighted when they are a bit light, funny, or playful when the time and circumstances allow for that. For example, we enjoy it when Superman or Clark Kent says something to Lois Lane to suggest that he knows about his secret identity, but she doesn't. Similarly, there's room in your origin story for you to reveal yourself as the multidimensional, well-balanced person you are, one who is both serious and light. Likewise, you can show balance in your origin story if you can include moments in your life when your plans changed. For example, maybe you carefully planned your career path but accidentally bumped into someone at a café, leading eventually to your deciding to go back to school and embark on a new path. If so, telling that story can suggest to listeners that you found a way to balance your planning and hard work with your openness to the chances and opportunities you encountered.

At their best, superhero origin stories provide us with models for coping with adversity, finding meaning in loss and trauma, and making good use of our strengths. Sometimes, they show us how we can work collaboratively with one another, as superheroes do when they team up to become the Avengers or the Justice League. Emmerson asks, "Isn't that what you want to do as a leader?"

WHERE TO DIG FOR ORIGIN STORY GOLD: 10 QUESTIONS

Your path to becoming a leader was filled with many moments, too many to recount in a brief origin story. Therefore, you will need to be selective. De Zoysa suggests that the following 10 questions can help you dig deeper into how you became who you are today and find your origin story gold:

1. What happened that had a significant, lasting effect on you? For example, did you lose your job, or did you come upon a very positive or negative role model?
2. Did anyone teach you something that changed your life? How did that lesson influence your leadership?
3. Did you experience an unexpected twist in your life trajectory? Consider both the big experiences and the "seemingly innocuous" ones, De Zoysa says.

4. Is there a story that you keep telling over and over? There must be a reason that the story matters to you enough to retell it. Lean into that reason.

5. Was there a moment when you took a leap of faith? Such moments may have empowered you to grow.

6. Was there a time when you didn't give up, but others had? De Zoysa suggests that stories that set you apart from the crowd can be very compelling.

7. What hurdles did you overcome to get where you are now? We love heroes who become who they are because of adversity.

8. Was there a time when you knew that all the risks you took were worth it? Compelling origin stories are about people who ultimately succeed. When was that for you?

9. What story can you tell that would make you consciously vulnerable? De Zoysa explains, "Being honest doesn't mean that you have to bare all your secrets or give excruciating or minute detail. It means choosing to be as open as you feel comfortable, right now." Keep in mind, though, that people may speculate on areas you don't reveal, or ask you questions you do not want to answer. De Zoysa says, "Rather than lie or cover-up, it is always best to preface your story with the boundaries you want to maintain."

10. When were you humbled? De Zoysa suggests that some of the best leaders are forged in their failures.

CHOOSE YOUR LEADERSHIP ORIGIN STORY THEME

When did you first feel like a leader? Researchers Alyson Meister, Wei Zheng, and Brianna Barker Caza[5] ask, "Would you start [your origin story] in childhood, or when you first took on that big position in your organization?" Was it when others started to follow you, or when you felt an obligation to your organization and the people you lead? Meister *et al.*, studied 92 leadership origin stories that converged around one of four dominant origin story themes. These themes, they say, determined both how the leaders told their origin stories and how they regarded their leadership today. Do you identify with one or more of these themes?

- *Being* **theme:** The leaders in the study who adopted this theme suggested that they have always thought of themselves as leaders. Meister *et al.*, explain, "They highlighted a natural call to leadership that started in childhood or early school years, perhaps organizing kids in the neighborhood, engaging in entrepreneurial activities, or becoming captains of sports teams." Leaders in the study who chose this theme often noted their personal qualities that have remained constant since childhood, such as their confidence, optimism, and inspirational leadership style.

- *Engaging* **theme:** Leaders who chose this theme highlighted their successful facilitation of others. They believed that their leadership originated when they were compelled to address an urgent need. For example, Meister *et al.*, cite the example of Jennifer in their study, who linked her leadership origin story to activities. Quoting Jennifer, they say, "It's not like I came out of the chute trying to be the natural-born leader…but I do like the idea of creating a vision, looking at what needs to get done, making something better than it is now." Leaders who viewed themselves through an engaging theme talked about how they changed unsatisfactory practices, started a new organization, brought disparate groups to a shared vision, tackled a challenge or crisis, or served as a liaison between conflicting groups. Meister *et al.*, say, "In the present day, these leaders gravitate toward a more facilitative leadership style, focusing on engaging others and enabling collective action."

- *Performing* **theme:** Do you feel a strong sense of duty to your healthcare organization and to your patients? Do you feel protective of the people you lead, and perhaps refer to them as "my people?" Meister *et al.*, suggest that leaders who adopted this theme often said that their leadership began when they felt a sense of duty and responsibility. They described themselves as having "paternalistic leadership styles," Meister *et al.*, say, citing examples of the ways they controlled, supported, and provided guidance for their team.

- *Accepting* **theme:** Leaders who described their leadership origin through an accepting theme didn't think of themselves as leaders until they realized that others were following them. They recalled suddenly noticing that people were coming to them for answers, guidance, and support. Meister *et al.*, say, "This group tended toward supporting or serving the needs of others above themselves, often with a low-key demeanor."

Meister *et al.*, concluded that there is a strong and reciprocal link between the stories leaders told about becoming leaders and their current leadership styles. They warn, "This means that rigidly using only one lens could limit your ability to experiment with different styles over time." For example, Meister *et al.*, say, if you see yourself only as a leader when and if others are following you (accepting theme), your identity may be highly tied to the perceptions of others. That could hold you back from volunteering for a new leadership role. Clinging only to one theme also may constrain who you seek as role models, and influence who you tap to take on new leadership roles. For example, if you "have always been a leader" (being theme), or if you believe that leaders are leaders only when others follow them (accepting theme), it may be difficult for you to support a new leader who has an engaging or performing theme.

Before crafting your leadership origin story, Meister *et al.*, suggest that you "experiment with different stories" that draw on different past experiences and memories of your leadership. Consider times when you stepped up during adversity to take needed action. Have others always considered you to be a leader? Did you find yourself assuming leadership roles in childhood? Meister *et al.*, suggest, "Practice constructing and telling your origin story through different lenses," and don't feel limited to one. The lenses or themes through which you tell your origin story can strengthen your identity and increase your adaptability.

Finally, Meister *et al.*, caution leaders to consider whether their gender has influenced the theme through which they regard their origin story and leadership. Women in their study more often said they felt like leaders when they were actively doing what they consider to be leadership activities (engaging theme). Men, on the other hand, more often believed they became leaders when they achieved a particular role and said that they felt like leaders when they were taking care of their teams and performing the duties and responsibilities assigned to that role (performing theme). These gender differences are subtle but can have significant implications for how women and men conceptualize their leadership and tell their origin stories. Meister *et al.*, suggest that leaders "try out new lenses" as they work on their origin stories and uncover potential blind spots that may limit their advancement.

HOW TO CRAFT YOUR ORIGIN STORY: 11 STRATEGIES

Now that you understand more about leadership origin stories, it's time for you to create the first draft of your own story. Here are 11 strategies:

1. **Put your audience first.** There's an implicit contract between storytellers and their audience that includes the promise that the audience's expectations, once aroused, will be fulfilled. Peter Guber[6] explains, "Listeners give the storyteller their time, with the understanding that he will spend it wisely for them. For most businesspeople, time is the scarcest resource; the storyteller who doesn't respect that will pay dearly." Guber calls fulfilling this promise "truth to the audience," and suggests that leaders commit to crafting origin stories that are worthy of their listeners' time. To meet the terms of this contract, and ideally overdeliver on it, great origin storytellers take time to understand what their listeners know about, care about, and want to hear. Guber says, "They then craft the essential elements of the story so that they elegantly resonate with those needs, starting where the listeners are and bringing them along on a satisfying emotional journey." Begin working on your origin story by learning as much about your listeners as you can.

2. **Position your story.** Reveal the context, place, and time within which your story takes place. For example, if your story happened in the 1970s when you were seven years old and you were going for your first plane ride, those details are important, because they set the context for the story. The same goes for any assumptions and biases you or others had at the time. De Zoysa says, "The listener can then listen to the story through the lens of the wide-eyed wonder of a child on a flight where smoking was not prohibited."

3. **Guide the audience's emotions.** Decide which emotions you want your origin story to provoke. For instance, Esther K. Choy[7] says, rags-to-riches origin stories prompt feelings of empathy, "overcoming the monster" origin stories provoke fear and anger, and quest stories instill "a sense of restlessness as the audience wishes for quests of their own." When you know the emotions that a certain plot is likely to inspire, you don't have to guess, "How will my audience feel after I share my origin story?" You can guide and predict their emotions with greater accuracy, Choy says.

4. **Share your feelings, not just the facts.** Ja'Bette Lozupone[8] urges you to let your audience see the truth of what was going on "by inviting them to experience your lows and highs." Don't minimize or try to put a positive spin on the extent of your emotions. Let your audience

see how the events you describe affected you emotionally, both in the moment and afterwards.

5. **Be honest.** Stick to the truth, and don't exaggerate or embellish. De Zoysa warns, "Really, don't make up facts," or they will come back to bite you.

6. **Include some magic.** The most engaging leadership origin stories have a little bit of magic in them. James Kerr[9] explains, "Magic keeps the audience interested. Most of the time, it's the hero's trusted advisor that gives them the magic needed." For example, when Kerr tells his own origin story, the magic comes in the form of his boss (a trusted advisor) who encouraged him to write an article describing his theory for solving a particular business problem he was facing. Kerr says, "I did, and it was published by a major periodical at the time. I didn't realize it immediately, but, I was about to learn firsthand about the power of the pen."

7. **Engage your audience's five senses.** Dane Stauffer[10] suggests that your audience wants to "hear the birds, smell the bread baking, feel the wind, be in the crowded subway," so provide them rich descriptions that will help them do that.

8. **Show rather than tell.** Your listeners want to draw their own conclusions. Therefore, don't tell them, "That's how I became a good leader," because that is just telling them the conclusion. Instead, De Zoysa says, "Share stories that demonstrate your actions and behaviors that reveal *how* you were a good leader," and let your listeners figure out the rest for themselves.

9. **Incorporate an element of surprise when possible.** Ideally, by the end of the story, your listeners will think, "We never expected that — but somehow, it makes perfect sense." Guber says, "A great story is never fully predictable through foresight — but it's projectable through hindsight."

10. **Exclude unnecessary details.** Part of what makes storytelling difficult is that the more we reflect on our stories, the more details we remember. Choy suggests that you streamline and stay close to your plot, which Choy says can "keep your story on a straight path instead of entangled in the weeds of extraneous details."

11. **End your story by emphasizing your transformation and the wisdom you gained.** Lozupone says, "Remember that you are still on your journey." Describe how you strive to apply that wisdom every day in your leadership.

HOW AND WHEN TO TELL YOUR LEADERSHIP ORIGIN STORY

It can be scary to share your origin story with others, especially at first. Disclosing our beginnings or the emotional, psychological, or even physical scars we carry can be the ultimate act of vulnerability. Lozupone explains, "No one wants to be judged for our choices, humiliated by embarrassing moments, or re-traumatized by our most painful experiences." When sharing your leadership origin story, have confidence in your audience and draw on what you know about them.

Sharing your leadership origin story can feel liberating because of the positive impact it can have. Lozupone says, "Your origin story just might be the message that inspires someone, changes someone's life, or delivers hope." Similarly, someone in your audience may think, "If they can do it, so can I." Consider how your origin story can help your listeners and how it can be useful to you, as it can be a powerful reminder of how far you've come and why you are the leader you are today. These additional tips will help to bolster your storytelling confidence and skill:

- **Rehearse your origin story until you feel comfortable and excited to tell it.** Rehearse alone at first, out loud. Try speaking into a mirror. Then try recording and listening to it. Do this until you know the story cold and feel ready to share it.
- **Try out your story on a few people.** Your first listener may be a trusted person close to you. However, Guber suggests also that you choose one or two people who "aren't already converts" to your leadership. That will give you a more realistic sense of how your real audience may respond.
- **Smooth over any rough spots.** As you rehearse, pay attention to any parts of your story that make you even a little uncomfortable. Are they boring? Unclear? Just not feeling right? Guber says, "Getting your story right…means working past a series of culs-de-sac and speed bumps to find the best path."
- **Tell your story like you are talking to a trusted friend, even when you are speaking to strangers.** Stauffer says, "Tell it like you talk." However, remember to stay on track. Stauffer warns, "Find a balance between clear details and over-explaining. Beware of 'ranting' about a subject — that can lead to losing a beginning, middle and end."
- **Seize key moments to share your leadership origin story.** We don't have to save our story only for dramatic, high-stakes occasions, Jim

Laughlin[11] says, "like the classic football half-time speech when the team is down by three touchdowns." Less dramatic opportunities to share your origin story occur all the time, and Laughlin suggests three of them: when taking on a new position, orienting a new direct report, and launching a new project. At these moments, Laughlin says, "Help people understand who you are and what motivates you" by sharing your leadership origin story with them. Some may have heard it once before, but that's OK. A well-crafted leadership origin story bears repeating. Just don't wear it out.

- **Be willing to drop the script and improvise when the situation calls for it.** Do not tell a memorized origin story word for word every time. That can sound contrived and mechanical. Guber says, "If you know your story well, you can riff on it without losing the thread or the focus."

———— **CHAPTER 15 BONUS FEATURE** ————

DISCOVERING YOUR LEADERSHIP SUPERPOWERS: 75+ POSSIBILITIES

Each of us brings unique gifts to our world — for example, our patience, enthusiasm, creativity, analytic ability, optimism, vision, and generosity. These are your superpowers, the attributes and traits that you've had for most of your life, or that you developed because of something that happened to you. Dede Henley[12] urges leaders to know their superpowers. She says, "The key is to know what they are…because once you have named them and claimed them, you can engage them at work more consciously. This is how you lead at a higher level with your team." Knowing your superpowers and where they came from also can help you develop your leadership origin story.

Leaders don't always recognize their superpowers, and many aren't aware of how they positively affect the people they lead. Some leaders are uncomfortable naming their superpowers because doing so may feel too much like boasting. However, you can't lead or craft your best leadership origin story without knowing your superpowers. Henley suggests that you ask five people who know you well to tell you what words describe you best. Henley says, "These people can be from your work or your home life — what matters most is that they know you well…because the people who know you best will know what your superpowers are."

The words people use to describe you may be adjectives, but they can easily be refashioned into superpower nouns. For example, if people tell you that you are curious, funny, and smart, your superpowers would be curiosity, humor, and intelligence. Henley suggests that you compile a complete list and then edit it down to the three to five words that you believe to be your top superpowers. Henley says, "Write them down and memorize them" because knowing and owning your superpowers is in itself, "an act of power."

The following list includes more than 75 possible leadership superpowers. You may see quite a few that you identify with, but which ones stand out to you the most? Do you know where those superpowers came from? If so, you may have just discovered your leadership origin story.

Accountability	Drive	Intelligence
Adaptability	Emotional intelligence	Inventiveness
Agility	Empathy	Judgment
Analytic ability	Empowerment	Kindness
Caring	Enthusiasm	Learning
Character	Fairness	Listening
Charisma	Flexibility	Logic
Clarity	Focus	Loyalty
Commitment	Generosity	Magnetism
Communication	Goal setting	Modesty
Community building	Gratitude	Observation
Confidence	Grit	Open-mindedness
Consistency	Honesty	Optimism
Courage	Hopefulness	Patience
Creativity	Humility	Passion
Curiosity	Humor	Perspective
Decisiveness	Inclusiveness	Persuasion
Delegating	Innovation	Positivity
Determination	Insight	Prioritizing
Diligence	Integrity	Problem solving

Relationship building	Sincerity	Tolerance
Resilience	Speaking	Transparency
Resourcefulness	Stamina	Trust
Respect	Strategy	Values
Responsibility	Strength	Vision
Self-awareness	Team building	Vulnerability
Self-discipline	Tenacity	Willpower
Service	Thoughtfulness	Writing

Healthcare Leadership in Times of Crisis

Being a healthcare administrator, leader, or manager in ordinary circumstances can be challenging. However, taking the helm at a time of crisis elevates the challenges of leadership to a whole new level. Henry Laker[1] says, "The coronavirus pandemic caused usual playbooks to be thrown away, with leaders around the globe having to think quickly on their feet." Many healthcare leaders felt as though COVID-19 had flung them headfirst into uncharted waters without the benefit of a nautical chart or life preserver. They had to make hard and fast decisions while swimming to the surface for air, all the while knowing that everyone they led, every patient they served — in fact, every person they knew — was in mortal danger.

Fortunately, a crisis of the magnitude of the coronavirus doesn't come knocking at our doors every day. Sreejith Balasubramanian and Cedwyn Fernandes[2] describe it as "a rare, long-haul health and economic crisis, which is global in nature, and no training or experience in previous crises could have prepared leaders for it." Although COVID-19 was one of the most difficult crises many healthcare leaders will ever face, it is likely that if you stay in the healthcare field long enough, you will lead your organization through another crisis or several crises. And, like COVID-19, you may have to do so with little or no warning. W. Timothy Cooms,[3] Gerald Lewis,[4] and Harvard Business Essentials[5] suggest that the crisis you may face someday can take many shapes and forms, including:

- Natural disasters
- Product recalls
- Environmental mishaps
- Accidents
- Protests against your organization

- Work-related deaths and injuries
- Disruptive and dangerous employees
- Security and data breaches
- Social media gaffes
- Product tampering
- Terrorist attacks
- Stock issues
- Corporate takeovers
- Ethical breaches
- Disruption of the supply chain and utilities access
- Corporate reorganizations
- Lawsuits
- Geopolitical turmoil
- Artificial intelligence issues

Waiting to see what happens and reacting to it is not a plan. Every health-care leader must plan for crisis leadership, even for crises we can't yet imagine. Zara Abrams[6] warns, "Disasters can make or break a leader," their organization, the people they lead, and the patients they serve. It is imperative that you prepare and train for leading your organization through whatever happens to it, even for events we can't foresee.

When the next crisis hits, you may not be able to wait to act until you have everything well in hand. The people you lead will be looking to you for strong leadership and reassurance, and you may find virtual and real microphones suddenly thrust at you for comment. Crises can be merciless to leaders who are unprepared for them. Some will say and do things they regret. Some may end up pouring oil onto the flames of an already raging crisis. Others may not make the decisions that were critically needed. One serious misstep in leadership during a crisis can have lasting, far-reaching, and regrettable consequences.

It can be extremely challenging to prepare for the unknown, but doing so should not be unfamiliar to you. The very practice of medicine often deals with the unknown, and people who work in healthcare are more prepared for medical crises than most people because of their study, training, and simulations. Likewise, leaders must prepare to deal with the unknown and shore up their leadership skills so they will be ready for the next crisis, whatever it may be. In the following sections we explore specifically what a crisis is and how to lead your organization through one.

WHAT IS A CRISIS?

While one could say that a crisis is in the eye of the beholder, a more specific definition is required. Steve Firestone[7] explains, "With a good understanding of the definition of a crisis, we can be better prepared to lead and respond when needed." Firestone defines *crisis* as "a situation that develops quickly and requires a response from a person or an organization in order to mitigate the consequences." That's a good beginning to a definition, but research suggests that there is more to it than that.

Three common denominators to the definitions of *crisis* can be found in scholarly literature. First, a crisis occurs quickly, even suddenly, or a problem reaches crisis level over time, sometimes without clear warning. Second, the event must imperil the organization's objectives and goals. And third, the event forces the organization to take steps to mitigate the possible consequences. Specifically, here are the ways that scholars and the U.S. military define *crisis:*

- **Perceived or actual threat.** Robert R. Ulmer, Timothy L. Sellnow, and Matthew W. Seeger[8] say that a crisis is "a specific, unexpected, and non-routine event or series of events that create high levels of uncertainty and threat or perceived threat to an organization's high priority goals." Notice Ulmer, *et al.'s,* emphasis on perceived versus actual threat. This definition suggests that leaders need to step into crisis mode while a threat is perceived as possible, not necessarily actualized. With such leadership, it may be possible to nip problems in the bud or at least reduce the impact of a crisis.
- **Sudden or evolving change.** Harvard Business Essentials[9] says, "A crisis is change — either sudden or evolving — that results in an urgent problem that must be addressed immediately. For a business, a crisis is anything with the potential to cause sudden and serious damage to its employees, reputation, or bottom line." Harvard Business Essentials emphasizes evolving change, suggesting that a crisis can evolve slowly but that its impact can be sudden. Leaders must become highly in tune with ongoing shifts and declines in their organizations that seem manageable in the present but that can skyrocket to crisis level through neglect and oversight.
- **Part of the human condition.** Ian I. Mitroff[10] suggests that crises "are more than an integral part of the human condition. They *are* the human

condition." This definition may sound grim. However, it is realistic and best to regard crises as an integral part of your job, not something you must handle on top of everything else you're tasked to do. If you embrace crisis leadership as your job, you won't feel resentful about what you must do when a crisis hits.

- **A 50-50 proposition.** Steven Fink[11] describes crisis as "an unstable time or state of affairs in which a decisive change is impending — either one with the distinct possibility of a highly undesirable outcome or one with the distinct possibility of a highly desirable and extremely positive outcome. It is usually a 50-50 proposition, but you can improve the odds." What stands out here is that Fink's emphasis is on improving the odds. Remembering that may help you to remain optimistic and to keep pushing the ball forward during a crisis, even if at first your efforts seem to be hopeless.

- **Crises leading to other crises.** The Joint Chiefs of Staff[12] define crisis as, "An incident or situation…that may occur with little or no warning. It is fast-breaking and requires accelerated decision making. Sometimes a single crisis may spawn another crisis elsewhere." Notice The Joint Chiefs' emphasis on the possibility of one crisis giving birth to another. That's sobering, but it's important for leaders to know this, yet not get bogged down because of fear of making bad decisions. Crises can multiply quickly and you don't want to set yourself up to play a game of crisis Whac-a-Mole.

Unfortunately, many — if not most — organizations have neither a defined concept of a crisis nor a list of what constitutes a crisis in their organization. Both would be helpful. Firestone explains, "By having a list of events describing what constitutes a crisis, the organization will be much quicker to recognize and respond and will be less likely to overreact when less severe events occur."

All of us probably have been in or heard of situations where an event occurred and only some people, or maybe only one person, viewed it as a crisis. Although a minority of the group may want to respond to the event as a crisis, it may not be able to do so if others don't grasp fully what the big deal is. This situation can be avoided when the organization develops a generally agreed-upon definition of a crisis. Therefore, your first act to prepare for a crisis will be to help your organization define the term, if it has not already done so, and to create a list of possible crisis events such as those listed in the bulleted points at the beginning of this chapter.

HOLD AND CONTAIN: THE PSYCHOLOGY OF CRISIS LEADERSHIP

When you think of crisis leadership, do you think of leaders who have strong vision? Or those who are especially inspiring? Or charismatic? Those leadership characteristics are dazzling so they get a lot of attention. However, the quieter, unsung hero during a crisis is the leader who is able to *hold* and *contain.*

The American Psychology Association[13] describes *holding* as the way another person, often an authority figure, interprets what's happening for us in times of uncertainty. *Containing* is the ability to help others make sense of a confusing predicament, and alleviate anxieties by acting as a container, or holding environment. Two psychoanalysts developed these theories in the early 1960s — Donald Winnicott[14] (holding), and Wilfred Bion[15] (containing). Their work focused largely on the mother–infant relationship, but it has useful application to leadership, especially during a crisis.

Gianpiero Petriglieri[16] explains, "When there's a fire in a factory, a sudden drop in revenues, a natural disaster, we don't need a call to action. We are already motivated to move, but we often flail. What we need is a type of holding, so that we can move purposefully." Think of a leader who, in a severe downturn, reassures employees that the organization has the resources to weather the storm and that most jobs will be protected, then helps them to interpret revenue data and gives clear directions about what must be done. That leader is *holding.* Petriglieri says that holding leaders "think clearly, offer reassurance, orient people, and help them stick together." Holding is as important as inspiring people, Petriglieri says. In fact, during a crisis, it is a precondition for inspiring others because people need to feel safe before they will feel inspired. Petriglieri explains, "When leaders cannot hold…anxiety, anger, and fragmentation ensue." Good holding, therefore, makes us feel more comfortable, reassured, courageous, and able to survive in a storm.

To hold during a crisis, Petriglieri suggests that leaders tell their employees what will happen to their salaries, health insurance, and working conditions. He suggests that you answer questions such as, "What will change about how they do their work? What are the key priorities now? Who needs to do what and in what order?" You may not be able to make predictions, but you can and should offer informed interpretations, Petriglieri says. You also can acknowledge and dispel rumors and encourage and protect everyone's participation as you work through the crisis. Holding, Petriglieri suggests, is what will make your employees feel secure. Without it, their anxiety, rumors, and speculation are likely to escalate, and some of your employees may shut down, panic, or jump ship.

To *contain* during a crisis, Marianna Sidiropoulou[17] says, leaders must create meaning out of chaos to "digest raw input/information and give it back in an intelligible form." Imagine a big, sturdy pot with lots of different ingredients going into it, Sidiropoulou says. *Containing* is the ability to hold the ingredients together without spilling them, and then, to let them cook into something different, "allowing the chemistry to happen." Specifically, Sidiropoulou says that you can contain during a crisis if you understand the root of the presenting problem, allow yourself to experience and not deny your own emotions, remain receptive and human, keep your center intact, prepare for change, and get the support you need. Fortunately, containing is what a good leader does unwittingly every day, Sidiropoulou says, adding, "It can range from a 'not losing it' attitude when faced with adversity to dealing with crises, office politics, and people problems to finding oneself in a 'sandwich crash' position between top and bottom misaligned strategy."

CRISIS LEADERSHIP VERSUS CRISIS MANAGEMENT

Crisis leadership and crisis management are both important during challenging times, but they are not the same thing. Indeed Editorial Team[18] explains, "The main distinction between crisis leadership and crisis management is that the former focuses on the organization's long-term strategy." Crisis management does not.

Crisis leadership in healthcare ensures positive public perception and trust during a crisis by preserving the organization's values and prioritizing the needs of patients and employees. Crisis management on the other hand, is a more reactive approach that strives to maintain an organization's normal operations. For instance, a natural disaster may make it challenging for your healthcare organization to obtain needed supplies. Indeed Editorial Team suggests, "Crisis managers can ration the company's current inventory, ensuring it lasts until vendors are once again operational." Crisis management also may involve adjusting procedures to maintain your organization's efficiency and ensuring that your organization can pay its employees. Managerial procedures such as these offer stability during challenging times and help crisis leaders maintain high morale.

25 WAYS TO PREPARE FOR AND LEAD THROUGH A CRISIS

The combination of preparation and strategic leadership will be your best defense against any crisis that comes your way. Here are 25 strategies:

1. **Define *crisis* for your healthcare organization and prepare a list of possible crisis events.** This chapter can provide a good start. However, work collaboratively with other stakeholders to create a definition and crisis list that is specific to your healthcare organization.

2. **Resolve smaller concerns before they escalate to crisis level.** Firestone suggests that more and more of the crises we see today are caused by human error. Firestone says, "Typically, it is not just a simple error by one person that leads to a major crisis. Instead, it is typically a chain of errors or an overall systemic error involving humans that leads to most of the crises we see in organizations." Keep your eyes always open to spot potential for errors and to provide training and management to help employees prevent mistakes. Trust your gut. If something doesn't feel right, it probably isn't.

3. **Learn to recognize a crisis early.** Crises with a gradual progression can be challenging to recognize before they impact an organization. It's far too easy to rationalize or miss small warnings or to be lulled into a false sense of security when you are in the calm before a storm. Indeed Editorial Team explains, "Even if a crisis develops rapidly, leaders may not recognize the extent to which it affects normal operations until later. You can implement an effective leadership style by practicing early recognition." A good practice is to research world and local events that could possibly impact your organization and become aware of your patients' attitudes, Indeed Editorial Team suggests. Then, work with your crisis managers as soon as you notice a potential issue so you can work together to reduce its effects on your organization.

4. **Increase your ability to remain calm.** Your ability to stay calm in the face of danger will allow you to recognize opportunities more clearly and develop solutions you may not think of when you are feeling stressed or anxious. Laker suggests that training and practice are the best ways to increase your ability to keep calm in stressful situations. Hypotheticals and simulations are excellent. Laker suggests, "In your future training, make sure to put examples of crisis in context to prepare for future obstacles."

5. **Express bounded optimism.** The term "bounded optimism" refers to having a positive attitude while acknowledging the severity of a challenge. Indeed Editorial Team explains, "This approach allows leaders to comfort employees and customers while remaining sensitive to how the event affects their lives." For example, consider a statement that a crisis leader would issue in response to a severe flood that affects the community. It would be unwise to ignore or minimize the devastating effects of the flood. Therefore, your statement might express your organization's condolences for families who have lost loved ones and property, while proclaiming that you are confident about your organization's and community's ability to persevere, Indeed Editorial Team suggests.

6. **See opportunities everywhere.** During a crisis, leaders must see opportunities everywhere and make the most of them. Glenn Liopis[19] says, "They must be open-minded enough to search within conversations and adverse circumstances for possibilities that will help better serve those they lead — beyond the obvious." For example, Liopis says, a crisis will demand that you respect different points of view to broaden your observations and perspectives about the reality that is right in front of you. That way, Liopis says, "You can see the glass half full, not half empty."

7. **Establish primary and secondary priorities.** Most leaders make the safety of customers and employees their first priority during a crisis, ensuring that every decision they make protects human life. However, it's important to establish secondary priorities as well. Indeed Editorial Team explains, "Companies can have various [secondary] values, with some of the most common being innovation, exceptional customer service, and commitment to the environment." An organization can feel free to implement new measures to uphold its core values but only after it has ensured that it is safe to do so.

8. **Learn how to recognize and manage your internal experience first.** Leaders who are hurled into a crisis may not think much about themselves. However, they will need to manage their internal experiences before they can provide the most effective direction to their teams and communities. One way to do that is to manage where your attention goes. Abrams suggests that you learn to become aware of what's happening in your body during a crisis so you can recognize your feelings and understand your physical responses. A leader who is locked in fear will have limited ability to develop creative solutions, Abrams warns. Training and practice can help you recognize and manage your emotions.

9. **Develop trust.** Leaders must strengthen trust before, during, and after a crisis so they will be able to break down barriers and forge strong bonds. Liopis says, "Trust during crisis is earned when leaders are reliable and they act on their word…when they commit to the needs of others before their own…when leaders are wise enough to enable their emotional intelligence by being vulnerable, open and honest."

10. **Learn how to communicate well.** You will need to disseminate information to your employees during a crisis by every good means possible. The information you provide will be powerful, because it can reduce emotional distress caused by the unknown, diminish fear, provide tactical guidance, and demonstrate to your employees that their leaders are concerned, involved, knowledgeable, and on top of the situation. An essential element of crisis leadership is clear and trustworthy communication. Abrams says, "Best practices for crisis communication, established through years of psychological and organizational research, include transparency, honesty and empathy." Communicating well starts with understanding the questions your audience has, then talking to experts and reviewing data to answer them accurately. Leaders need to develop and test their messages before issuing them to ensure they don't confuse people or inadvertently heighten their anxiety. Abrams says, "Leadership scholars agree that even in dire circumstances, honesty is the best policy." Abrams also suggests that leaders who withhold information essentially "shoot themselves in [the] foot" by breeding mistrust and uncertainty.

11. **Become more flexible.** Crisis leaders need to be flexible so they can revise their response plans as the crisis unfolds. For instance, they may use new research to adapt new procedures or revise an existing

policy. Indeed Editorial Team says, "This adaptability also allows leaders to analyze the effectiveness of their current approach and make the necessary adjustments to prepare for future crises." The Center for Creative Leadership[20] suggests that leaders develop three kinds of flexibility so they are ready for a crisis: cognitive flexibility (the ability to use different thinking strategies and mental frameworks); emotional flexibility (the ability to vary one's approach to dealing with one's own emotions and those of others); and dispositional flexibility (the ability to remain optimistic, yet realistic). The Center for Creative Leadership suggests, "Don't get too attached to a single plan or strategy. Have Plan B (and C) at the ready."

12. **Identify credible information sources.** Do you know which outlets will be your most reliable and truthful information sources about the crisis? That is very important because you may encounter different and conflicting reports about what is happening and what may happen in the future. Indeed Editorial Team[21] says, "Conflicting information can confuse both you and your team, so try to avoid finding information from unreliable sources such as social media and news organizations that are not well-respected." Instead, consult qualified experts about what is happening during a crisis, Indeed Editorial Team says, adding, "This can help to ensure that you don't feed staff with information that is untrue and could cause them to panic further."

13. **Develop circular vision.** Liopis defines circular vision as a leader's ability "to see around, beneath and beyond what they seek." For example, Liopis suggests that leaders explore employee engagement analytics. Liopis asks, "Who are those that you can rely on now and in the future?" Circular vision is especially useful when operating in an environment of uncertainty. It also is useful when you need to reset a strategy and prepare your organization to rebound after a crisis, Liopis says.

14. **Respect your organization's heritage and traditions.** Leadership legacies are born and made during a crisis. Liopis explains, "We discover the leaders that are most respected based on how well they reacted and responded to all the chaos and uncertainty around them." Leaders have a responsibility to uphold the heritage and traditions of the organizations they serve, but during times of crisis, they must equally hold themselves accountable for building on those traditions to strengthen the organization's culture and the communities they serve.

Liopis says, "Crisis puts our culture to the test." For leaders, crises are culture defining moments that either strengthen the culture for future legacies or awaken leaders to realize the importance of establishing a culture. Either way, leaders must learn how to ensure that a legacy platform is in place for the future.

15. **Learn about appropriate communication channels and frequency.** The channels you use to communicate during a crisis become extremely important so people will have access to the information they need when they need it. The Center for Creative Leadership suggests choosing, "face-to-face first, whether in person or through virtual channels." Also, repeating and reinforcing key information daily via multiple delivery channels will help it to sink in and be retained. The Center for Creative Leadership warns that when information regarding what is happening is scarce or non-existent, people will revert to gossip and rumors to fill the void, or they will invent things. Invariably, they add, what people make up will be much worse than reality, no matter how bad reality is.

16. **Be present, visible, and accessible.** Your first thought when thrown into a crisis may be to hunker down in your office and man the battle station from there. However, leaders need to be accessible to their employees during this vulnerable time. The Center for Creative Leadership says, "Let employees know how best they can reach you with status updates and questions." Also, let them hear from you frequently and be sure that you are on the premises whenever possible. The Center for Creative Leadership suggests that whoever is in charge during a crisis is whoever is there. If that means leaving a vacation early to return to work, that's what a leader will have to do. Your organization can't be hamstrung because a key player was not there when a crisis struck, the Center for Creative Leadership says.

17. **Develop and stick to healthy habits**. Laker suggests that every leader needs to maintain healthy habits all the time, including during times of uncertainty. These habits include pacing yourself, staying active, taking time to recover (sleep, rest, proper nutrition), and embracing your routines. Make it your habit to take care of yourself mentally and physically, especially during a crisis, by adding structure to your day and time to unwind.

18. **Take a wider view**. The human brain is programmed to narrow its focus in the face of a threat because narrowing is an evolutionary

survival mechanism designed for self-protection. The trap is that your field of vision during a crisis can become restricted to the immediate foreground. Eric J. McNulty and Leonard Marcus[22] suggest that leaders "intentionally pull back, opening your mental aperture to take in the mid-ground and background." They call this approach "meta-leadership" and define it as "taking a broad, holistic view of both challenges and opportunities." Properly focused meta-leadership fosters well-directed management, McNulty and Marus say. Leading through a crisis requires taking the long view, not just managing the present. Leaders need to anticipate what comes next week, next month, and next year to prepare the organization for the changes ahead. McNulty and Marcus add, "They also need to delegate and trust their people, provide support and guidance based upon experience, and resist the temptation to take over."

19. **Lead by example**. Volunteer first, before asking others to sacrifice. Erin Barr[23] suggests, "If there are sacrifices to be made, and there will be, then the leaders should step up and make the greatest sacrifices themselves." Everyone will be watching to see what the leaders do during a crisis. Will they stay true to their values? Bow to external pressures? Be seduced by short-term rewards? Or will they make near-term sacrifices so they can fix the long-term situation? Be the leader who is the exemplary team player you ask your employees to be during a crisis.

20. **Decentralize your response**. Risk and ambiguity increase during a crisis because so much is uncertain and volatile. Leaders may want to control everything, but doing so risks adding layers of approval required for minor decisions. McNulty and Marcus warn that the organization can become much less responsive when more control measures are put in place, and that frustration will grow with each new constraint. They say, "The solution is to seek order rather than control." Order means that people know what is expected of them and what they can expect of others. Leaders must acknowledge that they can't control everything. Instead, McNulty and Marcus suggest, "Determine which decisions only you can make and delegate the rest. Establish clear guiding values and principles while foregoing the temptation to do everything yourself."

21. **Take responsibility**. Reality starts with the person in charge. Therefore, recognize and take responsibility for your role in creating or contributing

to the problem. Barr says, "In order to understand the real reasons for the crisis, everyone on the leadership team must be willing to tell the whole truth." This is especially so when that truth is hard to face.

22. **Don't get seduced into managing**. Managing a crisis can feel thrilling, but managing can become a problem if you are doing it simply to return to your operational comfort zone. McNulty and Marcus warn, "Your adrenaline spikes as decisions are made and actions are taken. You experience a feeling of adding tangible value." Be mindful, though, that what you are experiencing when you manage a crisis can be a lot like a sugar high that will be followed quickly by a blood sugar crash.

23. **Request feedback.** Employees may believe that you expect them to keep their heads down and their mouths shut during a crisis, but the opposite is true. A crisis is the perfect time for them to tell you what's going on. Jennifer Herrity[24] says, "Ask your team to give you feedback on how they feel during the crisis and what more you can do to help them feel supported. "Your questions may be logistical, such as "How can we as an organization improve the services we are providing?" Or, they can be emotional, such as, "What can we do to make it easier or better for you to work during this challenging time?" Herrity suggests, "While you may not be able to alleviate all concerns, checking on your team confirms that you genuinely care about them beyond just their performance as an employee."

24. **Create an organization that is built to last.** It takes a lot for a healthcare organization to survive and thrive in a crisis. Create an organization for the long-haul that is designed to weather storms, just as you would if you were building a home in a region prone to hurricanes. Make sure, Laker says, that you have a strong enough foundation to endure whatever changes, stress, and challenges come your way.

25. **Don't waste a good crisis.** People often resist major changes or try to get by with minor adaptations when things are going well. Barr suggests, "A crisis provides the leader with the platform to get things done that were required anyway and offers the sense of urgency to accelerate their implementation." Assess how your policies and systems operate after a crisis. It's a good time to evaluate technological solutions that can help you facilitate consistent, multi-channel communication. Herrity adds, "Explore training programs that teach your employees techniques for developing their resilience, so that they can prepare for and persevere through future challenges." Also, introduce regular

team-building exercises to improve, strengthen, or possibly rebuild workplace connections after a crisis.

--------- **CHAPTER 16 BONUS FEATURE** ---------

4 KEY BEHAVIORS THAT WILL HELP LEADERS LEAD THROUGH A CRISIS

Do you lead leaders in your healthcare organization? The leadership firm ghSMART studied more than 21,000 leadership assessments among C-suite executives and found that four key behaviors help leaders to lead through a crisis. Chris Nichols, Shoma Chaterjee Hayden, and Chris Tendler[25] report, "Leaders need to cultivate four behaviors in themselves and their teams." Nichols, *et al.*, suggest that you: (1) employ the following behaviors and action steps yourself; and (2) teach them to the leaders you lead.

Behavior	Reason	Action Steps
Decide with speed over precision.	A crisis may change rapidly. Leaders may deal with cognitive overload, incomplete information, clashing interests and priorities, and high emotions, yet have to make timely decisions.	Define priorities. Make smart tradeoffs. Name the decision makers. Embrace action. Don't punish mistakes.
Adapt boldly.	Strong leaders get ahead of changing circumstances. They seek input and information from diverse sources, are not afraid to admit what they don't know, and bring in outside expertise when needed.	Decide what not to do. Throw out yesterday's playbook. Build and strengthen connections.
Deliver reliably.	Effective leaders take personal ownership in a crisis, even though many challenges and factors lie outside their control. They align team focus, establish new metrics to monitor performance, and create a culture of accountability.	Use a daily dashboard of priorities. Establish metrics. Keep your team in fighting shape.

Engage your team for impact.	No job is more important than taking care of your team. Effective leaders understand their teams' circumstances and distractions but find ways to engage and motivate them. Reiterate new priorities often to ensure continued alignment.	Connect with your team members. Dig deep to engage your team. Ask for help as needed. Focus on employees. Focus on customers. Amplify positive messages.

Leaders of leaders navigate extra challenges when priorities change and there is limited time to react. Nichols, *et al.*, say that moments of crisis reveal a great deal about the leaders below you. They suggest, "Some small investments in support and coaching can go a long way toward boosting your leaders' effectiveness."

Once the crisis is under control or over, Nichols, *et al.*, suggest that you think about who rose to the occasion, who struggled, and why. They say, "Consider how roles will change in the post-crisis world and whether your key executives are positioned for success." They add, "Ask yourself whom you want at the table both in the current crisis and in the longed-for tomorrow when you emerge to a new normal."

Healthcare Leadership Succession Planning

Healthcare organizations need to have the right leaders in the right roles at the right times. Yet most leaders are not sufficiently proactive and disciplined about creating and implementing an effective succession plan. This gap between the recognized need for succession planning and what happens in practice is not unique to healthcare leaders, but is common among leaders in other industries, too. For example, Kris Routch, Kelly Monahan, and Meghan Doherty[1] share the troubling findings of Deloitte's leadership succession planning study across industries. They say, "While 86 percent of leaders believe leadership succession planning is an 'urgent' or 'important' priority, only 14 percent believe they do it well." The Deloitte study found that most organizations are thwarted or derailed from succession planning because they fail to recognize and address the impact of human behavior on the succession planning process. Routch, *et al.*, explain, "More often than not, we found that companies [and leaders] were either avoiding succession planning altogether or were taking a dispassionate, process-oriented approach that minimizes, or even ignores, the very real impact that it has on the people involved."

The most obvious benefit of succession planning is that it will provide your healthcare organization with a steady pipeline of qualified leaders ready to step into new roles as needed. But there's more to it than that. The following sections explore the many reasons that succession planning matters, and then, what you need to do to create and implement an effective leadership succession plan.

WHAT IS SUCCESSION PLANNING AND WHY DOES IT MATTER?

Succession planning is the process an organization uses to ensure that every critical position is occupied by an employee with the right skills and experience. It aims to ensure workforce continuity by identifying and preparing suitable candidates so that positions aren't left vacant.

Organizations often focus succession planning among members of the senior leadership team. However, Orgvue[2] urges, "Succession planning should take a broader 'root and branch' approach that promotes candidates through the ranks, rather than rely on recruitment." This is particularly important today because many of the most in-demand skills are in short supply and expensive to acquire, Orgvue says.

Succession planning will help to future-proof your healthcare organization by ensuring its continuity and performance, particularly during times of shifting leadership and change. The National Institutes of Health (NIH)[3] explains, "Even when there is no identifiable successor within an organization, succession planning can help identify the knowledge, skills, and training needed in a future external candidate." Succession planning also is a process that organizations use to safeguard against lengthy and costly talent recruitments. Alexander Gillis *et al.*,[4] explain, "The hole created when an employee leaves his or her position can be profound, even at lower levels." Replacing employees can be difficult and costly, especially in industries with noted talent shortages and skills gaps, and it can take a long time to get a replacement employee to full productivity. A lack of succession planning can cripple or sink smaller organizations that don't have qualified internal candidates from which to choose, Gillis, *et al.*, warn.

There are several reasons that leadership succession planning matters. It can provide your organization with many benefits beyond a steady stream of qualified leaders. For instance, it can:

- **Keep you ahead of the curve.** You will want to be proactive, not reactive, when you must replace a key member of your leadership team. The process often takes time. For example, Eben Harrell[5] suggests that effective planning "takes years, not months" for organizations that are planning for a new CEO. When is it time to start thinking about a succession plan for a CEO or other top leadership position? Ideally, Harrell says, organizations should start planning for the next CEO "the moment a new CEO takes charge."
- **Bolster your organization's reputation as a talent destination.** The best job applicants will be attracted to organizations known to promote from within. Therefore, Gillis, *et al.*, suggest, being known for your

succession planning may help you to recruit more and better talent for all-level positions. Additionally, the Indeed Editorial Team[6] suggests that becoming a talent destination can help you retain your top performers by giving them "a clear career pathway." That, in turn, can boost employee engagement and help them to feel more valued.

- **Support your diversity, equity, and inclusion initiatives.** Leaders can address diversity gaps in their organizations and promote an inclusive workplace culture by prioritizing internal talent development and advancement. They can integrate diversity into their succession planning to ensure equitable access to career growth and to strengthen future leadership with diverse voices. This is highly desirable. Orgvue explains, "Identifying and promoting high-potential individuals from diverse backgrounds helps break barriers and enhances decision-making through varied perspectives." Routch, *et al.*, add that a more diverse portfolio of leaders will be "a natural outcome of an objective, unbiased identification process."

- **Help you deliver uninterrupted excellence.** Orgvue suggests that effective succession planning will provide smoother business operations that will benefit everyone, including your patients.

- **Maintain mission-critical knowledge.** Having no identifiable succession plan for critical roles poses an enormous risk to the organization. Healthcare organizations cannot afford to lose critical information every time an employee leaves. NIH asks, "If your organization lost its most critical employees today, would you have a successor with the knowledge, training, and skills needed to fill their shoes?"

- **Preserve brand integrity and reputation.** Healthcare organizations can be particularly vulnerable when they have vacancies in publicly visible positions. Orgvue warns, "There are many examples of failed C-level succession plans that have caused substantial reputational damage to the organizations concerned." Organizations that place emphasis on internal succession to senior positions may be able to minimize these threats. Leaders who are promoted from within are more likely than external hires to understand "what's right for the business and its people," Orgvue says.

- **Future-proof your staff.** Organizations may find it particularly challenging to deal with a vacancy during a time of crisis. Routch, *et al.*, suggest that effective succession planning can create "a 'future-proofed' workforce" that is better prepared to thrive in dynamic and different conditions.

- **Reveal vulnerabilities and highlight skills gaps.** Succession planning provides a risk assessment that will uncover vulnerabilities and gaps in your workforce and skills base. Orgvue suggests, "By reviewing your current organizational structure by department, you can begin to see points of weakness that could impact your business strategy."

- **Protect your leadership legacy.** Effective leaders who vacate their roles will want to ensure that the good work they've done is carried on. That means that they will want to leave their positions in the hands of well-chosen successors. Justus O'Brien[7] warns, "If by the end of your tenure you've failed to deliver stellar successors, your many other achievements…will be diminished, and your legacy will be tarnished." Legacy-building succession planning requires leaders' personal engagement early in their tenure. O'Brien says, "It requires a robust process that leaves little to chance, one that is intentional, well-thought-out and affords opportunities to develop your successor, or even better, several successors." [See the bonus chapter, "Crafting Your Leadership Legacy: A Template," for more information on leadership legacy planning.]

WHY IS SUCCESSION PLANNING DIFFICULT?

We can point to several reasons to explain why leaders who know the value of succession planning don't do it well. Chief among these is that it takes time. Leadership succession planning is a long-term discipline in a short-term world. A good succession plan will require years to bear fruit, while leaders typically are rewarded for shorter-term accomplishments. It's also a big task that will be added to a very long to-do list. Madeline Miles[8] warns, "And because it's not perceived as urgent, it may keep being moved to the back burner."

In some organizations, it's not clear who is accountable for succession planning. For example, there may be no clarity around whether the responsibility of planning for and grooming a successor sits with HR or with business or functional leaders. According to Routch, *et al.*, "Many of our surveyed leaders had no idea who was ultimately accountable for succession planning in their organizations." Routch, *et al.*, share that a current chair of the board for a large nonprofit in Deloitte's study said, "Even boards are often unclear on how CEO and executive succession accountability should be set — is it one of the committees? The whole board? An individual? In many cases there is no clarity for it and no one addresses it."

Leadership succession planning also can be a highly charged and sensitive topic. It can be uncomfortable to discuss a leader's departure or another person's capabilities, or lack thereof, to step into the role. Boardspan[9] explains, "Succession planning brings up emotions and often requires uncomfortable conversations." Conflict-avoidant individuals may be reluctant to start the succession planning process. Furthermore, some leaders may be vague about when they are planning to vacate their positions and may not want to talk about it. Miles suggests, "For some, succession planning may be seen as a lack of confidence in your current leadership team. And executives may hesitate to raise the issue of succession planning for fear of being perceived as having intentions of resigning." This destabilizing dynamic can have a negative effect on your succession planning efforts.

Another challenge to leadership succession planning is that good data are not always available, or are ignored, leading to subjective decisions. Many organizations still default to subjective or political succession decisions based on likeability and similar factors. Routch, *et al.*, report, "We heard many examples of organizations investing in obtaining solid data (for example, through an executive assessment), only to have it thrown out and replaced by pure opinion." As one executive from a large healthcare company in the Deloitte study lamented, "Even with a lot of data, subjectivity and politics come into play."

Leadership succession planning is further challenged because many organizations lack a methodology or the know-how needed to do it. Routch, *et al.*, found this to be the case among their research participants. One of their leaders reported, "Boards and senior executives don't know how to succession plan. If you ask them about financial oversight or executive compensation, they're clear on how it works. But ask them about succession planning, and you get blank stares."

Finally, leadership succession planning is about change, which many people will resist or reject in its own right. Human beings typically prefer to feel comfortable. Change that is thrust upon us often is unwelcome because people prefer to stick with the status quo if that status quo is one they like. Miles says, "There will be people who oppose any new initiative [such as succession planning] simply because it's new."

EFFECTIVE SUCCESSION PLANNING: 25 STRATEGIES

There is no way for any of us to know with certainty what the future holds. Yet, succession planning requires us to prepare for it. Here are 25 leadership succession planning strategies to help you prepare your organization for growth, challenges, and leadership vacancies, even if you don't know precisely what your future needs will be:

1. **Establish accountability.** Many organizations are unclear about who is accountable for succession planning. Who is responsible for identifying and developing top talent right now in your healthcare organization — your CEO, CHRO, direct managers, or board of directors? Find out if you don't know. Someone must be accountable for succession planning and have the time and resources they will need to do it well, or it may wither and die on the vine. If there is no one accountable, make that your first priority.

2. **Focus on preparing your organization for the future.** That may seem obvious. However, Routch, *et al.*, warn, "Ironically, many organizations build their succession processes around the needs of current roles, not what those roles will look like in the future." What is projected for your organization's future? What talent will you need? What is projected for your community? Do you anticipate that your demographics will shift? How? What is likely to happen to your infrastructure in the next 20 years? Effective succession planning focuses on these concerns. A future orientation is needed and makes succession planning discussions seem less threatening and more palatable for incumbent leaders who may fear for their self-preservation.

3. **Foster diversity, equity, inclusion, and belonging.** Remain open about whom you consider for moving up as you project your organization's future needs. Actively train your succession planning team to be more inclusive and help them uncover unconscious biases. Miles suggests, "A fresh viewpoint can sometimes be as valuable as an experienced one."

4. **Make succession planning worthwhile for incumbent leaders.** Asking them to engage fully in succession planning without an emphasis on their own interests is likely to result in apathy and avoidance. Organizations can make their incumbent leaders' participation financially worthwhile so that they will focus on succession. Routch,

et al., report, "Many leading organizations craft short- and long-term incentives that reward leaders for creating environments that develop successors, not just identify them."

5. **Prioritize your talent needs.** Outline your organization's objectives so you can best determine which jobs to train for. Identify positions that will be most in need of successors. The NIH suggests, "Two factors to consider when prioritizing the positions are vulnerability and criticality." Which positions have no identifiable successor? They are the ones most vulnerable to knowledge loss, the NIH says. A position is deemed critical if a vacancy would hinder your organization's ability to accomplish its mission. The NIH adds, "Critical positions often extend beyond senior leadership roles."

6. **Analyze each position.** It will be difficult to identify successors if you don't have a solid grip on what the position is. Consider what each position is now and what it can look like in the future. Atlassian[10] says, "While you might think you already understand what employees are up to each day, you'll probably be surprised by how many tasks and responsibilities are flying under the radar." Ask the person who holds the position what they do if you don't know. Head off their concerns that their jobs may be in jeopardy. Atlassian suggests, "Make it clear that succession planning isn't focused on replacing them right now." Explain that you are asking questions about the position as a reference guide that will be a huge help as you plan for your team to grow.

7. **Prepare for different types of departures.** A retirement announced three years before the date a person leaves differs significantly from a sudden vacancy after a firing or unexpected illness. Elizabeth Rubenstahl[11] urges leaders to consider the risk of turnover for each position and to develop a succession plan that accounts for both planned and emergency departures. Rubenstahl suggests, "To mitigate this risk, understand what skills team members who work closely with the specific role already have and what complementing talents are needed or desired in a successor."

8. **Break succession planning into a series of shorter-term steps.** Large tasks become less daunting and more manageable when you work in steps. Routch, *et al.*, describe a leader in the Deloitte study who explained, "We've broken [succession] into smaller pieces to create more focus and depth. We have nine executive talent review sessions per year — so we're doing this often and proactively." Leaders who

regard succession planning as part of their day-to-day tasks are likely to be more engaged in the shorter term while proactively pursuing long-term success.

9. **Assess potential.** Don't automatically earmark employees for training and promotion because they are the ones closest in rank for the roles that need to be filled. Gillis, *et al.*, say, "Other promising employees should be chosen if their skills have the most potential."

10. **Focus on the requirements of the position.** It's tempting to promote employees who have worked hard and been loyal. However, they must have the knowledge, skills, and abilities to fill the role. Don't fit the job to the person. Avoid succession plans where candidates are predetermined before a competitive process. The NIH says, "'Pre-selecting' and 'pre-determining' should be avoided." The NIH adds, "It is important to remind candidates that the position is not guaranteed to any one candidate because it depends on performance, and an employee may be removed from consideration should their performance fall below expectations."

11. **Guard your organization's reputation.** The stakes are especially high when you are succession planning for publicly visible positions. If your succession plan is to recruit a senior executive from the outside, take steps to ensure that the new appointee understands the values that bind your organization together, your culture, and the brand you have created. A new leader's rash attempts to impose change and make a mark could undermine your healthcare organization's mission and neglect the needs and expectations of your patients and employees. Orgvue suggests, "By placing the emphasis on internal succession to senior positions, these threats have less chance of materializing, as senior leaders are more likely to understand what's right for the business and its people."

12. **Be transparent.** Distrust can ensue when succession planning is held too close to the vest. Organizations will be most successful when they use simple, accessible, and transparent data collection processes for succession planning and clearly communicate their succession decisions using this data. Let your employees know what is going on so they don't fill in the gaps with speculation, rumors, and gossip.

13. **Conduct trial runs when possible.** A trial run occurs when potential successors assume some of the responsibilities of new roles while continuing to work in their current roles. That will give you an opportunity

to gauge whether the person is ready and if they are going to be a good fit. Also, Gillis, *et al.*, say, "This practice will allow the successor to gain potentially valuable experience." Robert Half[12] adds, "Don't wait until a crisis to test whether an employee has the right stuff to assume a more advanced role. The employee will…appreciate the opportunity to shine. And you can assess whether that person might need some additional training and development."

14. **Keep it simple.** Organizations sometimes add excessively complex assessment criteria to the succession planning process to improve the quality of the assessment. However, Marshall Goldsmith[13] warns, "Some of these criteria are challenging even for behavioral scientists to assess, much less the average line manager." Remember that the planning process is only a precursor to focus the development. Goldsmith says, "It doesn't need to be perfect," adding that more sophisticated assessments can be built into the development process and administered by a competent coach.

15. **Prepare new hires for succession planning.** Some leaders may regard succession planning as a threat. They may wonder if you are trying to replace them, or they may fear that talking about succession planning with you will put that idea into your head or suggest that they are thinking about resigning. Miles suggests that you begin talking about succession planning with your key executives during the onboarding process. Tell them that you want them to stay long-term, but that succession planning is part of your organization's strategy and that you will want them to participate in it. Miles adds, "Any strong and good leader will recognize the importance of succession planning."

16. **Tell the successor.** Don't identify a successor for a key role within your organization without telling that person. Jessica Leyshon[14] calls this an "age-old" mistake. She says, "Bosses too frequently utter the words, 'But I had great plans for you' when the earmarked successor hands their notice in." Informing an identified successor that they have been earmarked for a potential future role opens a conversation with the employee to establish if they are even interested in a future with your organization, and how they feel about the particular role you have in mind for them, Leyshon says. Telling them what you have in mind may help them to feel that they are valued and to stay with your organization longer. If not, learning their intentions early will tell you that you need to revise your succession plan.

17. **Recruit with your succession plan in mind.** Your succession planning process should start by recruiting great people. During the recruitment process, assess candidates' background, experience, and career plans to gauge how they could fit into your succession strategy long-term. Lucid Chart[15] says, "You don't necessarily have to recruit for a specific high-level opening — instead, look for the qualities and experience that would help you recruit employees that can be developed and groomed for future leadership roles."

18. **Help people let go.** One of the biggest challenges with succession planning is the difficulty many departing employees have letting go. Those who have been in a role for a long time may have mixed feelings about vacating it and believe that there are a lot of tasks only they can do. Emotions can run high, clouding judgment, and making it harder for departing employees to focus on coaching their successors and passing on knowledge. John Ramsden[16] suggests, "An objective third party can help keep these feelings out of the planning process."

19. **Think about your own successor.** Don't overlook yourself as you plan. Your own role will need to be filled someday. Half asks, "Which employee could step into your shoes someday? And what can you do, starting now, to help that person prepare for that transition?"

20. **Develop and publicize a fair selection process.** Employees sometimes feel that one of their colleagues has just been handed a promotion on a silver platter, without any formal selection process or succession plan. This is especially likely to happen when the role wasn't advertised. Leyshon suggests that you announce the vacancy internally to give other team members a chance to put their names forward for consideration. Or share your process and criteria for choosing successors with everyone, on a need-to-know basis, or only if employees ask. Leyshon says, "There's no right or wrong way to do this, but it can build trust and boost engagement if as a business you can share the reasons that a successor was chosen."

21. **Document.** Keep a detailed record of your succession planning efforts so you and others in your organization can learn from what you've done. Indeed Editorial Team suggests, "Consider those processes which went smoothly and those which may require improvement." Identify areas of miscommunication or confusion that your incoming candidates and other employees experienced. Reflect on and record lessons learned for future succession planning.

22. **Change the name.** Goldsmith suggests changing the name of the process from succession *planning* to succession *development*. Goldsmith says, "We see many companies put more effort and attention into the planning process than they do into the development process." Succession planning has lots of to-do's — forms, charts, meetings, due dates, and checklists. These tools sometimes create a false sense that the planning process is an end in itself rather than a precursor to real development. Goldsmith says, "Plans do not develop anyone — only development experiences develop people."

23. **Safeguard confidentiality.** Succession planning can involve sensitive issues as people leave your organization or leave one position within it for another. Emotions may escalate as a beloved colleague leaves, especially because of illness or other troubling circumstances, or if one person on the team is promoted but not another. You will need to balance transparency with discretion. Leyshon asks, "Does everybody need to know everything about the succession plan, and if so, do they all need to necessarily know at the same time?" Get your leadership team, the individual who is vacating a role, and the successor to agree about which types of information can be shared and which should be treated as confidential.

24. **Build interims into your succession plan.** Identify employees who could serve as interims should you find yourself with a sudden vacancy in a key position. Jon Jennings[17] suggests that you consider aligned responsibilities and core competencies between the two roles and which positions have similar day-to-day operations and functional areas. Jennings adds, "Remember that these interim employees could ultimately take over the role at some point, so they should be strong contenders." Be sure, however, that the interim understands from the start that the permanent position is not guaranteed and that you will be filling it according to your succession plan.

25. **Give yourself and your succession planning team some TLC.** It can feel daunting to hold in your hands the future of your organization and the careers of others. Allow your succession planning team to talk about their feelings and give them the feedback, support, and encouragement they need. Also be mindful of your own feelings as you work through the succession planning process. It is challenging work and the stakes are high. Seek the help and support you need and cut yourself some slack if the perfect candidates don't come to mind

right away. Succession planning is a tough job, but you can do it. And in the end, doing it well may be one of your most important contributions to your organization, to the people who work there today, and to those who come long after you are gone.

WHY SUCCESSION PLANNING FAILS

The right successors will be able to handle their new roles as well as or better than the people before them. Sometimes, however, that doesn't happen. Or the right person has been given the role but does not want to stay in it. Or you cannot find the right person for the role and find yourself having to compromise. There are several reasons succession plans fail, but fortunately, there also are steps you can take to failure-guard your plan.

One reason succession plans fail is that managers sometimes oppose it. They may find it challenging and unpleasant to think about letting go of their best performers who will ascend to a new position and leave a hole behind them. As a result, some may dig in their heels, resent succession planning, or otherwise not support it. To prevent this, set an expectation for your managers to develop their teams and hold them accountable for recognizing employees who excel. Create opportunities for them to feel engaged and supported at work so they don't feel that they are alone in the aftermath of losing a valued team member. Educate your managers on the benefits of succession planning, including how they will have their choice of internal candidates when they have vacancies to fill. Be transparent with them about your goal of keeping talent within the organization and solicit their help. Miles suggests, "Invest in your [management] team, helping them cultivate key management skills, along with the ability to make difficult leadership decisions."

A lack of time also can tank succession plans. Many leaders are rewarded chiefly for their short-term accomplishments and push long-term succession planning to the side. In too many organizations, Miles says, "The board only discusses CEO succession when a transition is looming." Start succession planning today, or if not, as soon as possible. Miles adds, "This means checking in with your leaders regularly on their career plans. It also might mean identifying future leaders by seeing their potential." Incentivize your leaders if you can and sell the urgency for and benefits of succession planning to them so they will be engaged in the task.

Another reason succession plans fail is that they are reactive rather than proactive. Linda Ginac[18] explains, "Many companies develop succession plans to find replacements in case an employee decides to leave. However, the right approach is to always have a pool of candidates/successors available." A proactive approach enables organizations to make changes according to their own planning while preparing them for abrupt changes outside of their control.

Succession plans fail, too, when they are too narrow. Organizations often focus on planning just for C-suite and other top leaders. Ginac says that most companies develop succession plans for only 25% of their workforce, at most, but that in reality, "it's more important to build succession plans for every other employee." Each department works like a well-oiled machine, and missing even one part of it can cause department-wide problems. Ginac says, "Ultimately, every employee is essential to ensure smooth business operations," and should be considered in your succession planning.

Succession plans also fail when they don't include prospective successors in the process. Planning for a person to ascend to a new position is not like moving a piece on a chess board. Human beings have their own ideas about their careers. Ginac warns, "The companies that develop succession plans for every employee often overlook whether an employee wants a role or not. Many employees can be qualified for a position, but only some of them would consider it an aspirational role." Work with your prospective successors by offering them "career pathing," Ginac says, so you know what they want their future roles to be.

A lack of integration is another reason that succession plans fail. Many organizations treat succession plans as a separate and independent process. Ginac warns, "As a result, even properly developed succession plans can have negative results when the successor doesn't perform well." There are two reasons for poor successor performance. First, succession plans are considered an HR function in many organizations when, in fact, it's more than that. Although HR may finalize a succession plan, the initial development of the successor should be the responsibility of each respective department. Second, succession plans often aren't tied to the organization's internal training, development, and coaching programs. Ginac suggests that you integrate your succession plan by including your training and development departments and other relevant entities. Consider every resource available to you that can help successors prepare for and transition into their new roles.

Finally, succession plans fail when organizations lack sufficient in-house talent. In some cases, organizations develop excellent succession plans but don't have the talent pool needed to enact them. However, you don't have to settle for less-than-ideal successors or seek external candidates for vacancies because the people who work in your organization right now are not suitable successors. You can create and improve your own talent pool. Talentguard[19] says, "The easiest way to ensure you have the best successors is to develop an organizational talent pool depending on the qualification, skills, and preferences of employees." Recruit at every level in your organization to create a team of the right mix of employees for today and for the future.

HOW TO HANDLE EMPLOYEES WHO DIDN'T GET THE PROMOTION

Succession plans focus on identifying and preparing successors to take on new roles. That's how it should be. However, you also must keep in mind that for every succession there is likely to be at least one person who is not happy about being passed over for the promotion. Madeleine Burry[20] says, "Being passed over for a promotion — particularly when you feel like you deserved it, or if someone you believe is less qualified receives one instead — can be demoralizing and discouraging."

Typically, little more is said to candidates passed over for the promotion other than some polite form of, "You didn't get it." Or worse, candidates are left to figure out on their own that they didn't get the job when the successor is announced. Employees may become bitter or jaded when they are passed over, especially when they were a final contender for the position and it was a long recruitment process. Some may be tempted to quit. Employers can manage the situation in a much more effective and sensitive way to prevent this from happening. Jathan Janove[21] says, "When employees don't know the facts, they will speculate about what the truth may be. And that speculation is invariably worse than reality."

Employees who were passed over for a promotion need to know three things: why they were not chosen; that they are still valued; and what they can do to improve their chances for future promotion. Be specific about the qualifications, experience, and certification(s) of the selected candidate when promotions or new hires are announced. Explain how that individual was a better fit for the position. Often, this information helps less-qualified internal applicants understand why the selection decision was made. Have regular performance discussions with the employee and offer appropriate guidance about their strengths and weaknesses. Teach them effective interview strategies if you felt that their interview performance could have been better. Review their personal development plans and suggest training opportunities. Janove says, "Sometimes, it's helpful to be direct and honest with people you think won't ever be promoted for that type of position. If you know you're never going to hire Jane or Jim into that senior management role, talking with them about their interests and other options may ultimately be the kindest thing you can do."

Often the conversations we don't want to have are the most important to have. Explaining promotion decisions to disappointed candidates falls into this category. Janove warns, "Beware the avoidance instinct. The sooner you engage the candidates and share reasons for the decision, the better."

———— CHAPTER 17 BONUS FEATURE ————

HOW TO USE A NINE-BOX MATRIX FOR SUCCESSION PLANNING

High Potential Low Performance	High Potential Moderate Performance	High Potential High Performance
Moderate Potential Low performance	Moderate Potential Moderate performance	Moderate Potential High Performance
Low Potential Low performance	Low Potential Moderate Performance	Low Potential High Performance

The nine-box matrix is a popular tool for assessing employees' performance and potential, team composition, and candidates for training and development. Managers typically use the nine-box matrix in preparation for performance reviews, reorganizing employee responsibilities, and other managerial duties. In addition, the Indeed Editorial Team[22] suggests, "If you're a manager who takes part in succession planning, the nine-box matrix can be a useful tool to help you assess members of your team for a promotion."

The nine-box matrix offers several benefits. It is an easy-to-use tool that enables managers to compare team members and assess them by the same yardstick. It can help them monitor changes in team composition over time and give them a holistic approach to reviewing talent. And it can be used by managers across the organization, standardizing their evaluations. Employees who are assessed as having high potential and high performance will be promising candidates for succession. In addition, Profit Co.[23] offers the following guidelines for using the nine-box matrix for succession planning:

- **Low performers.** Do not consider low performers for your succession planning.
- **Moderate performers.** Consider those with high potential for development programs, but not for succession planning at this time. Do not consider those with moderate or low potential for your succession planning.
- **High performers.** Recognize and reward all high performers. Those with high potential are ideal candidates for succession planning and other advanced development opportunities. Those with moderate potential are good candidates for development but are not ready for succession planning at this time. Do not consider low potential for succession planning.

Crafting Your Leadership Legacy: A Template

Perhaps the ultimate test of a leader is not what you are able to do in the here and now, but instead what continues to grow long after you're gone.

—Tom Rath and Barry Conchie[1]

Every administrator, leader, or manager who works in a healthcare organization will leave a leadership legacy. Robert M. Galford and Regina Fazio Maruca[2] suggest, "It won't be a record of how you behaved or a report card of your company's performance (although that is how it might be summed up by the press)." Instead, your leadership legacy will be revealed in how your colleagues, employees, and others think and behave because of the time they spent working with you. It will also be found in the works you created, the patients you helped to serve, and the improvements you made that stand the test of time.

Most of us never deliberately attempt to learn much about the full scope and scale of our influence at work. Instead, we strive to do our best and leave our legacy to luck or chance. However, the time to start thinking about your leadership legacy is now, not shortly before you change jobs or retire, and certainly not at the end of your life. If you start now, you will greatly increase the odds of leaving the leadership legacy that you want, rather than one that happens organically. With clear legacy intentions, you will move through every day, week, month, and year throughout your career purposely, with the end in mind. You will know in specifics the long-term impact you'd like to have through your leadership and continually assess the changes you need to make to achieve your intended legacy. MindTools[3] suggests, "This enables you to work toward your legacy throughout your life, rather than considering it only in retrospect."

Some leaders don't like to think about the end. It's hard for some of us to imagine a world without us in it. Some are so overcome by day-to-day tasks that they can't see the forest for the trees. Some procrastinate because they believe that there is plenty of time later to worry about leaving a legacy, even when they know that tomorrow is not promised to us. Becoming a legacy thinker now, regardless of your age, health, or where you are in your career progression, can make you a happier and better leader throughout your career, and even change the trajectory of your professional life. If you're a leader who tries to take on too much, for instance, legacy thinking will reveal to you where your influence is having a lasting effect, and where it is not. James M. Kouzes and Barry Z. Posner[4] say, "Thinking about leadership in the context of your legacy helps you establish — and reestablish — your priorities." Legacy thinking also locates you in the history of your healthcare organization. It can help you recognize when you are wasting time in a job and identify the right time to make a move. As well, it can help you put succession planning into perspective and enable you eventually to let go and seed the success of your successor.

Perhaps the most important benefit of legacy thinking is that it can help you bring purpose to your work and place the actions you take today in a wider context. MindTools says, "Chances are, the knowledge that you're building something to last will make you more focused, motivated, empowered, and satisfied." Legacy thinking focuses your eyes on the prize. Galford and Maruca explain, "You will gain a better understanding of yourself in your role as leader, and you will better understand how the big-picture view of your role is fueled by your actions on a daily basis." Legacy thinking can help you become a more positive role model and encourage others to consider their own legacies. It can make you more decisive, more patient under trying circumstances, and more caring about the people you lead. It can help you to identify gaps in your knowledge and skills that you will need to fill to achieve your legacy. It can help you to stay focused despite myriad distractions and your own shortcomings and weaknesses. And it can help you gain self-knowledge and become more generative, that is, more able to plant seeds for future generations. Kimberly Wade-Benzoni[5] explains, "Thinking about your legacy is a great way to ensure that you are taking into account the long-term perspective of your organization and resisting the temptation to make myopic decisions that are overly focused on short-term gain."

We all are familiar with a mission statement that defines the purpose or goal of a business or organization. A clearly written mission statement can be a powerful tool to guide our thoughts and behaviors. Similarly, a leadership legacy statement can become a powerful tool to guide what you think and do as a healthcare leader. It can capture and articulate an intentional legacy that you design, and provide you with specific, customized targets and benchmarks so you can track your progress. Keep in mind, however, that writing a legacy statement is much more than a description of actions and accomplishments. Instead, a good one focuses on a leader's values, behaviors, and approaches to leading others, as well as what they will leave behind that outlives them.

A well-crafted leadership legacy statement can describe your concept of your healthcare organization 20 or 30, or even 50 years from now. It can record your authentic aspirations, strivings, and passions. However, a leadership legacy statement is neither a to-do list nor a report card upon which you will be judged when you retire or pass. It is a living, breathing document that will establish your self-imposed standards and goals, with the hope that you will take them seriously and act on them.

The culminating feature of this chapter, and this book, is my leadership legacy statement template, a tool I developed for my legacy workshops. This easy-to-use template, coupled with the sample legacy statement that I have written and provided for you, will help you write your own leadership legacy statement. My template will help you to encapsulate your legacy intentions quickly and relatively easily. However, let's be sure that you have a legacy mindset before you begin to work with it.

SEVEN WAYS TO DEVELOP A LEGACY MINDSET

Legacy thinking is not a substitute or synonym for a leader's organizational vision, mission, and strategy. Galford and Maruca say, "Legacy thinking is grounded in the individual." Legacy thinking provides leaders with a lens through which to see what they do in the big picture. It provides them with an honest look at their own strengths and limitations, desires, and aversions. Viewing leadership through a legacy lens helps leaders decide how best to allocate their time and attention. It also enables them to see if they are living the professional life they want to lead.

You will answer specific questions in my template about the lasting impact you want to have on your healthcare organization and the people in it, and the ways you want to be remembered because of your leadership. You will be more effective at answering these questions if first you spend some time thinking broadly about legacies. Here are seven ways to do that:

1. **Commit to starting now.** It takes time to build a legacy. MindTools says, "The sooner you begin, the more time you'll have to craft your legacy, and the longer you'll have to align your actions with your aims."

2. **Ask your friends, family, and colleagues to explain how your past behavior has affected them.** Other people often see our strengths more clearly than we can. Look for patterns that identify your strengths. How can you build on them?

3. **Reflect on the difference you want to make.** An effective (though admittedly morbid) technique is to draft your own eulogy. MindTools suggests that you write it in a "lighthearted, upbeat style" and describe what you hope your colleagues will say about you after you're gone. List what you hope your concrete accomplishments will be, but also, the lasting effect you will have had on the people you worked with.

4. **Think about what previous generations have done for you.** Wade-Benzoni says, "While you can't always reciprocate the deeds of prior generations because they are no longer part of the organization, you can pay it forward by behaving similarly to the next generation of organizational actors." What inspiration can you draw from your predecessors? What lessons did they teach you? How did they improve your healthcare organization? What did they contribute to make both your healthcare organization and you what you are today?

5. **Think about what's missing.** What programs, trainings, services, resources, and facilities are lacking in your healthcare organization? What problems need to be addressed? In what ways would you like to leave your healthcare organization better than you found it?

6. **Consider the burdens and benefits of leadership legacies.** Sometimes, a leader's decision leaves behind a burden that others will have to live with long after they are gone. For example, think about decisions others have made that have left behind a negative environmental impact, debt, hazardous waste, high-cost maintenance, and litigation. Wade-Benzoni says, "Highlighting the burdensome aspects of long-range decisions can help leaders to recognize the negative legacies that such decisions can create." It can prevent them from making burdensome decisions that will leave them with guilt and shame.

7. **Contemplate your own death.** This will not come easily to everyone. Some people find it difficult and even unsettling to come face-to-face

with the prospect of their own mortality. However, Wade-Benzoni says, "Reminding people of death motivates them to consider their legacy and causes them to act in ways that benefit future generations, thus improving the overall quality of their long-term decisions." People fare better in the face of death when they feel that they have been part of something good that will live on after them. Having a positive impact on future generations through your leadership legacy can help you fulfill that need. Think about how you want to be remembered by other people when you're gone and act on those thoughts. Wade-Benzoni says, "Ultimately, your legacy is all you've got…Give the Grim Reaper a run for his money by creating something meaningful that will outlive yourself."

QUIZ: YOUR STRENGTHS AND WEAKNESSES FOR LEAVING THE LEGACY YOU INTEND

Your ability to achieve your intended legacy will depend upon several factors. Although some of them may be at the organizational level and, therefore, beyond your control, a great many of them will depend on your attitudes and beliefs. Take the quiz below. Use your answers to determine whether your attitudes and beliefs support your achieving your intended leadership legacy, even if you haven't yet figured out precisely what you want that legacy to be. If you are disappointed in what you find in your answers, use this quiz to help you identify the additional work you may need to do before moving forward.

Answer True or False to each statement:

_____ 1. I care about what will happen to my healthcare organization after I'm gone.

_____ 2. The work I do every day at my healthcare organization matters.

_____ 3. I can make important contributions to my healthcare organization.

_____ 4. What I do at my healthcare organization can have a lasting impact.

_____ 5. I care how I will be remembered at my healthcare organization.

_____ 6. I am good at setting goals.

_____ 7. I am a visionary thinker.

_____ 8. I do not shy away from hard work.

_____ 9. I take great satisfaction in achieving my goals.

_____ 10. I am not easily derailed from my goals.

_____ 11. I am generally a positive person.

_____ 12. I have knowledge worth passing on to others.

_____ 13. It's possible to achieve an intended leadership legacy.

_____ 14. It's possible to improve things at my healthcare organization.

_____ 15. It's possible to make a lasting difference in other people's lives.

_____ 16. I care about the impact I have on others.

_____ 17. I want to leave the world a better place than I found it.

_____ 18. I cherish the leadership legacy of at least one person.

_____ 19. One person can make a difference.

_____ 20. I can see the big picture.

_____ 21. I take myself and my leadership seriously.

_____ 22. My leadership means a lot to me.

_____ 23. I want my leadership to have mattered.

_____ 24. I can determine and shape my leadership legacy.

_____ 25. I can achieve the legacy I wish to leave behind.

Your score is based on the number of times you answer "False":

- **0–1:** Your attitudes are strong for crafting and achieving an intended leadership legacy.
- **2–4:** Overall, you have good attitudes about crafting and achieving your intended legacy. Focus on your few False answers. Work toward shifting your attitudes about them.
- **5–7:** Some of your attitudes may interfere with your ability to craft or achieve an intended legacy. Spend time thinking about your False answers and how you can shift your attitudes about them. Seek help as needed.
- **8 or more:** Your attitudes are likely to interfere with your ability to craft an intended leadership legacy or to achieve it. You probably will benefit

from working with a leadership coach or other helping professional to shift your attitudes.

HOW TO USE THE LEADERSHIP LEGACY STATEMENT TEMPLATE

Writing your legacy statement is not a task to be taken lightly. In fact, you may feel intimidated by it. Kouzes and Posner explain, "A heartfelt quest to leave a lasting legacy is a journey from success to significance." That's a huge and bold goal. Yet, as lofty as "significance" may sound, leadership legacies usually are much harder to think about in the abstract than in the concrete, and harder to write on a blank page, rather than by answering questions.

That is why I created a legacy statement template in my legacy workshops and provided it and a sample legacy statement at the end of this bonus chapter. The template leads you through simple questions to guide your leadership legacy thinking. It will help you shape and capture your best ideas. The template also will help you organize your thinking into an outline so you can write your leadership legacy statement easily and relatively quickly. However, before you delve into the questions, here are nine final tips to help you make better use of my template:

1. **Don't worry about sounding too idealistic.** Start with high legacy aspirations, not safe ones. Gordon Tredgold[6] explains, "Big goals can inspire us to take action. They can fit well with our aspirations and desires to achieve greatness. We all want to be recognized, and we get recognized for big achievements, not small ones." Work at the template's questions until you feel excited and enthusiastic about your answers.

2. **Don't stress about your precise word choices.** You can edit your leadership legacy statement later. Keep in mind as you work that your legacy statement is not a legal document. No one is going to test it in court and you don't have to share it with anyone if you don't want to.

3. **Tie your leadership legacy statement to your lifetime of work.** Think backward and forward in time. Kouzes and Posner suggest, "Legacies encompass past, present, and future, and when pondering our legacies, we are forced to consider where we've been, where we are now, and where we're going." Consider your intended legacy beyond your current job, even if you don't yet know what or where your next leadership position may be.

4. **Distinguish between your professional and personal legacies.** Your character and values should parallel closely in your professional and personal lives. However, the legacy you leave your children will not be identical to the one you leave your employees. Everyone may remember you as a kind and patient person, for instance, but the way you exercise your kindness and patience will be different in different circumstances.

5. **Focus on the time you have left.** If you had to leave your healthcare organization right now, you would already have left a legacy. If that is not the legacy you intend, think about how much time you may have left. Your legacy statement can help you make the most of the time you have and spur you to make the changes you will need to make to seal your intended legacy.

6. **Customize the template and your leadership legacy statement to meet your needs.** Eliminate questions from the template that don't suit you and add new ones that are unique to you. As you'll see, my legacy statement is structured according to the questions in the template. It provides some imagined answers. Sticking to this format makes easy and quick work of the legacy statement writing task, but don't feel locked into it. Write your statement however you like.

7. **Embrace the process.** Writing your leadership legacy statement may require you to stretch in ways you haven't before. However, if you do it well, both the process and your completed legacy statement will give you the push you need to try something new or to improve or repair an important interpersonal relationship. You can grow a lot by writing a well-crafted leadership legacy statement.

8. **Block out time in your schedule without interruption to answer the template questions**. Allow yourself time to think of the big picture and to imagine a future in your healthcare organization without you in it. Schedule time off site if that will help you think more clearly. Write honestly about what you want, not what you think sounds good. When you're done, put your answers away for at least a couple of days, longer if possible. Then, re-read what you wrote with fresh eyes. Continue to edit your answers until you feel satisfied that you have captured how you want to be remembered and what you want to have accomplished. If you get stuck or are having trouble expressing your thoughts, discuss sticking points with a trusted individual who can help you complete the template.

9. **Ask a trusted person who knows you well for feedback on your leadership legacy statement.** MindTools suggests, "They can help you to 'raise your sights' if the aspirations on your legacy statement are too modest or encourage you to rethink objectives that may be out of reach." The opinion you receive from someone you trust will help you test your intended legacy with minimal risk. You can find out if you are missing something that belongs in your legacy and whether you need to revise, discard, or rewrite your legacy statement. Ask for feedback about how closely your leadership legacy statement reflects who you are with questions such as:

- Do I believe that my goals are authentic and self-driven? Do they seem to be expectations generated by other people and not by me?
- Are my aspirations realistic?
- Have I identified real areas for potential growth and accomplishment?
- Have I aimed too high? Too low?
- Do I connect with what I have written?
- Is my legacy statement clear? Are there areas that need further or better explanation?
- How can I improve my leadership legacy statement?

LIVE YOUR LEADERSHIP LEGACY

Write and edit your leadership legacy statement until you are satisfied with it. Then, keep it in a place where you will see it often. MindTools suggests creating a treasure map to keep your aims visible. A legacy treasure map, also known as a *vision board*, will be a physical representation of your legacy goals. MindTools explains, "It's a collage of images and text that acts as a reminder of what you want to accomplish, and how you will do it. It intensifies the effects of visualization — a technique which acts on your subconscious mind to motivate and encourage you toward reaching those goals." Treasure maps work because language, not images, is the medium in which you rationalize. Language leaves you vulnerable to negative self-talk, which can undercut your motivation. Treasure maps, on the other hand, bypass language. You don't have to talk yourself into believing what you want to achieve because you can see it as though it already exists. That makes it easier and more likely for us to believe that what we seek is possible. MindTools says, "Creating and focusing on a physical image of yourself in your desired state, you can build confidence and belief in your own abilities to achieve what you set out to do." Place your completed treasure map where you can see it daily — either physically or digitally, or both — and look at it often.

Your leadership legacy statement will not be set in stone. You created it, and you can change it. Therefore, review it periodically to see if it is still current. You may find that what matters to you today may not matter in the same way years from now. New situations and opportunities will arise that can change your thinking. The hard knocks you take in life and the losses you experience may alter your goals. You may be influenced by new people you meet, new challenges you face, and new ways in which you grow. Continue to learn and remain agile and open minded. Commit to revisiting your leadership legacy statement at least annually throughout the remainder of your career to see if it continues to reflect your current legacy intentions. If it doesn't, solicit feedback and revise your statement so it remains current and accurate and continues to motivate you.

Begin to live your leadership legacy statement immediately. Start by looking for ways to make a difference to the people around you. Strive to align your behavior with your aims and look for discrepancies between the legacy you want and what you do. Consider what may need to change about your leadership style, behavior, and working methods. Also identify the hard and soft skills you may need to improve. Set goals with deadlines for learning those skills and choose the methods you will use to learn them. Start the process of learning or improving at least one needed skill right away.

A leader's ability to achieve their intended legacy will depend on the people who remain at the healthcare organization after they are gone. Those who live after the leader, in fact, will have the final word on the matter, because it will be in their hearts, minds, and behaviors that a leader's legacy will endure. Therefore, leaders who wish to leave their intended legacies must not operate in a vacuum. Check in with others, often, to see if you are on course for achieving your intended legacy. Use periodic evaluations to determine if you should maintain the status quo or if you need to make mid-course corrections to achieve your intended legacy.

Explore other ways to solicit some feedback. Asking others what they believe you will be remembered for and why can be illuminating. A 360-feedback, also known as *multi-rater feedback, multisource feedback,* or *multisource assessment,* can be a more systematic tool for gathering the opinions of others. In addition, schedule annual legacy statement audits. Using this technique, you will ask key people around you to help you judge your progress toward your intended legacy and give you feedback. MindTools[3] warns, "Even with careful planning, your legacy-building will probably remain fragile, at least initially." It is easy to get blown off course by everyday demands, short-term crises, inattention, inaction, inertia, or attempting to be something that you're not. Take a step back if you find that you are not living your legacy. Revisit this chapter, your leadership legacy statement, and your legacy treasure map if you've created one, and try to figure out why you are missing the mark. If you don't know, seek the help of a leadership coach or other professional to help you reset priorities and get back on track. With purpose, steadfast commitment, and the gift of good health and sufficient time, you will be able to achieve your intended legacy.

WORKING COLLABORATIVELY TO ACHIEVE YOUR INTENDED LEADERSHIP LEGACY

There are several ways that healthcare leaders can work together to develop, support, and achieve their intended leadership legacies. These include forming legacy learning communities, working with a legacy buddy, honoring and preserving the legacies of other leaders, and sharing legacy intentions with supervisors and direct reports:

- **Legacy learning communities.** The purpose of a legacy learning community is to help leaders become legacy thinkers and to provide them with the education and support they need to shape and achieve their intended legacies. Healthcare leaders and those who develop leaders at healthcare organizations may find that forming a legacy community is very worthwhile. A legacy learning community can help leaders craft and refine their legacy statements, clarify and articulate their legacy goals, and work through obstacles and threats to achieving their intended legacies.
- **Legacy buddy programs.** Two healthcare leaders can pair up to share their leadership legacy statements with one another and meet regularly to discuss legacy progress, challenges, and strategies. Well-matched buddies can become accountability partners and help keep one another on track and focused on their legacy intentions.
- **Honoring and preserving legacies of other leaders.** Attending awards ceremonies and memorial services for past leaders can be personally

valuable and meaningful. Healthcare leaders are encouraged to take part in such programs as a community and to embrace them as opportunities to preserve and cherish the legacies of others.

- **Sharing legacy intentions with bosses and direct reports.** Bosses can shape tasks and new initiatives that are beneficial both to the healthcare organization and to the leaders they supervise. Healthcare leaders also may want to share their intended legacies with their direct reports, depending on the situation and the people involved. Personnel who report directly to the leader may be, in fact, the individuals who are in the best position to support the leader's legacy intentions.

COMMIT TO LEAVING A POSITIVE LEADERSHIP LEGACY

A leader may intend a particular legacy and articulate it clearly through a legacy statement. However, that alone does not guarantee that they will achieve it. Healthcare organizations can greatly influence whether their leaders succeed in achieving their intended legacies, or even, whether they are legacy thinkers. Those that offer top-down support, tools, resources, and communication avenues for legacy thinking will create environments that are conducive for legacy thinking and for working toward, achieving, and preserving leadership legacies. Unfortunately, healthcare organizations also can thwart a leader's legacy motivations and intentions, even if inadvertently, by stretching their leaders so thin that they leave them little time for legacy thinking. They also can limit or discourage legacy thinking if they don't recognize the contributions of their leaders, both present and past. Healthcare organizations whose leaders are overwhelmed, that have poor communication channels, and where bureaucracy and negativity take center stage are environments where legacy thinking may be particularly challenged.

Of course, a great deal of the responsibility for achieving a leader's legacy also resides within the leader. Crafting and regularly updating a leadership legacy statement is a good place to begin one's efforts to shape an intentional legacy and to achieve it. However, the leader's personal commitment to their legacy and their ability to work through the challenges and obstacles that come their way also are hugely important factors in whether they will succeed in leaving an intended legacy. As you've learned in this chapter, shaping and living your leadership legacy promises many benefits. You've learned, too, that crafting a leadership legacy statement is an important step in the process. You may finish reading this chapter and this book with good intentions to work on your legacy and to write your leadership legacy statement. However, you will need more than that to achieve your legacy. You also will need your absolute, unwavering commitment.

Leaving a positive professional legacy is arguably the most important thing you will ever do as a leader. Caring for others and the environment is what matters most. Keep your eyes on what you are doing and always remember that leaders come and go. Policies and procedures that are meticulously built by leaders today can be swept away by successors in a heartbeat. What you do for your healthcare organization's culture and people — the recruitment choices you make, the people you develop, the inspiration and encouragement you provide to others, and the values and mindsets you instill in their hearts — *that* will be what endures.

Make your legacy your priority, because when we are gone, leaving a positive legacy is all we have. It's also our job. As Jim Rohn[8] aptly puts it, "All good men and women must take responsibility to create legacies that will take the next generation to a level we could only imagine. What makes good and honorable leaders is having a foundational part of our lives based on the goal of leaving a positive legacy." You've *got* to concern yourself not only with what you are doing today, tomorrow, and in the coming year, but with what you will leave behind for future generations. Nothing matters more than this.

Your ability to achieve your intended legacy will depend upon the people who will remain at your healthcare organization after you are gone. Those who live after us, in fact, will have the final word on the matter. Your legacy will be in their hearts, minds, and behaviors. Therefore, don't work on your intended legacies alone, closeted away in your office. Invite others along with you on your journey. Check in with them, often, to let you know if they think you are on course. Consider the ways that you can help develop *their* careers and help *them* generate meaningful legacies. Take the focus away from your mortality and put it where it belongs — on the people you will leave behind.

When I've worked with leaders on their legacy intentions and strivings, I've suggested that they keep in mind a remark attributed to Groucho Marx, who said, "I plan to live forever. So far, so good." Groucho humorously hit upon a basic and very serious tenet of the human condition. We know we are going to die. Yet, most of us don't want to or plan to. Quoting my scholarly work, Laura Hills[9] says, "In our youth, we typically push away thoughts of our own passing. That's relatively easy for most of us when we look in the mirror and see all the time in the world ahead of us. But as we grow older, we revisit our mortality in a new way. We come to terms with it." That coming to terms powerfully motivates most of us to want to take action to leave something behind for future generations while there's still time.

We cannot be immortal in the way Groucho suggested. However, we can ensure our immortality by leaving an enduring legacy. Your leadership legacy, captured and articulated in a clear legacy statement that guides your behavior and thoughts, is the best place to begin.

LEADERSHIP LEGACY STATEMENT TEMPLATE

Answer the questions below. Take your time. If you don't know the answers right away, come back to them later after you've had time to think about them. Discuss them with someone you trust if you think that will help. Write what is true for you, not what you think sounds good or what others might like to hear.

1. How do you wish to be remembered by those inside and outside your healthcare organization, in your current role and in your career?
   A. For which two or three *characteristics* would you like to be remembered?

   • _____

   • _____

   • _____

   How would you like these *characteristics* to manifest themselves? How will they show up?

   _____

   _____

   _____

B. For which two or three *behaviors* would you like to be remembered?

- _____

- _____

- _____

How would you like these *behaviors* to manifest themselves? How will they show up?

_____

_____

_____

C. For which two or three *skills* would you like to be remembered?

- _____

- _____

- _____

How would you like these *skills* to manifest themselves? How will they show up?

_____

_____

_____

D. For which two or three core *values* would you like to be remembered?

- _____

- _____

- _____

How would you like these *core values* to manifest themselves? How will they show up?

_____

_____

_____

2. What have you learned in your work and in your life thus far that you would most like to pass on?

_____

_____

_____

How will you convey that learning?

_____

_____

_____

3. What remains for you to accomplish? Why is that important to building or completing your legacy?

_____

_____

_____

4. Aside from more time, what will help or impede you in completing what remains to be accomplished?

_____

_____

_____

5. How do you believe that completing this template will affect what you do daily in the next week and in the next few months?

_____

_____

_____

SAMPLE LEADERSHIP LEAGACY STATEMENT

The legacy statement below was drawn from the questions in my leadership legacy template. It is a fictional example I wrote to demonstrate the scope, language, and possible format of a leadership legacy statement. Customize your legacy statement to your leadership legacy intention and strivings. Write the best legacy statement you can. Then, edit your writing. Replace ho-hum words like *good* and *excellent* with robust, energizing words like *extraordinary, vigorous,* and *fierce.* Write a compelling statement that makes you feel enthusiastic about your intended legacy. It's your life and your career. Write a leadership legacy statement that lights a fire under you.

These are the ways in which I wish to be remembered by those inside and outside my healthcare organization, in my current role, and in my career:

Characteristics. I want to be remembered as a leader who possessed extraordinarily creative vision, who made the tough decisions when they had to be made, and who didn't pass the buck. I want to be remembered for being an inspiring and encouraging teacher and mentor, and an astute, voracious learner. I also want to be remembered as a leader who was not afraid to take chances and who genuinely cared about others.

Behaviors. I want to be remembered as a leader who honored deadlines and promises, no matter the personal cost, and who always had an open door. When people think of me, I want them to remember my hearty laughter and my smile. I want to be remembered for my professional presence that was manifested in the professional way I dressed, carried myself, kept my cool when the pressure was on, and maintained my workspace. I want the people I led to say that our organization was a better place to work because of my leadership and that together, we accomplished amazing things. I want them to say that I brought out the best in them and that I treated them with respect, no matter the circumstances.

Skills. I want to be remembered as a leader who communicated accurately, thoughtfully, and compellingly both in speaking and in writing. I especially want to be remembered for being an interested listener, one who gave people my time and attention whenever they spoke. I want the people I led to feel that I fostered their creativity, teamwork, and professional development. I want my colleagues to remember me for my technical know-how and sharp analytical ability, but also for my people smarts. I want them to point with pride to specific things I helped them to accomplish, and to say that I helped them to do work that mattered and continues to matter to them.

Values. I want to be remembered as a leader who was honest, transparent, and fiercely loyal. I want people to remember that I was extremely kind and generous with praise, and that I appreciated them. I want them to be glad that they worked with me and to feel that I enriched their lives. I want to be remembered as a leader who was unselfish, who was not ego-driven, and who had a vigorous work ethic. I also want people to remember that I valued excellence and produced extraordinary results, and that good things happened on my watch.

Here is what I have learned in my work and life thus far that I would most like to pass on:

I've learned that people have the capability to do fantastic things, sometimes more so than they know themselves. I've learned that toughing it out and persevering is usually the key to success. I'd like to pass on that you really can't judge a book by its cover. I've learned, too, that failures make us stronger and that often our anticipation of a dreaded event is much worse than the event itself. I've learned that people matter most in everything we do.

This is how I will convey that learning:

I will convey that learning by mentoring others and by my own example. I will convey that learning explicitly to my direct reports by creating and facilitating an annual workshop for them. I also will convey that learning by writing and publishing my memoir.

This is what remains for me to accomplish:

I have yet to write and publish my memoir. I also intend to mentor at least five more individuals before I retire. As well, I need to teach my lessons learned explicitly to my direct reports by developing and facilitating an annual workshop for them.

Aside from more time, these are the things that will help or impede me in completing what remains for me to accomplish:

I must identify individuals who could be my mentees and establish mentoring relationships with at least five of them. I must learn how to write my memoir and do the writing. I must learn about publishing and secure a book contract to publish my memoir. As well, I need to get the help I need to develop and facilitate an annual lessons-learned workshop for my direct reports.

This is how I believe that completing this legacy statement will affect what I will do daily in the next week and in the next few months:

This legacy statement has reminded me that my time as a healthcare leader is finite and that I have much left to do to realize my intended legacy. It has reminded me to live the characteristics, behaviors, skills, and values that I want to be remembered for. It has motivated me to learn about memoir writing and publishing and to be more proactive about finding new employees to mentor. It has also motivated me to get the help I need to plan, schedule, and facilitate an annual lessons-learned workshop for my direct reports.

References

PART 1:
Next-Level Healthcare Leadership
Begins with Self-Leadership

1. Dennison K. The importance of self-leadership, and how it makes you a great leader. *Forbes* blog, April 18, 2024. www.forbes.com/sites/karadennison/2024/04/18/the-importance-of-self-leadership-and-how-it-makes-you-a-great-leader/?sh=137415e37ff6. Accessed April 29, 2024.

2. Neuhaus M. What is self-leadership? theory, models, and examples. *Positive Psychology* blog, March 18, 2024. https://positivepsychology.com/self-leadership/. Accessed April 29, 2024.

3. Manz CC. Improving performance through self-leadership. *National Productivity Review*, 1983; 2:288-297. https://doi.org/10.1002/npr.4040020308

4. Manz CC. Self-leadership: toward an expanded theory of self-influence processes in organizations. *The Academy of Management Review*. 1986;11(3):589. https://doi.org/10.2307/258312

5. Manz CC, Sims HP. SuperLeadership: Beyond the myth of heroic leadership. *Organizational Dynamics*. 1991;19(4):18-35. https://doi.org/10.1016/0090-2616(91)90051-A

6. Birdi K, Clegg C, Patterson M, *et al*. The impact of human resource and operational management practices on company productivity: A longitudinal study. *Personnel Psychology*. 2008;61:467-501. https://doi.org/10.1111/j.1744-6570.2008.00136.x

7. Du Plessis M. Positive self-leadership: a framework for professional leadership development. In: Van Zyl LE, Rothman S Sr, eds. *Theoretical Approaches to Multi-cultural Positive Psychological Interventions*. New York: Springer International Publishing; 2019:450. https://doi.org/10.1007/978-3-030-20583-6_20

8. Carver CS, Scheier MF. *Attention and Self-regulation*. New York: Springer; 1981.

9. Bandura A. *Social Foundations of Thought and Action: A Social Cognitive Theory*. Englewood Cliffs, New Jersey: Prentice-Hall; 1986.

10. Deci EL, Ryan RM. *Intrinsic Motivation and Self-determination in Human Behavior*. New York: Springer; 1985.

11. Goleman D. *Emotional Intelligence*. New York: Bantam Books; 2005.

12. Eurich T. You aren't actually self-aware. *Science of Success* podcast, May 21, 2020. www.successpodcast.com/show-notes/2020/5/20/you-arent-actually-self-aware-with-tasha-eurich. Accessed May 2, 2024.

13. Initiative One. 21 leadership challenges and how to overcome them. *Initiative One* blog, January 24, 2023. www.initiativeone.com/post/leadership-challenges. Accessed May 14, 2024.

14. Jeffrey S. How to cultivate self-leadership. *CEOsage* blog, April 10, 2024. https://scottjeffrey.com/self-leadership/#10_Self-Leadership_Skills. Accessed May 14, 2024.

15. Kristenson S. How to improve your visualization skills and mental imagery. *Develop Good Habits* blog, March 5, 2022. www.developgoodhabits.com/improve-visualization/#:~:text=How%20

to%20Improve%20Visualization%201%201.%20Don%E2%80%99t%20overthink,5.%20 Visualize%20with%20a%20sense%20of%20expectation.%20. Accessed May 15, 2024.

16. Elizabeth A. What is grit and how to develop it for a successful life. *LifeHack* blog, April 18, 2024. www.lifehack.org/884651/what-is-grit. Accessed May 15, 2024.

17. Valcour M. Anyone can learn to be a better leader. *Harvard Business Review* blog, November 4, 2020. https://hbr.org/2020/11/anyone-can-learn-to-be-a-better-leader. Accessed May 16, 2024.

18. Rath T, Conchie B. *Strengths Based Leadership: Great Leaders, Teams, and Why People Follow.* Washington, DC: Gallup Press, 2008.

19. Kelly M. *The Rhythm of Life: Living Every Day with Passion and Purpose,* 3rd ed. North Palm Beach, Florida: Blue Sparrow Books; 2015.

20. Schwartz R. Internal family systems and coaching: self-leadership and internal complexity. Coaches Rising podcast, July 2, 2020. www.coachesrising.com/podcast/internal-family-systems-and-coaching/. Accessed May 21, 2024.

21. Freedman M. What is self-leadership? Your guide to unlocking excellence. *Fellow App* blog, November 3, 2022. https://fellow.app/blog/leadership/the-ultimate-guide-to-self-leadership/?v2=1. Accessed May 21, 2024.

22. Sullivan J & IFS Institute. The 8-C's of self-leadership wheel. IFS Foundation, 2020. https://foundationifs.org/images/banners/pdf/The_8_Cs_of_Self_Leadership_Wheel.pdf. Accessed May 21, 2024.

PART 2:
Advanced Topics for Healthcare Administrators, Leaders, and Managers

Chapter 1: Assessing and Changing Work Culture

1. Schein EH. *Organizational Culture and Leadership*, 4th ed. San Francisco: Jossey-Bass, 2010.
2. Cameron KS & Quinn RE. *Diagnosing and Changing Organizational Culture.* San Francisco: Jossey-Bass, 2006.
3. Martin J. *Organizational Culture: Mapping the Terrain.* Thousand Oaks, CA: Sage, 2002.
4. Rhodes A & Shepherdson N. *Built on Values: Creating an Enviable Culture that Outperforms the Competition.* San Francisco: Jossey-Bass, 2011.

Chapter 2: Servant Leadership in the Healthcare Organization

1. Lyon A. Servant leadership vs. traditional leadership. Communication Skills Coach (video). May 5, 2018. www.communicationskillscoach.com/home/servant-leadership-vs-traditional-leadership. Accessed January 24, 2020.
2. Servant Leadership Centre of Canada. So what is servant leadership anyway? Servant Leadership Centre of Canada website. www.servantleadership.ca/servant-leadership-defined. Accessed January 24, 2020.
3. Greenleaf RK. *The Servant as Leader.* Indianapolis, IN: The Robert K. Greenleaf Center; 2008.
4. Tzimas E. Top 5 reasons behind the popularity of servant leadership. StepChange blog. January 23, 2019. www.stepchangelearning.co.nz/top-5-reasons-behind-the-popularity-of-servant-leadership-today/. Accessed January 27, 2020.

5. Stone AG, Russell AF, & Patterson K. Transformational vs. servant leadership: a difference in leader focus. Regent University School of Leadership Studies article, August 2003. https://regentparents.regent.edu/acad/global/publications/sl_proceedings/2003/stone_transformation_versus.pdf. Accessed January 27, 2020.

6. Lichtenwalner B. Servant leadership companies list. Modern Servant Leader website. www.modernservantleader.com/featured/servant-leadership-companies-list/. Accessed January 27, 2020.

7. Online Staffing. How a servant leadership style can benefit your business. Online Staffing blog, February 21, 2019. www.ontimestaffing.com/2019/02/21/servant-leadership-style-benefit-business/. Accessed January 28, 2020.

8. Sherman F. The advantages of servant leadership style. *Chron*, October 23, 2019. https://smallbusiness.chron.com/advantages-servant-leadership-style-11693.html. Accessed January 28, 2020.

9. Luthor J. The advantages of the servant leadership style. AZ Central blog. August 5, 2019. https://yourbusiness.azcentral.com/advantages-servant-leadership-style-5282.html. Accessed January 28, 2020.

10. Tarallo M. The art of servant leadership. SHRM blog, May 17, 2018. www.shrm.org/resourcesandtools/hr-topics/organizational-and-employee-development/pages/the-art-of-servant-leadership.aspx. Accessed January 28, 2020.

11. Spiro J. How to become a servant leader. *Inc.* blog, August 31, 2010. www.inc.com/guides/2010/08/how-to-become-a-servant-leader.html. Accessed January 30, 2020.

12. Zisa J. Listen to serve: servant leadership and the practice of effective listening. Robert K. Greenleaf Center for Servant Leadership blog. June 20, 2013. www.greenleaf.org/listen-to-serve-servant-leadership-and-the-practice-of-effective-listening/. Accessed January 30, 2020.

13. Percy S. Are you ready to become a servant leader? *Forbes* blog, August 2, 2018. www.forbes.com/sites/sallypercy/2018/08/02/are-you-ready-to-become-a-servant-leader/#53cbac57bc7d. Accessed January 30, 2020.

14. Modern Servant Leader. Academic programs for servant leadership. Modern Servant Leader website. www.modernservantleader.com/academic-programs-list/. Accessed January 30, 2020.

15. *Fortune* Magazine. 100 best companies to work for in 2016. *Fortune*. https://fortune.com/best-companies/2016/. Accessed January 27, 2020.

16. Fox M. Trying to grow servant leaders? Here's 3 myths that can get in the way. Berrett-Kohler Publishers blog. May 9, 2019. https://ideas.bkconnection.com/trying- to-grow-servant-leaders-heres-3-myths-that-can-get-in-the-way. Accessed January 27, 2020.

17. Riley J. The myths of servant leadership. Robert K. Greenleaf Center for Servant Leadership. September 26, 2013. www.greenleaf.org/the-myths-of-servant-leadership/. Accessed January 27, 2020.

18. Blanchard K. Let's clear up some misunderstandings about servant leadership. How We Lead blog. February 7, 2018. https://howwelead.org/2018/02/07/lets-clear-up-some-misunderstandings-about-servant-lead. Accessed January 27, 2020.

19. Rosetta Technology Group. Yes, servant leaders do actually lead. Rosetta Technology Group blog, May 4, 2018. www.rosettatg.com/blogtoon/2018/5/2/yes-servant-leaders-do-actually-lead. Accessed January 27, 2020.

20. Spears L. Ten characteristics of a servant-leader. The Spears Center for Servant Leadership website. www.spearscenter.org/46-uncategorised/136-ten-characteristics-of-servant-leadership. Accessed January 30, 2020.

Chapter 3: How to Become a More Visionary Leader

1. Cornell D. 15 Visionary leadership examples. Helpful Professor blog, October 23, 2022. https://helpfulprofessor.com/visionary-leadership-examples/. Accessed February 20, 2023.
2. Meinert D. How to be a visionary leader. SHRM *HR Magazine*, November 1, 2015. www.shrm.org/hr-today/news/hr-magazine/pages/1115-execbrief.aspx. Accessed February 20, 2023.
3. De Jong R-J. *Anticipate: The Art of Leading by Looking Ahead.* New York: American Management Association, 2015.
4. Trevino L. Brainy Quotes website. www.brainyquote.com/quotes/lee_trevino_160664. Accessed February 21, 2023.
5. Lucas S. Visionary leadership. The Balance blog, September 27, 2021. www.thebalancemoney.com/visionary-leadership-4174279. Accessed February 27, 2023.
6. Collins J & Porras JI. *Built to Last: Successful Habits of Visionary Companies (Good to Great 2).* New York: HarperCollins, 1994.
7. Lindberg C. The importance of visionary leadership and why we need it. Leadership Ahoy blog, July 27, 2022. www.leadershipahoy.com/the-importance-of-visionary-leadership-and-why-we-need-it/. Accessed February 28, 2023.
8. Indeed Editorial Team. What is visionary leadership? (characteristics and benefits). Indeed blog, September 7, 2021. https://ca.indeed.com/career-advice/career-development/what-is-visionary-leadership. Accessed February 27, 2023.
9. MasterClass. 5 qualities of visionary leaders. MasterClass blog, January 24, 2022. www.masterclass.com/articles/visionary-leadership. Accessed February 28, 2023.
10. Lewis A. Good leadership? It all starts with trust. Harvard Business Publishing blog, October 26, 2022. www.harvardbusiness.org/good-leadership-it-all-starts-with-trust/. Accessed February 27, 2023
11. De Jong R-J. *Anticipate: The Art of Looking Ahead.* New York: AMACOM, 2015.
12. Life Coach Spotter. 9 steps to help you become a visionary leader at work. Life Coach Spotter blog. www.lifecoachspotter.com/9-steps-to-help-you-become-a-visionary-leader-at-work/. Accessed March 1, 2123.
13. Stillman J. The science of why you do your best thinking while walking. *Inc.* blog, April 11, 2016. www.inc.com/jessica-stillman/the-science-of-why-you-do-your-best-thinking-while-walking.html. Accessed March 6, 2023.
14. Jahr F. Why walking helps us think. *The New Yorker,* September 3, 2014. www.newyorker.com/tech/annals-of-technology/walking-helps-us-think. Accessed March 6, 2023.
15. Christensen T. Writing ideas down is a phenomenal idea. Creative Something blog, April 25, 2008. https://creativesomething.net/post/32852038/writing-ideas-down-is-a-phenomenal-idea. Accessed March 6, 2023.
16. Stevenson T. 5 keys to become a visionary leader. Lead Communicate Grow blog, August 21, 2020. https://leadcommunicategrow.com/becoming-a-visionary-leader/. Accessed March 6, 2023.
17. Bibri SE. A methodological framework for futures studies: integrating normative backcasting approaches and descriptive case study design for strategic data-drive sustainable

city planning. *Energy Informatics.* 2020;3:31. https://energyinformatics.springeropen.com/articles/10.1186/s42162-020-00133-5#citeas. Accessed March 7, 2023. https://doi.org/10.1186/s42162-020-00133-5

18. Gold A. 5 steps to developing a visionary mindset. LinkedIn blog, July 12, 2015. www.linkedin.com/pulse/5-steps-developing-visionary-mindset-andrea-gold-www-goldstars-com-. Accessed March 7, 2023.

19. Sutton J. What is intuition and why is it important: 5 examples. Positive Psychology blog, August 27, 2020. https://positivepsychology.com/intuition/. Accessed March 7, 2023.

20. Rankin L. 18 ways to develop and strengthen your intuition. MBG Mindfulness blog, March 1, 2021. www.mindbodygreen.com/articles/how-to-strengthen-your-intuition. Accessed March 7, 2023.

21. Cooke P. The courage required of visionary leaders. *Outreach Magazine,* November 24, 2019. https://outreachmagazine.com/features/leadership/49047-the-courage-required-of-visionary-leaders.html. Accessed March 7, 2023.

22. Zetlin M. 8 really effective tricks to boost your courage. *Inc.* blog, May 8, 2014. www.inc.com/minda-zetlin/8-really-effective-tricks-to-boost-your-courage.html, Accessed March 7, 2023.

23. Menghello K. Three ways to get more curious as a leader. *Forbes* blog, February 17, 2021. www.forbes.com/sites/forbescoachescouncil/2021/02/17/three-ways-to-get-more-curious-as-a-leader/?sh=4f0f2c49b32a. Accessed March 7, 2023.

24. Leslie I. *Curious: The Desire to Know and Why Your Future Depends on It.* New York: Basic Books, 2014.

25. Adams M. *Change Your Questions, Change Your Life: 12 Powerful Tools for Leadership, Coaching, and Results.* Oakland, CA: Berrett-Koehler Publishing, 4th ed., 2022.

26. Sonita. 5 mistakes visionary leaders make with their teams (and how to fix them). First by Five blog. https://firstbyfive.com/5-mistakes-visionary-leaders-make-with-their-teams-and-how-to-fix-them/. Accessed March 10, 2023.

27. Orrock W. Three mistakes visionaries, idealists, and optimists make (and how to avoid them). The 3 Movement blog. https://thev3movement.org/2014/08/07/3-mistakes-visionaries-idealists-and-optimists-make-and-how-to-avoid-them/. Accessed March 20, 2023.

28. Ates NY, Taracki M, Porch JP, van Knippenberg D, & Groenen P. Why visionary leadership fails. *Harvard Business Review.* February 28, 2019. https://hbr.org/2019/02/why-visionary-leadership-fails. Accessed March 10, 2023.

29. Schwartz T. The bad behavior of visionary leaders. *The New York Times,* June 26, 2015. www.nytimes.com/2015/06/27/business/dealbook/the-bad-behavior-of-visionary-leaders.html. Accessed March 10, 2023.

Chapter 4: Management Fads: How to Resist Shiny Object Syndrome

1. Perina K. When the novelty wears off. *Psychology Today* blog, July 3, 2020. www.psychologytoday.com/us/blog/moments-matter/202007/when-the-novelty-wears. Accessed May 19, 2021.

2. Toggl Track. Shiny object syndrome: what entrepreneurs need to know. Toggl Track, January 14, 2019. https://toggl.com/blog/shiny-object-syndrome. Accessed May 18, 2021.

3. James G. 17 management fads almost as dumb as the open-plan office. *Inc.* bog, March 28, 2019. www.inc.com/geoffrey-james/17-management-fads-almost-as-dumb-as-open-plan-office.html. Accessed May 19, 2021

4. Dsouza M. Shiny object syndrome: how to stop chasing different goals. Productive Club blog. https://productiveclub.com/shiny-object-syndrome/. Accessed May 19, 2021

5. Miller D, Hartwick J. Spotting management fads. *Harvard Business Review* blog October 2002. https://hbr.org/2002/10/spotting-management-fads#. Accessed May 18, 2021.

6. Stokes S. How to cure shiny object syndrome. Medium blog, February 27, 2019. https://medium.com/the-business-of-being-happy-and-healthy/how-to-cure-shiny-object-syndrome-c6dc884d3f7. Accessed May 20, 2021.

7. Finkel D. Entrepreneurs may be particularly susceptible to shiny object syndrome: here's how to cure it. *Inc.* blog, January 16, 2020. https://www.inc.com/david-finkel/entrepreneurs-may-be-particularly-susceptible-to-shiny-object-syndrome-heres-how-to-cure-it.html. Accessed May 20, 2021.

8. Shaw D. The cure for shiny object syndrome. Douglas Shaw & Associates blog, January 11, 2015. www.douglasshaw.com/the-cure-for-shiny-object-syndrome/. Accessed May 20, 2021.

9. Butcher S. Is shiny object syndrome sabotaging your success? Calmpreneur blog. https://calmpreneur.com/shiny-object-syndrome-sabotaging-success/. Accessed May 20, 2021.

10. Fingerprint for Success. 6 simple tips to overcome 'shiny object syndrome.' Fingerprint for Success blog. www.fingerprintforsuccess.com/blog/shiny-object-syndrome. Accessed May 20, 2021.

11. The Highlands Company. What to do about a boss with shiny object syndrome? The Highlands Company blog, May 23, 2017. www.highlandsco.com/boss-shiny-object-syndrome/. Accessed May 24, 2021.

12. Kislik L. What to do if your boss gets distracted by every new thing? *Harvard Business Review* blog. November 20, 2017. https://hbr.org/2017/11/what-to-do-if-your-boss-gets-distracted-by-every-new-thing. Accessed May 24, 2021.

13. Sakas K. "Too much" initiative: what to do when your employee keeps burying you in bright ideas? Sakas and Company blog, January 6, 2014. https://sakasandcompany.com/too-much-initiative/. Accessed May 24, 2021.

14. Sid S. Entrepreneurs, save yourself from shiny object syndrome and stay productive. 101 Productivity blog, April 2, 2020. https://101productivity.com/save-yourself-from-the-shiny-object-syndrome/. Accessed May 25, 2021.

15. *Entrepreneur*. Do you have 'shiny object' syndrome? *Entrepreneur* blog. February 9, 2017. www.entrepreneur.com/article/288370. Accessed May 25, 2021

Chapter 5: Managing the Isolation and Loneliness of Leadership

1. Edmonson R. Seven pitfalls of leadership. *RE blog,* January 10, 2013. http://www.ronedmondson.com/2013/01/7-pitfalls-of-leadership.html. Accessed November 23, 2015.

2. Blom R. Nine healthy ways to deal with leadership loneliness. ChurchLeaders blog. www.churchleaders.com/youth/youth-leaders-articles/158376-9-healthy-ways-to-deal-with-leadership-loneliness.html. Accessed November 24, 2015.

3. Thinking Partners, Inc. Exceptional leaders . . . exhibit self control. Thinking Partners, Inc. blog. www.leadershipmasterymap.com/ExhibitSelfControl_000.htm. Accessed November 23, 2015.

4. Nelson S. Guest post: there's a reason it's lonely at the top. *Psychology Today* blog, March 4, 2011. www.psychologytoday.com/blog/the-friendship-doctor/201103/guest-post-there-s-reason-it-s-lonely-the-top. Accessed November 22, 2015.

5. *Psychology Today.* The dangers of loneliness. *Psychology Today* blog, July 1, 2003. www.psychologytoday.com/articles/200307/the-dangers-loneliness. Accessed November 23, 2015.

6. Weintraub K. Dangers of loneliness. *Boston Globe* blog, April 24, 2015. www.bostonglobe.com/lifestyle/2015/04/24/loneliness/WMyewgKBU5cBjVnbkH9bVK/story.html. Accessed November 24, 2015.

7. Hedges K. Do you feel lonely as a leader? Study says you're not alone. *Forbes* blog, February 23, 2012. www.forbes.com/sites/work-in-progress/2012/02/23/if-mark-zuckerberg-is-lonely-heres-my-solution/. Accessed November 23, 2015.

8. Luna A. 17 habits of the self-destructive person. LonerWolf. http://lonerwolf.com/self-destructive-person/. Accessed December 1, 2015.

9. Hall K. Accepting loneliness. *Psychology Today* blog, January 13, 2013. www.psychologytoday.com/blog/pieces-mind/201301/accepting-loneliness. Accessed November 27, 2015.

10. George B. Psychology today: overcoming the loneliness of leadership. Bill George blog, October 30, 2015. www.billgeorge.org/page/psychology-today-overcoming-the-loneliness-of-leadership. Accessed November 28, 2015.

11. Brown B. The power of vulnerability. TED, June 2010. www.ted.com/talks/brene_brown_on_vulnerability?language=en#t-745230. Accessed November 28, 2015.

12. Rokach A. Leadership and loneliness. *International Journal of Leadership and Change*, 2014;2(1): 6:46-58. http://digitalcommons.wku.edu/cgi/viewcontent.cgi?article=1014&context=ijlc. Accessed November 30, 2015.

13. Lomenick B. 10 reasons leaders need a confidant. *Ministry Today*, November 20, 2013. http://ministrytodaymag.com/leadership/pastoral-care/20510-10-reasons-why-leaders-need-a-confidant. Accessed November 30, 2015.

14. Kearns K. Top 7 ways to combat being lonely at the top. Christopher M. Knight's Top 7 Business, November 23, 2005. http://top7business.com/?Top-7-Ways-to-Combat-Being-Lonely-at-The-Top&id=1199. Accessed December 1, 2015.

15. Korkki P. Building a bridge to a lonely colleague. *The New York Times*, January 28, 2012. www.nytimes.com/2012/01/29/jobs/building-a-bridge-to-a-lonely-colleague-workstation.html. Accessed December 1, 2015.

Chapter 6: Developing a Thicker Skin as a Leader

1. Ma L. The thick skinned: it's not all about you, so stop picking on yourself. *Psychology Today blog*, June 9, 2016. www.psychologytoday.com/us/articles/200409/the-thick-skinned. Accessed July 22, 2019.

2. Licht A. Seven ways to develop a thick skin in the office. *Forbes* blog, May 4, 2017. https://www.forbes.com/sites/alizalicht/2017/05/04/7-ways-to-develop-a-thick-skin-in-the-office/ Accessed July 22, 2019.

3. Hughes AJ. The secret to developing thicker skin. M: Mission Originals blog, July 25, 2018. https://medium.com/the-mission/the-secret-to-developing-thick-skin-a6151c33ceb1. Accessed July 23, 2019.

4. Weingarten R. How to develop a thicker skin at work without being obnoxious. Ladders blog, January 1, 2019. www.theladders.com/career-advice/how-to-develop-a-thicker-skin-at-work-without-being-obnoxious. Accessed July 26, 2019.

5. Hendrickson E. How to grow a thick skin and handle criticism. Quick and Dirty Tips blog, January 21, 2016. www.quickanddirtytips.com/health-fitness/mental-health/how-to-grow-a-thick-skin-and-handle-criticism. Accessed July 26, 2019.

6. Dinwiddie M. Dealing with criticism: 5 tools to develop thick skin. Tiny Buddha blog. https://tinybuddha.com/blog/dealing-criticism-5-tools-develop-thick-skin/. Accessed July 29, 2019.

7. Young SH. How to develop a thicker skin. Scott H. Young blog. October 2008. www.scotthyoung.com/blog/2008/10/20/how-to-develop-a-thicker-skin/. Accessed July 29, 2019.

8. Brenner G. It's not personal. Dr. Gail Brenner blog, September 10, 2013. https://gailbrenner.com/2013/09/its-not-personal/. Accessed July 26, 2019.

9. Awosika A. How to develop obnoxiously thick skin: 10 tips for facing your fear of criticism and social rejection. Ayo the Writer blog, January 12, 2016. https://byrslf.co/how-to-develop-obnoxiously-thick-skin-10-tips-for-facing-your-fear-of-criticism-and-social-dabe32a23163. Accessed July 25, 2019.

Chapter 7: Telling Stories to Lead, Teach, Influence, and Inspire

1. Fryer B. Storytelling that moves people. *Harvard Business Review*, June 2003. https://hbr.org/2003/06/storytelling-that-moves-people. Accessed January 23, 2021.

2. Hazell C. Leading through story: how great business leaders use narrative to inspire and lead others. Point Loma Nazarene University blog. www.pointloma.edu/resources/business-leadership/leading-through-story-how-great-business-leaders-use-narrative. Accessed January 24, 2021.

3. Byrne D. Steve Jobs' lesson about storytelling. Pulse/LinkedIn blog. July 31, 2020. www.linkedin.com/pulse/steve-jobs-lesson-storytelling-dave-byrne/?articleId=6694940202449956864. Accessed January 25, 2021.

4. American Society of Administrative Professionals (ASAP). Learn what makes stories so powerful—and meet three powerful storytellers. ASAP blog, March 1, 2019. www.asaporg.com/what-makes-stories-so-powerful. Accessed January 25, 2021.

5. Smith P. The leader as storyteller: 10 reasons it makes a better business connection. TLNT blog, September 12, 2012. https://www.tlnt.com/the-leader-as-storyteller-10-reasons-it-makes-a-better-business-connection/. Accessed January 25, 2021.

6. Boris V. What makes storytelling so effective for learning? Harvard Business Publishing Corporate Learning, December 20, 2017. www.harvardbusiness.org/what-makes-storytelling-so-effective-for-learning/. Accessed January 25, 2021

7. Smith P. *Lead with a Story: A Guide to Crafting Business Narratives that Captivate, Convince, and Inspire.* AMACOM; 2012.

8. Yellis N. Why stories: 10 characteristics of effective stories. Leadership Institute blog, July 10, 2014. www.leadershipinstitute.org/news/?NR=10570. Accessed January 25, 2021.

9. BB & Co. Strategic Storytelling. Lessons from Lincoln on how to persuade with storytelling. BB & Co. blog, February 1, 2013. https://bbcostorytelling.com/blog/lessons-from-lincoln-on-how-to-persuade-with-storytelling/. Accessed January 26, 2021.

10. Choy E. Why is leadership storytelling so powerful? Leadership Story Lab blog, February 14, 2020. www.leadershipstorylab.com/why-is-leadership-storytelling-so-powerful/. Accessed January 27, 2021

11. Thompson S. Storytelling for leaders: craft stories that matter. Virtual Speech blog, November 9, 2017. https://virtualspeech.com/blog/storytelling-for-leaders-craft-stories-that-matter. Accessed January 26, 2021.

12. Shattuck R. Why it's important for great leaders to tell great stories. *Forbes* blog, September 26, 2017. www.forbes.com/sites/forbesagencycouncil/2017/09/26/why-its-important-for-great-leaders-to-tell-great-stories/?sh=6afa447b6f99. Accessed January 27, 2021.

13. Choy E. Don't overlook key leadership storytelling moments. Leadership Story Lab blog, December 8, 2019. www.leadershipstorylab.com/don-t-overlook-these-key-leadership-storytelling-moments/. Accessed January 27, 2021.

14. Kipman S. 15 highly successful people who failed on their way to success. Life Hack blog, January 20, 2021. www.lifehack.org/articles/productivity/15-highly-successful-people-who-failed-their-way-success.html. Accessed January 27, 2021.

15. Grossman D. Share stories to connect with employees. The Grossman Group blog, January 29, 2020. www.yourthoughtpartner.com/blog/share-stories-to-connect-with-employees. Accessed January 27, 2021.

16. Denning S. *The Leader's Guide to Storytelling: Mastering the Art and Discipline of Business Narrative.* Jossey-Bass; 2011.

17. Peck S. 11 ways to improve your business and personal storytelling. One Month blog, July 12, 2019. https://learn.onemonth.com/11-ways-to-improve-your-business-and-personal-storytelling/. Accessed January 28, 2021.

18. Biesenbach R. 10 fatal mistakes storytellers make. Biesenblog. https://robbiesenbach.com/10-fatal-mistakes-storytellers-make/. Accessed January 28, 2021.

Chapter 8: Healthcare Leadership for Introverts

1. Berkun S & Ho L. Interview with Scott Berkun. Lifehack. www.lifehack.org/articles/lifehack/interview-with-scott-berkun.html. Accessed March 24, 2022.

2. Cain S. *Quiet: The Power of Introverts in a World that Can't Stop Talking.* New York: Crown Publishers; 2012.

3. Monych B. The surprising reasons why introverts make exceptional leaders. Insperity blog. www.insperity.com/blog/the-surprising-reasons-why-introverts-make-exceptional-leaders/. Accessed March 21, 2022.

4. Harvard Division of Continuing Education. Introverts as leaders: quiet power as a leadership strength. Professional Development Program. https://professional.dce.harvard.edu/programs/introverts-as-leaders-quiet-power-as-a-leadership-strength/#outcomes. Accessed March 21, 2022.

5. Rampton J. 23 of the most amazingly successful introverts in history. *Inc.* blog, July 20, 2015. www.inc.com/hannah-hall/radio-flyer-hero-wagon-design-innovation.html. Accessed March 21, 2022.

6. Kahlweiler JB. *The Introverted Leader: Building on Your Quiet Strength.* 2nd ed. Oakland, CA: Berrett-Kohler Publishers; 2018.

7. Belknap T. *Leadership for Introverts: The Power of Quiet Influence.* Takoma, WA: Port Bell; 2018.

8. Inam H. The good news for introverted leaders. *Forbes* blog. April 15, 2018. www.forbes.com/sites/hennainam/2018/04/15/the-good-news-for-introverted-leaders/?sh=160a244c192f. Accessed March 22, 2022.

9. Ellis RR. Introvert personality. WebMD, June 24, 2020. www.webmd.com/balance/introvert-personality-overview. Accessed March 22, 2022.

10. Miller B. 7 reasons why introverts make great leaders. About Leaders blog. https://aboutleaders.com/introverts-great-leaders/. Accessed March 24, 2022.

11. Wakowski A. 4 weaknesses introverted leaders can turn into strengths. Healthline blog. https://aboutleaders.com/introverted-leaders/. Accessed March 25, 2022.

12. Cornes J. The strengths and weaknesses of being an introvert. Jason Cornes blogs. www.jasoncornes.co.uk/blog/the-strengths-and-weaknesses-of-being-an-introvert. Accessed March 28, 2022.

13. Elkins K. 7 disadvantages of being an introvert. Insider blog, May 7, 2015. www.businessinsider.com/disadvantages-of-being-an-introvert-2015-5. Accessed March 25, 2022.

14. Crockett Z. 65% of execs think introverts are bad leaders. Here's why that's BS. Hustle blog, May 16, 2022. https://thehustle.co/65-of-execs-think-introverts-are-bad-leaders-heres-why-thats-bs/. Accessed March 28, 2021.

15. Tekeli C, Miller-Merril J, Lederman M, Garnett L, Guthrie L, Forbes Coaches Council. 12 challenges introverted leaders face and how to overcome them. Forbes Coaches Council. https://www.forbes.com/sites/forbescoachescouncil/2016/03/08/12-challenges-introverted-leaders-face-and-how-to-overcome-them/?sh=352739cf57bb. Accessed March 28, 2022.

16. Ma S. How I've used these 4 "flaws" to my advantage as an introverted leader. Fast Company blog, September 6, 2018. www.fastcompany.com/90232320/how-ive-used-these-4-flaws-to-my-advantage-as-an-introverted-leader. Accessed March 28, 2022.

17. Markow J. Nine tips to help introverted leaders succeed in the workplace. Forbes Coaches Council. www.forbes.com/sites/forbescoachescouncil/2018/03/02/nine-tips-to-help-introverted-leaders-succeed-in-the-workplace/?sh=30d145a24300. Accessed March 28, 2022.

18. Friedman S. 10 survival tips for introverted leaders. Introvert, Dear blog, May 7, 2021. https://introvertdear.com/news/10-survival-tips-for-introverted-leaders/. Accessed March 28, 2022.

19. Maguire A. How to start an affinity group at work, according to real people who did it. The Muse blog www.themuse.com/advice/how-to-start-an-employee-resource-affinity-group-in-the-workplace. Accessed March 29, 2022.

20. Bainbridge C. The difference between being shy and introverted. Very Well Family blog, February 25, 2021. www.verywellfamily.com/the-difference-between-being-shy-and-being-introverted-1448616. Accessed March 22, 2022.

21. Curtin M. Are you shy or are you introverted? Science says this is the difference between them. *Inc.* blog, May 31, 2018. www.inc.com/melanie-curtin/are-you-shy-or-introverted-science-says-this-is-1-primary-difference.html. Accessed March 22, 2022.

22. Healthline. What you should know about shyness. Healthline blog. www.healthline.com/health/shyness#signs. Accessed March 26, 2022.

Chapter 9: The Pros and Cons of Transparency in Healthcare Leadership

1. Clarke S. Importance of transparent leadership. Leaderonomics blog, May 23, 2020. www.leaderonomics.com/articles/leadership/importance-of-transparent-leadership. Accessed July 13, 2022.

2. Welch J. *Winning.* New York: HarperCollins; 2005.

3. Iste C. Do leaders need to be transparent? Multi Briefs blog, July 5, 2017. https://exclusive.multibriefs.com/content/do-leaders-need-to-be-transparent/business-management-services-risk-management. Accessed July 20, 2022.

4. Birkinshaw J & Cable D. The dark side of transparency. *McKinsey Quarterly*, February 1, 2017. www.mckinsey.com/business-functions/people-and-organizational-performance/our-insights/the-dark-side-of-transparency. Accessed July 13, 2022.

5. Sugiarto HA. Pros and cons of transparency in the workplace. Rock Paper Scissors blog, November 2019. https://learn.rps.asia/pros-and-cons-of-transparency-in-the-workplace/. Accessed July 13, 2022.

6. Perucci D. The importance of transparency in leadership – what you need to know. Bamboo HR blog, January 23, 2020. www.bamboohr.com/blog/importance-of-transparency-in-leadership. Accessed July 19, 2022.

7. Caucci S. Transparency in leadership: why it's so important. 1Huddle blog, October 4, 2021. https://1huddle.co/blog/transparency-in-leadership/. Accessed July 18, 2022.

8. Liopis G. 5 powerful things that happen when a leader is transparent. *Forbes*, September 10, 2012. www.forbes.com/sites/glennllopis/2012/09/10/5-powerful-things-happen-when-a-leader-is-transparent/. Accessed July 18, 2022.

9. Ahmed T. Why new CEOs should practice transparent leadership. Vantage Circle blog, March 1, 2022. https://blog.vantagecircle.com/transparent-leadership/. Accessed July 18, 2022.

10. Dames K. 6 ways to become a more transparent leader. *People Development Magazine*, October 27, 2021. https://peopledevelopmentmagazine.com/2021/10/27/transparent-leader/. Accessed July 18, 2022.

11. Ellwood C. Building trust through transparency. The Myers-Briggs Company blog, March 25, 2020. www.themyersbriggs.com/en-US/Connect-with-us/Blog/2020/March/Trust-and-Transparency. Accessed July 19, 2022.

12. NeuroLeadership Institute. Why transparency is the secret to improving employee experience. Neuroleadership blog. October 26, 2018. https://neuroleadership.com/your-brain-at-work/transparency-secret-employee-experience. Accessed August 26, 2024.

13. Coleman J. Is there such a thing as too much transparency? Fast Company blog, June 19, 2012. www.fastcompany.com/1840647/there-such-thing-too-much-transparency. Accessed July 25, 2022.

14. Harrington S. You can't build trust through transparency. The People Space blog. November 14, 2018, www.thepeoplespace.com/ideas/articles/you-cant-build-trust-through-transparency. Accessed July 25, 2022.

15. Bernstein E. The transparency trap. *Harvard Business Review*, October 2014. https://hbr.org/2014/10/the-transparency-trap. Accessed July 25, 2022.

16. Botsman R. *Who Can You Trust? How Technology Brought Us Together and Why It May Drive Us Apart*. New York: Hachette Book Group; 2018.

17. Jouany V & Martic K. How does information overload affect your business and how to stop it. Haiilo blog. https://haiilo.com/blog/how-does-information-overload-affect-your-business-how-to-stop-it/. Accessed July 25, 2022.

18. Executive Velocity. Does your leadership fear transparency? Executive Velocity blog, https://executive-velocity.com/does-your-leadership-fear-transparency/. Accessed July 26, 2022.

19. Bennett M. Are you a transparent leader? Niagara Institute blog, March 16, 2022. https://www.niagarainstitute.com/blog/transparent-leader. Accessed July 25, 2022.

20. Advanced Resources. Transparency in leadership. Advanced Resources blog, July 7, 2020. https://blog.advancedresources.com/the-importance-of-transparency-in-leadership. Accessed July 27, 2022.

21. Nevogt D. How to be a transparent leader (and why). Hubstaff blog, October 29, 2020. https://blog.hubstaff.com/transparent-leader/. Accessed July 27, 2022.

22. Youshael J. 3 ways to be a more transparent leader. *Forbes*, November 19, 2021. www.forbes.com/sites/jonyoushaei/2021/11/19/3-ways-to-be-a-more-transparent-leader/. Accessed July 22, 2022.

23. Klass T. Can a leader be too transparent? Terri Klass Consulting blog, January 30, 2022. www.terriklassconsulting.com/2022/01/30/can-a-leader-be-too-transparent/. Accessed July 26, 2022.

24. Paterson K. The risk of being the bearer of bad news. Leader's Edge blog, October 30, 2020. www.leadersedge.com/brokerage-ops/the-risk-of-being-the-bearer-of-bad-news. Accessed July 26, 2022.

Chapter 10: The Challenge of Being a Positive Role Model for Your Employees

1. Miller JV. Leaders as role models—what the research tells us. People Equation blog, September 28, 2021. https://people-equation.com/leaders-as-role-models-research/. Accessed September 15, 2022.

2. Ready Training Online. 6 traits of an effective role model. Ready Training Online blog. https://readytrainingonline.com/articles/effective-role-model-traits/. Accessed September 22, 2022.

3. Ingram D. Behavior modeling in the workplace. *Chron* blog, April 24, 2019. https://smallbusiness.chron.com/behavior-modeling-workplace-10980.html. Accessed September 22, 2022.

4. Pangelinan DR. The problem with leading by example. Vunela blog, August 20, 2017. https://magazine.vunela.com/the-problem-with-leading-by-example-e87fbc803d2c. Accessed September 19, 2022.

5. Blanchard K. 7 common reactions to change and how to react to them. Ken Blanchard Linkedin blog, March 12, 2020. www.linkedin.com/pulse/7-common-reactions-change-how-respond-them-ken-blanchard. Accessed September 15, 2022.

6. Cancel D. The three types of role models everyone needs in their career. *Forbes,* January 2, 2019. www.forbes.com/sites/forbesbostoncouncil/2019/01/02/the-three-types-of-role-models-everyone-needs-in-their-career/. Accessed September 16, 2022.

7. Latson A. When employees disappoint; how effective leaders respond. Latson Leadership Group blog, November 4, 2014. www.latsonleadershipgroup.com/employees-disappoint-effective-leaders-respond/. Accessed September 20, 2022.

8. Tu M-H, Bono JE, Schum C, Montagne L. Breaking the cycle: the effects of role model performance and ideal leadership self-concepts on abusive supervision spillover. *J Appl Psychol.* 2018;103:689-702. https://digitalscholarship.unlv.edu/cgi/viewcontent.cgi?article=1193&context=hotel_fac_articles. Accessed September 21, 2022.

9. Porath C & Porath M. How to thrive when everything feels terrible. *Harvard Business Review*, October 30, 2020. https://hbr.org/2020/10/how-to-thrive-when-everything-feels-terrible. Accessed September 21, 2022.

10. Folkman J. How to spot and eliminate poor role models in your organization. *Forbes,* April 28, 2021. www.forbes.com/sites/joefolkman/2021/04/28/how-to-spot-and-eliminate-poor-role-models-in-your-organization/. Accessed September 21, 2022.

11. Csizik T. What to do when leadership role modeling fails? Symblify blog. www.symblify.net/magazine/what-to-do-when-leadership-role-modeling-fails/. Accessed September 22, 2022.

12. Krach K. What is the most counterintuitive leadership superpower? Never look too good or talk too smart. *Forbes,* November 19, 2018. www.forbes.com/sites/keithkrach/2018/11/19/what-is-the-most-counterintuitive-leadership-superpower-never-look-too-good-or-talk-too-smart/. Accessed September 22, 2022.

13. Blount J. Leaders are always on stage. Jeb Blount's LinkedIn blog, January 30, 2019. www.linkedin.com/pulse/leaders-always-stage-jeb-blount. Accessed September 23, 2022.

14. Lykken D. Quiet time: leadership and rejuvenation. National Mortgage Professional blog, January 20, 2015. https://nationalmortgageprofessional.com/blog/quiet-time-leadership-and-rejuvenation. Accessed September 26, 2022.

15. Preston C. "Take a vacation": Three words all leaders need to embrace in the workplace. Fast Company blog, July 11, 2022. www.fastcompany.com/90765794/take-a-vacation-three-words-all-leaders-need-to-embrace-in-the-workplace. Accessed September 26, 2022.

16. Edelman MW. You can't be what you can't see. Children's Defense Fund blog, August 21, 2015. www.childrensdefense.org/child-watch-columns/health/2015/its-hard-to-be-what-you-cant-see/. Accessed September 26, 2022.

17. Bastian R. The power of representation in leadership roles. *Forbes,* November 9, 2020. www.forbes.com/sites/rebekahbastian/2020/11/09/the-power-of-representation-in-leadership-roles/. Accessed September 26, 2022.

18. Busch M. How to find role models when you don't see any around you. May Busch blog, https://maybusch.com/find-role-models/. Accessed September 26, 2022.

19. Hills L. *Lasting Female Educational Leadership: Leadership Legacies of Women Leaders.* New York: Springer, 2013.

Chapter 11: Leading Your Healthcare Organization with Charisma

1. Antonakis J, Fenley M, & Liechti S. Learning charisma. *Harvard Business Review,* June 2012. https://hbr.org/2012/06/learning-charisma-2. Accessed November 14, 2022.

2. Potosyan M. Is charisma a gift—or can it be trained? *Psychology Today,* February 22, 2019. www.psychologytoday.com/us/blog/between-cultures/201902/is-charisma-gift-or-can-it-be-trained. Accessed November 14, 2022.

3. Mattone J. Is charisma a learned leadership skill? John Mattone Global blog, January 25, 2018. https://johnmattone.com/blog/is-charisma-a-learned-leadership-skill/. Accessed November 14, 2022.

4. Lyon A. Charismatic leadership theory. YouTube video, February 8, 2021. www.youtube.com/watch?v=kI5va5ptQgM. Accessed November 15, 2022.

5. Flora C. The X-factors of success: the mysterious qualities that make people shine. *Psychology Today.* www.psychologytoday.com/us/articles/200505/the-x-factors-success. Accessed November 15, 2022.

6. Northouse PG. *Leadership Theory and Practice,* 9th ed. Thousand Oaks, CA: SAGE Publications; 2022.

7. Status Net. Charismatic leadership: the good, the bad, and best practices. Status.net blog. https://status.net/articles/charismatic-leadership/. Accessed November 16, 2022.

8. Western Governors University What is charismatic leadership? WGU blog, March 23, 2021. www.wgu.edu/blog/charismatic-leadership2103.html#close. Accessed November 16, 2022.

9. Miller K. Charismatic leadership style advantages, disadvantages and characteristics. Future of Working blog. https://futureofworking.com/charismatic-leadership-style-advantages-disadvantages-and-characteristics/. Accessed November 16, 2022.

10. Hills L. Telling stories to lead, influence, teach, and inspire. *J Med Pract Manage.* 2021;36: 305-311.

11. Barot H. 8 essential tips on voice modulation and tonality. Frantically Speaking blog. https://franticallyspeaking.com/8-essential-tips-on-voice-modulation-and-tonality/. Accessed November 18, 2022.

12. Cuddy AJC, Kohut M, & Neffinger J. Connect, then lead. *Harvard Business Review.* https://hbr.org/2013/07/connect-then-lead. Accessed November 18, 2022.

13. Hills L. *They'll eat out of your hand if you know what to feed them: the 30 essential communication skills that give highly successful career professionals their edge.* Fairfax, Virginia: Blue Pencil Institute; 2014.

14. Graham AR. Dark side of charismatic leadership. Penn State Leadership PSYCH 485 blog, November 15, 2015. https://sites.psu.edu/leadership/2015/11/15/dark-side-of-charismatic-leadership/. Accessed November 21, 2022.

Chapter 12: Why and How to Become a More Resilient Leader

1. Gleeson B. Resilience in leadership: how to change and win despite obstacles. *Forbes.* April 13, 2021. www.forbes.com/sites/brentgleeson/2021/04/13/resilience-in-leadership-how-to-lead-and-win-despite-change-and-obstacles/. Accessed December 8, 2022.

2. Gair J. How to lead by modeling resilience. LinkedIn blog, June 16, 2020. www.linkedin.com/pulse/how-lead-modelling-resilience-work-janice-gair-pcc-cphr-shrm-scp. Accessed December 8, 2022.

3. Folkman J. New research: 7 ways to become a more resilient leader. *Forbes.* April 6, 2017. www.forbes.com/sites/joefolkman/2017/04/06/new-research-7-ways-to-become-a-more-resilient-leader/. Accessed December 8, 2022.

4. Southwick FS, Martini BL, Charney DS, Southwick SM. Leadership and resilience. In: Marques J, Dhiman S (eds.) *Leadership Today.* Springer; 2017:315-333.

5. American Psychological Association. Resilience. APA website. www.apa.org/topics/resilience. Accessed December 13, 2022.

6. Kohlrieser G, Orlick AL, Perrinjaquet M, Rossi RL. Resilient leadership: navigating the pressures of modern working life. IMD blog, February 2015. www.imd.org/research-knowledge/articles/resilient-leadership-navigating-the-pressures-of-modern-working-life/. Accessed December 13, 2022.

7. Peterson C, Seligman MEP. *Character, Strengths, and Virtues: A Handbook and Classification.* New York: Oxford University Press; 2004. Washington, DC, American Psychological Association.

8. Gavin M. How to become a more resilient leader. Harvard Business School blog, December 17, 2019. https://online.hbs.edu/blog/post/resilient-leadership. Accessed December 14, 2022.

9. Spillane J. 10 ways to become a more resilient leader. Business 2 Community blog, December 20, 2019. www.business2community.com/leadership/10-ways-to-become-a-more-resilient-leader-02270379. Accessed December 16, 2022.

10. Dohaney J, de Róiste M, Salmon RA, Sutherland K. Benefits, barriers, and incentives for improved resilience to disruption in university teaching. Int J Disaster Risk Reduct. 2020

Nov; 50: 101691. Published online 2020 May 29. www.ncbi.nlm.nih.gov/pmc/articles/
PMC7256496/. doi: 10.1016/j.ijdrr.2020.101691. Accessed December 20, 2022.

11. Suarez FF, Montes JS. Building organizational resilience. *Harvard Business Review,* November-December 2020. https://hbr.org/2020/11/building-organizational-resilience. Accessed December 21, 2022.

12. Overby S. Change management: 9 ways to build resilient teams. The Enterprisers Project blog, November 16, 2021. https://enterprisersproject.com/article/2021/11/change-management-9-ways-build-resilient-teams. Accessed December 21, 2022.

13. Ferrazzi K, Race M-C, Vincent A. 7 strategies to build more resilient teams. *Harvard Business Review,* January 21, 2021. https://hbr.org/2021/01/7-strategies-to-build-a-more-resilient-team. Accessed December 21, 2022.

Chapter13: Developing and Using Your Core Leadership Values

1. Steinhorst C. Rethinking the value of core values. *Forbes.* October 17, 2019. www.forbes.com/sites/curtsteinhorst/2019/10/17/rethinking-the-value-of-core-values/. Accessed May 9, 2023.

2. Gamb M. *Values-based Leadership for Dummies.* Hoboken, NJ: John Wiley & Sons, 2018.

3. Falcone P. Values-based leadership in action. SHRM blog. June 9, 2022. www.shrm.org/resourcesandtools/hr-topics/employee-relations/pages/values-based-leadership-in-action.aspx. Accessed May 10, 2023.

4. Gleeson B. 5 attributes (and benefits) of values-based leadership. *Forbes.* July 19, 2021. www.forbes.com/sites/brentgleeson/2021/07/19/5-attributes-and-benefits-of-values-based-leadership/. Accessed May 10, 2023.

5. Kraemer HM Jr. *From Values to Action: the Four Principles of Values-Based Leadership.* San Francisco: Jossey-Bass, 2011.

6. Kouses JM, Posner BZ. *The Leadership Challenge: How to Make Extraordinary Things Happen in Organizations,* 7th edition. Hoboken, NJ: John Wiley & Sons, 2023.

7. Copeland MK. The emerging significance of values-based leadership: a literature review. *International Journal of Leadership Studies.* 2014;8(2). www.regent.edu/journal/international-journal-of-leadership-studies/significance-of-values-based-leadership/. Accessed May 10, 2023.

8. Olli-Pekka V. Intra-organizational challenges of values-based leadership. *Electronic Journal of Business Ethics and Organization Studies (EJBO).* 2009;14(2). http://ejbo.jyu.fi/pdf/ejbo_vol14_no2_pages_6-13.pdf. Accessed May 15, 2023.

9. Androscoggin Bank. Putting values first: what it means to be a values-based leader. Androscoggin Bank blog. www.androscogginbank.com/blog/leadership/putting-values-first-what-it-means-to-be-a-values-based-leader/. Accessed May 11, 2023.

10. Ralph P. The benefits of values-based leadership. The Leadership Sphere blog. August 3, 2022. https://theleadershipsphere.com.au/insights/the-benefits-of-values-based-leadership/. Accessed May 11, 2023.

11. Wambi. Why are company values important for healthcare organizations? WAMBI blog. October 11, 2022. https://wambi.org/blog/why-are-company-values-important-for-healthcare-organizations/. Accessed May 16, 2023.

12. Baskin E. Ask employees to define your corporate values. *Forbes.* March 24, 2022. www.forbes.com/sites/forbescommunicationscouncil/2022/03/24/ask-employees-to-define-your-corporate-values/. Accessed May 16, 2023.

13. Enochson H. What are core values? 40 core values examples to consider. On Strategy blog. https://onstrategyhq.com/resources/core-values/. Accessed May 24, 2023.

14. Boston Medical Center. Values. Boston Medical Center website. www.bmc.org/mission. Accessed May 24, 2023.

15. Indeed Editorial Team. How to write a value statement (with template and example). Indeed blog. June 24, 2022. www.indeed.com/career-advice/career-development/how-to-write-value-statement. Accessed May 24, 2023.

16. Under Armour. Mission, vision, and values. Under Armour website. https://about.underarmour.com/en/Purpose/Mission-Vision-Values.html. Accessed May 24, 2023.

17. Graber DR, Kirkpatrick AO. Establishing values-based leadership and value systems in healthcare organizations. *J Health Hum Serv Adm.* 2008;31(2):179-197, 2008. www.jstor.org/stable/41288084. Accessed May 15, 2023

18. Kraemer HM Jr. *From values to action: the four principles of values-based leadership.* San Francisco: Jossey-Bass, 2011.

19. Hook B. A guide to values-based decision making. Values Institute blog. Last modified March 12, 2023. https://values.institute/a-guide-to-values-based-decision-making/. Accessed May 24, 2023.

20. Patry M. Values, finding your North Star. LinkedIn blog. October 23, 2019. https://iteffectivity.com/blog-1/2019/10/22/values-finding-your-north-star/. Accessed May 24, 2023.

21. Mayo Clinic. About Mayo Clinic: Mayo Clinic mission and values. Mayo Clinic website. www.mayoclinic.org/about-mayo-clinic/mission-values. Accessed May 16, 2023.

22. Johns Hopkins Medicine. Johns Hopkins mission, vision and values: our core values. Johns Hopkins Medicine website. www.hopkinsmedicine.org/about/mission.html. Accessed May 16, 2023.

23. Cleveland Clinic. Mission, vision and values. Cleveland Clinic website. https://my.cleveland clinic.org/about/overview/who-we-are/mission-vision-values. Accessed May 16, 2023.

24. Northwestern Medicine. Our mission, vision, and core values. Northwestern Medicine website. www.nm.org/about-us. Accessed May 16, 2023.

25. Ascension Medical Group. Our mission and values. Ascension website. https://about.ascension.org/en/our-work/ascension-medical-group-our-mission-values. Accessed May 16, 2023.

26. Seattle Children's Hospital. Our mission, vision and values. Seattle Children's Hospital website. www.seattlechildrens.org/about/mission-vision-values/. Accessed May 24, 2023.

Chapter 14: Overcoming Impostor Syndrome in Healthcare Leadership

1. Rihanna. Rihanna's tips for confidence. YouTube shorts. www.youtube.com/shorts/d3kp3 eMcBco. Accessed September 13, 2023.

2. Ibottson A. R.I.P. "fake it till you make it." *Wisdom You Didn't Ask For* video series. www.youtube.com/watch?v=CQz8VtiUrJY&list=PLIycDTbdCaGs3IAIRI6ICrIx8dipQ4Suj&index=2. Accessed September 13, 2023.

3. White A. How imposter syndrome became the new normal. *AOL News.* August 31, 2023. www.aol.com/news/imposter-syndrome-normal-those-don-053000347.html. Accessed September 13, 2023.

4. *Psychology Today*. Imposter syndrome. *Psychology Today* blog. www.psychologytoday.com/us/basics/imposter-syndrome. Accessed September 11, 2023.

5. Kets de Vries MFR. The dangers of feeling like a fake. *Harvard Business Review*, September 2005. https://hbr.org/2005/09/the-dangers-of-feeling-like-a-fake. Accessed September 11, 2023

6. Clance PR, Imes SA. The imposter phenomenon in high achieving women: dynamics and therapeutic intervention. *Psychotherapy: Theory, Research, & Practice*. 1978;15:241-247. http://mpowir.org/wp-content/uploads/2010/02/Download-IP-in-High-Achieving-Women.pdf. https://doi.org/10.1037%2Fh0086006. Accessed September 12, 2023.

7. Langford J, Clance PR. The imposter phenomenon: recent research findings regarding dynamics, personality and family patterns and their implications for treatment. *Psychotherapy*. 1993;30:495-501. https://paulineroseclance.com/pdf/-Langford.pdf. https://doi.org/10.1037/0033-3204.30.3.495. Accessed September 23, 2023

8. Badawy RL, Gazdag BA, Bentley JR, Brouer RL. Are all imposters created equal? Exploring gender differences in the imposter phenomenon-performance link. *Personality and Individual Differences*. 2018;131:156-163. www.sciencedirect.com/science/article/abs/pii/S0191886918302435. https://doi.org/10.1016/j.paid.2018.04.044 . Accessed September 18, 2023

9. Cleveland Clinic. Imposter syndrome: what it is and how to overcome it. *Cleveland Clinic Health Essentials*. April 4, 2022. https://health.clevelandclinic.org/a-psychologist-explains-how-to-deal-with-imposter-syndrome. Accessed September 12, 2023.

10. Charleson K. What is impostor syndrome? *Very Well Health*. August 26, 2023. www.verywellhealth.com/impostor-syndrome-5089237. Accessed September 12, 2023.

11. Mint. What is imposter syndrome and how much does it cost us? *Intuit Mint Life*. July 28, 2022. https://mint.intuit.com/blog/early-career/imposter-syndrome/. Accessed September 13, 2023.

12. Friedman A. Overcoming impostor syndrome as an emerging leader. *Forbes*. September 3, 2020. www.forbes.com/sites/forbescoachescouncil/2020/09/03/overcoming-impostor-syndrome-as-an-emerging-leader/. Accessed September 13, 2023.

13. Belton J. The cost of faking it: impostor syndrome's silent struggle in organizational culture and leadership. *LinkedIn*. September 6, 2023. www.linkedin.com/pulse/cost-faking-impostor-syndromes-silent-struggle-judith-belton-phd/. Accessed September 13, 2023.

14. Benisek A. What is imposter syndrome. *WebMD*. February 15, 2022. www.webmd.com/balance/what-is-imposter-syndrome. Accessed September 18, 2023

15. Cuncic A. Imposter syndrome: why you may feel like a fraud. *Very Well Mind*. May 22, 2023. https://www.verywellmind.com/imposter-syndrome-and-social-anxiety-disorder-4156469. Accessed September 18, 2023.

16. Duszynski-Goodman L. Imposter syndrome: what it is, causes, and how to overcome it. *Forbes*. September 11, 2023. www.forbes.com/health/mind/imposter-syndrome/. Accessed September 28, 2023.

17. Shaikh M. The link between depression and imposter syndrome. Healthy Place blog October 28, 2020. www.healthyplace.com/blogs/workandbipolarordepression/2020/10/the-link-between-depression-and-imposter-syndrome. Accessed September 18, 2023.

18. Lee E. What is the relationship between imposter syndrome and depression? *Clinicians of Color*. August 29, 2021. www.cliniciansofcolor.org/clinician-articles/what-is-the-relationship-between-imposter-syndrome-and-depression/. Accessed September 18, 2023.

19. Gottlieb M, Chung A, Battaglioli N, Sebok-Syer SS, Kalantari A. Impostor syndrome among physicians and physicians in training: a coping review. *Med Educ.* 2020;54:116-124. https://doi.org/10.1111/medu.13956. Accessed September 19, 2023.

20. Edwards-Maddox S. Burnout and imposter phenomenon in nursing and newly licensed registered nurses. *J Clin Nurs.* 2023;32:653-665. https://doi.org/10.1111/jocn.16475. Accessed September 19, 2023.

21. Aubeeluck A, Stacey G, Stupple EJN. Do graduate entry nursing students experience 'imposter phenomenon'?: an issue for debate. *Nurse Education in Practice.* 2016;19:104-106. www.sciencedirect.com/science/article/abs/pii/S1471595316300415. https://doi.org/10.1016/j.nepr.2016.06.003. Accessed September 19, 2023.

22. LaDonna KA, Ginsburg S, Watling C. "Rising to the level of your incompetence": what physicians' self-assessment of their performance reveals about imposter syndrome in medicine. *Acad Med.* 2018;93:763-768. https://doi.org/10.1097/ACM.0000000000002046. Accessed September 19, 2023.

23. Armstrong MJ, Shulman LM. Tackling the imposter phenomenon to advance women in neurology. *Neurology Clinical Practice,* April 2019. First published March 5, 2019. https://cp.neurology.org/content/9/2/155. https://doi.org/10.1212/CPJ.0000000000000607. Accessed September 19, 2023.

24. Moskal E. Physicians experience impostor syndrome more often than other U.S. workers. *Stanford Medicine.* September 15, 2022. https://med.stanford.edu/news/all-news/2022/09/physicians-imposter-syndrome.html. Accessed September 19, 2023.

25. Watt W. Imposter syndrome is common in healthcare—how can you combat it? *Good RX Health.* March 27, 2022. www.goodrx.com/hcp/students/imposter-syndrome-healthcare. Accessed September 19, 2023.

26. Davis M. Impostor syndrome in healthcare professions. *Cummings Graduate Institute for Behavior Health Studies.* September 9, 2019. https://cgi.edu/news/impostor-syndrome-in-healthcare-professions/. Accessed September 19, 2023.

27. Mattone J. What is imposter syndrome in leadership and how can you address it? John Mattone Global blog. May 24, 2022. https://johnmattone.com/blog/what-is-imposter-syndrome-in-leadership-and-how-can-you-address-it/. Accessed September 21, 2023.

28. Cherry H. Leadership when you have imposter syndrome. *Forbes.* February 1, 2021. https://www.forbes.com/sites/womensmedia/2021/02/01/leadership-when-you-have-imposter-syndrome/?sh=20639b227195. Accessed September 21, 2023.

29. Laozi. Laozi quotes about leadership. AZ Quotes. www.azquotes.com/author/19615-Laozi/tag/leadership. Accessed September 21, 2023.

30. Smith DD, Grandey AA. The emotional labor of being a leader. *Harvard Business Review.* November 2, 2022. https://hbr.org/2022/11/the-emotional-labor-of-being-a-leader. Accessed September 21, 2023.

31. Vistage staff. How to deal with imposter syndrome as a new leader. *Vistage.* January 26, 2021. www.vistage.com/research-center/personal-development/20210126-imposter-syndrome/. Accessed September 21, 2023.

32. Von Born J. First-time leaders: here's how you can avoid feeling like a fraud. *Ready Set More.* May 24, 2023. https://readysetmore.com/2023/05/24/first-time-leaders-heres-how-you-can-avoid-feeling-like-a-fraud/. Accessed September 21, 2023.

33. Clance PR. Clance IP Scale. Paulineroseclance.com. https://paulineroseclance.com/pdf/IPTestandscoring.pdf. Accessed September 21, 2023.

34. Manning-Schaffel V. Fake it till you make it: good advice or a setup for failure? *Shondaland.* February 18, 2022. www.shondaland.com/live/money/a39125630/fake-it-till-you-make-it-good-advice-or-a-setup-for-failure/. Accessed September 22, 2023.

35. Bennett J. How to overcome 'impostor syndrome.' *The New York Times.* www.nytimes.com/guides/working-womans-handbook/overcome-impostor-syndrome. Accessed September 22, 2023.

36. Saymeh A. What is imposter syndrome? Definitions, symptoms, and overcoming it. Better Up blog. February 22, 2023. www.betterup.com/blog/what-is-imposter-syndrome-and-how-to-avoid-it. Accessed September 22, 2023.

37. Richards C. Learning to deal with the impostor syndrome. *The New York Times.* October 26, 2015. www.nytimes.com/2015/10/26/your-money/learning-to-deal-with-the-impostor-syndrome.html. Accessed September 12, 2013.

38. BBC News. I still have impostor syndrome. *BBC News.* December 4, 2018. www.bbc.com/news/uk-46434147. Accessed September 12, 2023.

39. Stevenson G. 11 times celebrities have talked about impostor syndrome. *Insider.* April 19, 2023. www.insider.com/celebrities-who-talked-about-having-impostor-syndrome-2023-4. Accessed September 12, 2023.

40. Locke T. Why Barbara Corcoran "felt like an absolute fraud" after selling her business for $66 million. *CNBC Make It.* February 27, 2020. www.cnbc.com/2020/02/27/why-barbara-corcoran-felt-like-a-fraud-after-selling-her-business.html. Accessed September 13, 2023.

41. Leadem. 12 leaders, entrepreneurs, and celebrities who have struggles with impostor syndrome. *Entrepreneur.* November 8, 2017. www.entrepreneur.com/leadership/12-leaders-entrepreneurs-and-celebrities-who-have/304273#3. Accessed September 13, 2023.

42. Allen S. 6 notable people who experienced impostor syndrome. Grammarly blog. July 17, 2017. www.grammarly.com/blog/notable-people-impostor-syndrome/. Accessed September 13, 2023.

43. Kajabi. 10 famous people who deal with impostor syndrome. Kajabi blog. https://kajabi.com/blog/celebrities-with-impostor-syndrome. Accessed September 13, 2023.

44. Ludden J. Sotomayer: 'always looking over my shoulder.' *NPR.* May 26, 2009. www.npr.org/2009/05/26/104538436/sotomayor-always-looking-over-my-shoulder. Accessed September 13, 2023.

45. Woznicki S. Quotes from 9 successful and powerful women with impostor syndrome. Sandy Woznicki blog. July 14, 2020. https://stressandanxietycoach.com/quotes-from-9-successful-and-powerful-women-with-impostor-syndrome/. Accessed September 13, 2023.

46. Davies J. What is imposter syndrome and how to know if you suffer from it. *Learning Mind.* July 24, 2016. https://www.learning-mind.com/imposter-syndrome/. Accessed September 13, 2023.

47. Marie Claire. 16 celebrity quotes on suffering with impostor syndrome. *Marie Claire UK.* November 10, 2015. www.marieclaire.co.uk/entertainment/celebrity-quotes-on-impostor-syndrome-434739. Accessed September 13, 2023.

Chapter 15: Discovering Your Leadership Superpowers and Origin Story

1. Bennett JB. Discovering your leadership superpowers and "origin story" on the journey to becoming an effective leader. Healthcare Financial Management Association blog. August

21, 2019. www.hfma.org/leadership/discovering-your-leadership-superpowers-and-origin-story/. Accessed November 1, 2023.

2. De Zoysa M. Your origin story matters. Life and Leadership. August 30,2021. https://medium.com/life-and-leadership/your-origin-story-matters-2e9a85401a6f. Accessed November 6, 2023.

3. Emmerson S. Why origin stories matter and how to tell yours. Echostories blog. February 22, 2018. www.echostories.com/how-to-tell-origin-story/. Accessed November 1, 2023.

4. Rosenberg R. The psychology behind superhero origin stories: how does following the adventures of Spider Man and Batman inspire us to cope with adversity? Smithsonian Magazine blog. February 2013. www.smithsonianmag.com/arts-culture/the-psychology-behind-superhero-origin-stories-4015776/. Accessed November 2, 2023.

5. Meister A, Zheng W, Caza BB. What's your leadership origin story? *Harvard Business Review.* August 10, 2020. https://hbr.org/2020/08/whats-your-leadership-origin-story. Accessed November 6, 2023.

6. Guber P. The four truths of the storyteller. *Harvard Business Review.* December 2007. https://hbr.org/2007/12/the-four-truths-of-the-storyteller. Accessed November 8, 2023.

7. Choy E. Leadership is hard; crafting origin stories shouldn't be—here's how. *Forbes* blog. August 7, 2018. www.forbes.com/sites/estherchoy/2018/08/07/leadership-is-hard-crafting-origin-stories-shouldnt-be-heres-how/?sh=68aad81b2e78. Accessed November 9, 2023.

8. Lozupone J. Why your origin story matters and how to tell yours. Wishful Doings blog. May 15, 2022. https://wishfuldoings.com/your-origin-story/. Accessed November 8, 2023.

9. Kerr J. How to shape your origin story in a winning way. CEO World blog. June 23, 2021. https://ceoworld.biz/2021/06/23/how-to-shape-your-origin-story-in-a-winning-way/. Accessed November 9, 2023.

10. Stauffer D. Telling our stories: a guide to writing your own story. Next Avenue blog. July 24, 2020. www.nextavenue.org/telling-our-stories-writing-your-own-story/. Accessed November 9, 2023.

11. Laughlin J. Your leadership story: develop it and share it often. Best Practice Institute blog. https://blog.bestpracticeinstitute.org/leadership-story-develop-share-often-leadership-development-innovation/. Accessed November 13, 2023.

12. Henley D. What's your leadership superpower? Forbes blog. July 10, 2022. www.forbes.com/sites/dedehenley/2022/07/10/whats-your-leadership-superpower/?sh=2868a9cc531e. Accessed November 13, 2023.

Chapter 16: Healthcare Leadership in Times of Crisis

1. Laker B. 5 crucial ways to lead during crisis. *Forbes* blog, February 9, 2021. www.forbes.com/sites/benjaminlaker/2021/02/09/5-crucial-ways-to-lead-during-a-crisis/?sh=6092c1ef5e63. Accessed January 3, 2024.

2. Balasubramanian S, Fernandes C. Confirmation of a crisis leadership model and its effectiveness; lessons from the COVID-19 pandemic. *Cogent Business and Management.* 2022;9(1). https://doi.org/10.1080/23311975.2021.2022824. Accessed January 3, 2024.

3. Coombs WT. *Ongoing Crisis Communication: Planning, Managing, and Responding,* 6th ed. Los Angeles: Sage; 2022.

4. Lewis G. *Organizational Crisis Management: The Human Factor.* New York: Auerbach Publications; 2006. https://doi.org/10.1201/9781420013184

5. Harvard Business Essentials. *Crisis Management: Master the Skills to Prevent Disasters.* Boston: Harvard Business School Press; 2004.

6. Abrams Z. Leadership in times of crisis. *Monitor on Psychology.* 2020;51(5):July 1. www.apa.org/monitor/2020/07/leadership-crisis. Accessed January 3, 2024.

7. Firestone S. What is crisis leadership? *Biblical Principles of Crisis Leadership.* May 29, 2020. www.ncbi.nlm.nih.gov/pmc/articles/PMC7254531/#CR2. Accessed January 3, 2024.

8. Ulmer RR, Sellnow TL, Seeger MW. *Effective Crisis Communication: Moving From Crisis to Opportunity,* 5th ed. Los Angeles: Sage; 2022.

9. Harvard Business Essentials. *Crisis Management: Master the Skills to Prevent Disasters.* Boston: Harvard Business School Press, 2004.

10. Mitroff II. *Crisis Leadership: Planning for the Unthinkable.* Hoboken, NJ: Wiley; 2004.

11. Fink S. *Crisis Management: Planning for the Inevitable.* Lincoln, NJ: iUniverse; 2000.

12. Joint Chiefs of Staff. JP 5-0 Joint operations planning. Washington, DC: 2011.

13. American Psychological Association. Holding environment. *APA Dictionary of Psychology.* https://dictionary.apa.org/holding-environment. Accessed January 15, 2024.

14. Winnicott D. Holding and containing. *UK Essays,* 1960. www.ukessays.com/essays/psychology/holding-and-containing-winnicott.php#citethis. Accessed January 15, 2024.

15. Bion W. *Learning from Experience.* London: Routledge; 2023. https://doi.org/10.4324/9781003411840

16. Petriglieri G. The psychology behind effective crisis leadership. *Harvard Business Review* blog, April 22, 2020. https://hbr.org/2020/04/the-psychology-behind-effective-crisis-leadership. Accessed January 15, 2024

17. Sidiropoulou M. Succeed softly: the "containing" leader. LinkedIn blog, July 16, 2014. www.linkedin.com/pulse/20140716113821-89831881-the-containing-leader/. Accessed January 15, 2024.

18. Indeed Editorial Team. Crisis leadership: definition and 6 essential components. Indeed blog, June 24, 2022. www.indeed.com/career-advice/career-development/crisis-leadership. Accessed January 17, 2024.

19. Liopis G. 6 leadership principles to guide you during crisis. *Forbes* blog, April 13, 2020. www.forbes.com/sites/glennllopis/2020/04/13/6-leadership-principles-to-guide-you-during-crisis/?sh=16e354a78237. Accessed January 17, 2024.

20. Center for Creative Leadership. Adapting to change requires flexible leaders. Center for Creative Leadership blog, August 24, 2021. www.ccl.org/articles/leading-effectively-articles/adaptability-1-idea-3-facts-5-tips/. Accessed January 17, 2024.

21. Indeed Editorial Team. How to provide leadership in crisis (plus tips and advice). Indeed blog, March 19, 2023. https://uk.indeed.com/career-advice/career-development/leadership-in-crisis. Accessed January 17, 2024.

22. McNulty EJ, Marcus L. Are you leading through the crisis…or managing the response? *Harvard Business Review* blog, March 25, 2020. https://hbr.org/2020/03/are-you-leading-through-the-crisis-or-managing-the-response. Accessed January 22, 2024.

23. Barr E. How to lead in a crisis. *The Wall Street Journal,* April 7, 2009. www.wsj.com/articles/how-to-lead-in-a-crisis. Accessed January 22, 2024.

24. Herrity J. How to lead your team through a crisis. Indeed blog, December 20, 2023. www.indeed.com/career-advice/career-development/how-to-lead-through-a-crisis#:~:text=How%

20to%20lead%20through%20a%20crisis%201%201.,8%208.%20Evaluate%20your%20 policies%20...%20More%20items. Accessed January 22, 2024.

25. Nichols C, Hayden SC, Tendler C. 4 behaviors that help leaders manage a crisis. *Harvard Business Review* blog, April 2, 2020. https://hbr.org/2020/04/4-behaviors-that-help-leaders-manage-a-crisis. Accessed January 16, 2024.

Chapter 17: Healthcare Leadership Succession Planning

1. Routch K, Monahan K, Doherty M. The holy grail of effective leadership succession planning: how to overcome the succession planning paradox. Deloitte blog, September 27, 2018. www2. deloitte.com/us/en/insights/topics/leadership/effective-leadership-succession-planning. html. Accessed February 20, 2024.

2. Orgvue. What are the benefits of succession planning? Orgvue website. www.orgvue.com/ resources/articles/what-are-the-benefits-of-succession-planning/. Accessed February 20, 2024.

3. National Institutes of Health Office of Management. Succession planning: a step-by-step guide. https://hr.nih.gov/sites/default/files/public/documents/2021-03/Succession_Planning_ Step_by_Step_Guide.pdf. Accessed February 20, 2024.

4. Gillis AS, Daniel D, Snider E. Succession planning. Tech Target blog, last updated November 2021. www.techtarget.com/searchhrsoftware/definition/succession-planning. Accessed February 20, 2024.

5. Harrell E. Succession planning: what the research says. *Harvard Business Review*. December 2016. https://hbr.org/2016/12/succession-planning-what-the-research-says. Accessed February 20, 2024.

6. Indeed Editorial Team. The importance of succession planning and how to prepare. Indeed blog. August 23, 2022. https://au.indeed.com/career-advice/career-development/importance-of-succession-planning. Accessed February 20, 2024.

7. O'Brien J. Succession planning is legacy building. Russel Reynolds blog, May 6, 2022. https:// www.russellreynolds.com/en/insights/articles/succession-planning-is-legacy-building. Accessed February 21, 2023.

8. Miles M. 4 reasons why you can't afford to skip succession planning. BetterUp blog, November 18, 2022. https://www.betterup.com/blog/succession-planning. Accessed February 26, 2024.

9. Boardspan. Management succession planning: why it's hard, how to fix it. Boardspan blog. at https://boardspan.com/resources/article/management-succession-planning-why-its-hard-how-to-fix-it. Accessed February 26, 2024.

10. Atlassian. A manager's ultimate guide to effectives succession planning. Atlassian blog, October 29, 2021. www.atlassian.com/blog/leadership/guide-to-effective-succession-planning. Accessed March 6, 2024.

11. Rubenstahl E. How and why to make a succession plan. Positive Impact blog. https:// positiveimpact.me/how-and-why-to-make-a-succession-plan/. Accessed March 6, 2024.

12. Half R. What is succession planning? 7 steps to success. Robert Half blog, May 9, 2023. at www.roberthalf.com/us/en/insights/management-tips/7-steps-to-building-a-succession-plan-for-success. Accessed June 6, 2024.

13. Goldsmith M. 4 tips for efficient succession planning. *Harvard Business Review* blog, May 12, 2009. https://hbr.org/2009/05/change-succession-planning-to. Accessed March 6, 2024.

14. Leyshon J. 7 tips for an effective succession planning strategy. Sage blog, October 13, 2020. www.sage.com/en-gb/blog/succession-planning-strategy-effective/. Accessed March 6, 2024.

15. Lucid Chart. Succession planning best practices: 9 steps to prepare your org for change. Lucid Chart blog. www.lucidchart.com/blog/succession-planning-best-practices. Accessed March 6, 2024.

16. Ramsden J. 10 tips for successful succession planning. Investors in People blog, January 28, 2019. www.investorsinpeople.com/knowledge/10-tips-for-successful-succession-planning/. Accessed March 7, 2024.

17. Jennings J. A comprehensive guide to the leadership succession planning process. *Forbes* blog, October 26, 2022. www.forbes.com/sites/forbesbusinesscouncil/2022/10/26/a-comprehensive-guide-to-the-leadership-succession-planning-process/?sh=70e1ceb031aa. Accessed March 7, 2024.

18. Ginac L. Why succession plans fail. Advisorpedia blog, June 16, 2021. https://www.advisorpedia.com/advisor-tools/why-succession-plans-fail/. Accessed March 7, 2021.

19. Talent Guard. Why succession plans fail. Talent Guard blog. www.talentguard.com/blog/succession-plans-fail. Accessed March 7, 2024.

20. Burry M. What to do if you don't get the promotion. Balance Money blog, November 9, 2022. www.thebalancemoney.com/what-to-do-after-you-don-t-get-a-job-promotion-4692181. Accessed March 7, 2023.

21. Janove J. Passed over for promotion—now what? SHRM blog, September 30, 2021. https://www.shrm.org/topics-tools/news/humanity-hr-compliance/passed-promotion-now. Accessed March 7, 2024.

22. Indeed Editorial Team. How to use the 9-box matrix for succession planning. Indeed blog, February 3, 2023. www.indeed.com/career-advice/career-development/9-box-matrix. Accessed March 7, 2024.

23. Profit Co. Strategic talent management with a 9-box matrix. Profit Co. blog. www.profit.co/blog/performance-management/strategic-talent-management-with-the-9-box-matrix/. Accessed March 7, 2024.

Bonus Chapter: Crafting Your Leadership Legacy Statement: A Template

1. Roth T, Conchie B. *Strengths-Based Leadership: Great Leaders, Teams, and Why People Follow*. New York: Gallup Press; 2008.

2. Galford RM, Maruca RF. *Your Leadership Legacy: Why Looking Toward The Future Will Make You a Better Leader Today*. Boston, MA: Harvard Business School Press; 2006.

3. MindTools Content Team. What is legacy thinking? Beginning with the end in mind. MindTools blog. www.mindtools.com/a3axrm1/what-is-legacy-thinking. Accessed July 13, 2013.

4. Kouzes JM, Posner BZ. *A Leader's Legacy*. San Francisco: Jossey-Bass; 2006.

5. Wade-Benzoni K. How to think about building your legacy. Inc. blog, December 15, 2016. https://hbr.org/2016/12/how-to-think-about-building-your-legacy. Accessed July 13, 2023

6. Tredgold G. Secret to success: aim high, start small, and keep going. Inc. blog, October 10, 2016. www.inc.com/gordon-tredgold/secret-to-success-aim-high-start-small-and-keep-going.html. Accessed July 12, 2023

7. MindTools Content Team. Treasure mapping. MindTools blog. www.mindtools.com/ansbhwc/treasure-mapping. Accessed July 21, 2023.

8. Rohn J. Rohn: 5 undeniable reasons to leave a legacy. *Success* blog, July 13, 2016. www.success.com/rohn-5-undeniable-reasons-to-leave-a-legacy/. Accessed July 21, 2023.

9. Hills L. *Lasting Female Educational Leadership: Leadership Legacies of Women Leaders.* New York and London: Spring Dordrecht-Heidelberg, 2013. https://doi.org/10.1007/978-94-007-5019-7

www.ingramcontent.com/pod-product-compliance
Lightning Source LLC
Chambersburg PA
CBHW060331220326
41598CB00023B/2671